MAXI MIZE

**29 Strategies to
Turbocharge Your Business
With the Power of the Internet**

Matthias Mazur
Internet Entrepreneur and Marketing Maven

About the Author

Matthias Mazur is an entrepreneur, author, speaker and investor with past and present interests in diverse businesses. He is a former Swiss national tennis champion, having trained alongside Roger Federer, the Swiss and Belgian Davis Cup teams and has competed with Rafael Nadal, Novak Djokovic and many other top players. He was ranked the #1 tennis player in Switzerland before suffering a career-ending injury, which forced him to reevaluate his entire life. He swiftly turned his focus to entrepreneurship.

Starting from scratch, he built a multimillion-dollar internet marketing business in less than 36 months and his strategies have generated over 50 million dollars for his companies and clients. He has written 3 books on the topics of internet marketing, business growth, sales and entrepreneurship and is invited to share his experience and strategies as a keynote speaker in front of thousands of attendees for corporations and business events. He currently runs ZuraMedia, an online marketing, sales & social media agency, helping clients with turnkey and hands-free solutions to increase exposure, leads and sales. Matthias is also involved in the movie business as an actor, producer and investor. He spends most of his time in London.

To my parents and to my sister, for all their unconditional love and support.

Table of contents

PREFACE

This book is not about doing things the way traditional businesses operate. This book is about using real-life and profit-producing online strategies to MAXIMIZE profits, turbocharge any business and win in your industry.

I was recently reading an article about the failure rate of businesses in our current economy and it was mentioned that:

- According to Bloomberg, 8 out of 10 entrepreneurs who start a business fail within their first 18 months.
- 96% of ALL companies fail within 10 years.
- A study done by Deloitte revealed that only 16% of busi nesses have an effective online presence and use the internet to grow their business.
- Approximately 543,000 new businesses get started each month.
- 94% of B2B buyers research the internet for purchase de cisions.
- 89% of consumers use online search engines for pur chase decisions.

To me, this means 3 things:

1. The majority is always wrong.
2. Most business refuse to ADAPT to how consumers be have and buy in today's economy and end up suffering the consequences.
3. Entrepreneurs accept to run mediocre businesses, blaming the economy for slow business and low (or non-existent) growth and profits.

In the past 10 years of working with thousands of entrepreneurs and companies, speaking at dozens of seminars in Europe and in North America, I've seen the evolution of the internet first-hand and the impact it has on the life of every single business and CEO I've met.

Just a few years ago, most businesses were skeptical about using the internet for business. Today, it is a necessity. If you're not online, you don't exist to the modern consumer who walks around with his smartphone, searches Google and social networks for solutions and product reviews and asks his friends which restaurant to go to and which ones to avoid.

Social media has built and brought down brands faster than anything we could have imagined. Online advertising strategies allow you to pinpoint specifically who you want to target and place your marketing message in front of your ideal customers. And best of all, the majority of all the strategies I share in this book can be automated to scale your business in a matter of weeks. The promise of this book is that you will learn cutting-edge internet marketing strategies you can implement immediately in your business. The main lesson I've learned in my sports career is that having a solid foundation is an absolute necessity. But to out-compete others in your market and dominate, you need to do MORE and use strategies and tactics they don't. You will get these strategy and all you need in this book to generate more exposure for your business, explode your marketing results, boost your sales and build a raving fan base.

If you're an entrepreneur wanting to turn an idea into a lucrative business or a business owner looking to increase profits fast, welcome to my universe of rebellious online methods that make a lot of money.

Since the majority of businesses fail in less than 36 months, doesn't it make sense to look for strategies the majority of businesses are not applying? Of course it does. And this book is all about that.

In this book, I hope to empower and give you the most effective and proven business strategies combined with cutting-edge online marketing techniques to out-grow, out-perform and out-profit your competition without them knowing what happened.

These strategies are not known to the masses and will demand you to go above and beyond what you have been doing until now. If you keep on doing what you've always done, you will always end up with the same results. Growing and increasing your business' performance will require you to expand you comfort zone, implement new strategies and be ready to act fast.

CAUTION!

Let me warn right from the start: some of the information you will find in this book goes against everything you've ever heard in your business and entrepreneurial life. You might be tempted to discard some of the advice you discover because of its lack of "social popularity", but make no mistake: these strategies are supremely powerful if integrated the right way.

I pull no punches and make no excuses for being blunt and telling it like it is.

This book is not a compilation of "feel-good" theories and fluffy anecdotes. This book is loaded with street-smart strategies I have been using on a daily basis for the last 10+ years in my different businesses and that have generated over $50 million in dozens of industries.

If you are truly dedicated to growing a business into a highly profitable venture or maximizing the results of your current business, you will need to tolerate some of the discomfort related to the strategies I expose here. Before long, you'll understand that everything I cover in this book really does turn average businesses into cash-rich companies.

Throughout this book, you'll come across various concepts and methodologies that generate multiple millions of dollars in extra revenue every year for those who apply them. These concepts are not complicated. On the contrary, they are rather simple. But like Albert Einstein said it so eloquently: "Any dumb person can make something complicated. The genius is in simplifying it."

I will also be sharing my personal experiences and those of the clients who have authorized me to share their stories and results.

I firmly believe that entrepreneurs are the light of our society because they are the solution to many of the economic disasters our world has faced lately. So, congratulations to you. Picking up this book is your first step to building a highly profitable money machine that will support your lifestyle for years to come and enable you to do whatever you wish to do. No matter how successful you are, I'm confident you'll find several ideas in this book that can benefit you enormously. And having consulting with billion-dollar brands over the past 10 years, I can also say that even massive multinational companies could increase their sales with the strategies I share.

Reach out to me on social media and let's connect!

Website: **www.MatthiasMazur.com**

Facebook: Facebook.com/MatthiasMazur
Twitter: @MattMazur
Instagram: @MatthiasMazur
LinkedIn: http://linkedin.com/in/MatthiasMazur
Snapchat: MatthiasMazur
Medium: @MattMazur
Tumblr: http://MatthiasMazur.tumblr.com

Notes

If you are easily offended and do not have an open mind to new ideas and profitable strategies, you should probably not read this book.

Throughout this book, you will see me referring to the business owner, client or other people using the masculine form "him" or "he", etc. I don't mean this as lack of respect to women, only as a convenience for the reader.

In some instances, I've been authorized to use the names of companies, individuals and actual case studies throughout this book. In a few cases, individuals' names have been withheld on request.

While every effort has been made to ensure factual accuracy, no warranties concerning such acts are made. This book is published for general information and entertainment purposes only. It is sold with the understanding that no party is engaged in rendering legal, accounting, or other professional services. If legal advice or other expert assistance is required, the services of a competent professional person should be sought.

1

TENNIS, INJURY AND REBIRTH

To give you some context on how the strategies in this book came along, I believe it's important to explain what happened to me and what led me to building and operating multimillion dollar businesses without any formal business education and starting from scratch without any contacts or "easy way" in.

My first "business venture" involved publishing and selling a monthly printed magazine I wrote at the age 8. My parents had a subscription for National Geographic, so I would read and summarize my favorite articles (usually about animals, travel and unexplored parts of the world) every month, type and format them and sold my very own monthly magazine to schoolmates, teachers and neighbors. It made me about $20/ week, which is like a billion at that age.

From the earliest I can remember, my entire life revolved around sports – ice hockey (which I *loved* and still love), judo and swimming (which I hated) – but mainly, tennis.

That's when I fell in love with competition, focus and dedication and it's also where I got my first taste of challenges and my love and addiction for winning.

After being deemed "not talented enough" by tennis coaches at age 12, I set my goals on becoming the best player in the country (Switzerland). To accomplish that, my plan was simple: outwork and practice twice as much as everybody I was competing against. And it worked.

At age 14 and for the following years, I won the national championships and was ranked the number 1 junior in Switzerland and represented the country on the World Junior Tour and at multiple European and World Junior Championships. It enabled me to achieve an all-time high ranking in the top 15 European players of my age group and gave me the opportunity to compete against players like Novak Djokovic, Rafael Nadal, Stan Wawrinka and others.

After a string of solid results on the European Tour, I was recruited by Peter Carter (Roger Federer's coach and mentor at the time) to join the Swiss Tennis Federation and train full-time alongside other top professional players.

During that time, I was fortunate enough to train with "The Master" himself: Roger Federer. After Peter's passing in a tragic car accident that year, I suffered a career-halting leg injury, which forced me to reevaluate my tennis goals and ambitions.

It was a crushing injury: I tore my thigh muscle over 9 inches wide and wasn't allowed to move for weeks. It took almost 9 months just to be able to walk normally again and almost 2 years to be able to trust my body again.

Being away from the courts during the recovery process gave me a lot of time to look within and dig into one of my other passions: entrepreneurship. I started my first internet business (in the online advertising and publishing space) at the age of 17 while I was lying in my bed, injured.

After recovering, I went back and played on the pro tour (in the Future and Challenger categories) for a few years and got to travel the world again and meet and compete with amazing people.

But in the spring of my 21st birthday, I contracted a severe case of pneumonia (twice in the span of 3 months) that forced me to go through 47 days of antibiotics due to the disease not being well diagnosed by the first doctor I consulted.

It was a tough, tough time and I felt like suffocating every time I was walking up the stairs.

Being a pro athlete dedicating every day of your life for years to reach the goal of having a long and successful career and experiencing two major health issues made me realize how fast life can change from one minute to the next.

It also made me realize that my body was not the "unstoppable machine" I once thought it was. Shortly after recovering from pneumonia a few months later, I decided to retire from tennis and focus 100% on the business I had started a few years earlier.

Transitioning from pro sports to running and growing my business full-time didn't leave me any time to dwell or feel sorry for myself.

Over the years that followed, the internet companies I launched and grew resulted in operating hundreds of websites and numerous collateral businesses in 3 different continents, ranging from an online publishing company with over 25,000 customers, a call center business with over 30 telephone sales agents and over 60 employees, and an online advertising and media company.

My core expertise lies in growing businesses using online marketing and advertising strategies, expanding brands (through social media marketing) and multiplying revenue with direct response marketing and sales (through online advertising, phone sales, webinar sales, framing and positioning offers, etc.) which have generated multiple millions of dollars for my companies and for my clients and partners.

I've written books and publications about business and entrepreneurship and have spoken at dozens of conferences in the United States, the U.K., the Netherlands, France and Switzerland.

I've also scripted and given thousands of live teleseminar and webinar sales presentations and have advised hundreds of businesses ranging from start-ups to billion-dollar corporations and CEOs.

Currently, I run ZuraMedia, an agency that helps brands increase exposure through social media marketing and that helps businesses boost sales with hands-free marketing and sales systems as well as online advertising strategies to generate unlimited amounts of leads and customers in any market.

And this stuff works. The strategies I've applied over the last 10 years have generated over 50 million dollars in extra revenue for our companies and our clients. No fluff or theory here.

I did all this without attending a single formal business education class in college and without getting an MBA or any fancy degree. Actually, I dropped out of college after 3 months because I realized the "conventional education system" was way too slow and inefficient for me. I love speed. I love implementing things fast and executing while others are still "thinking about it".

This book is a product of my mindset, the way I do business and my experience of selling products and services using the internet for last 10 years. This is the book I wished someone would have given me when I was just starting out, because it merges everything you need to supercharge any business with the power of the internet and gain an unfair advantage in your market.

Now, let's get to it.

Why this is different

Let's talk about why this is material is different than anything you've ever seen and why I'm so proud of what I share here. Well, first of all, I don't just teach this - I actually use these strategies in my own companies.

These online marketing and advertising strategies have generated hundreds of thousands of leads for our businesses and clients in the past few years.

I'll share concrete examples of what we do and what we've done not only in the English-speaking market, but also markets in markets in Europe and in other languages.

I'll also share case studies of some of our clients and some of my own companies and show you how to grow your business not by 10%... but by 100%, 500% and even 1,200% in the next 12 months, dominate your market, generate thousands of leads a month and reduce your work hours. The goal of all this is to help you achieve predictable income and insane growth results.

Here's what we'll be covering. I'll be sharing 29 profit-producing strategies to turbocharge your business using solid offline growth concepts combined with cutting-edge online marketing strategies. Depending on the current situation of your company, this might result in millions of dollars in extra revenue in the upcoming months, like it has for many of our clients.

Does this sound like you?

Sometimes you have some great months, and sometimes you have some bad months. And you have completely unpredictable income. You don't know where the next batch of clients will come from. You don't know how to position yourself in the marketplace. Maybe you don't know how to create irresistible and high-converting offers that turn prospects to buyers.

If you're selling services of any kind, you don't know how to predictably generate new clients and you don't have a system to attract a flow of ongoing and motivated leads and prospects who want what you have to offer.

Maybe you're trapped selling cheap products and services and you're afraid that people won't pay if you raise your prices. Maybe you're stuck on a treadmill at the moment and if feels like the more money you want to make the more you need to work. And it feels like the business controls you instead of your business working FOR you and you know that something needs to change. Even though you might be a delivering an incredible product or service to your market or have an idea that might change the world, you're not hitting your income goals.

Or if you're currently hitting your income goals, you're just working way too hard and you know that it's not sustainable. Maybe you're putting in 40, 50, 60-hour weeks and running a good business, but you know you can't keep doing that for months and years and being a slave to your company.

Once you start implementing these strategies one by one, this is how the situation will evolve, as it has for my own companies and for our clients.

You'll have an automated way of attracting new and qualified prospects who want what you have to offer and who are happy to pay the price to get the solutions you provide without having to negotiate or offer special discounts.

You'll have a system to convert leads into loyal and high-paying clients and you'll be able to attract the right clients - those who are happy to sign up and pay you without asking 10,000 questions - and be able to repel those annoying clients who make your life a nightmare.

If you want to get more exposure and visibility for your message and your brand but feel like you're completely clueless about all the "social media stuff", this will help you clarify what you need to do and the best way to go about it, without stress or overwhelm.

And best of all, it's also going to help you decrease your work hours by at least 25% compared to what you're doing at the moment.

The Entrepreneur's Lifestyle

With pop culture depicting entrepreneurship as a fun and super profitable way of life in movies such as "The Social Network", "The Wolf of Wall Street" and documentaries about high-level entrepreneurs who made it big like Mark Cuban, Jay-Z and P. Diddy, people seem to forget that being an entrepreneur involves a lot of risk. Risking time, money and energy, raising money, hiring and managing staff, building a sales force, paying bills, managing cash flow, staying updated with the trends in your marketplace and dealing with the day-to-day fires and chaos of building and running a business is no walk in the park.

Let's have a look at a few concepts I use to be clear on my mission and the direction where my companies are heading.

Be the architect of your own life

I often share this concept with audiences during speeches because it has allowed me to literally change my life. I firmly believe that everyone has the choice to create a life that they want and if you don't like your current situation, you have the power and opportunity to change that at any moment.

My belief is that everyone has the power to create and be the architect of his own life and that 90% of success in business doesn't depend on "the market", "the competition" or "the economy", but rather on the mindset that you adopt in your business on a daily basis and the actions that you take to reach your goals.

I've met thousands of entrepreneurs over the last 10 years and I noticed that people who know how to take responsibility for their wins and losses and refuse to feel like a victim of any given situation or make excuses often succeed much faster than others.

Winners don't make excuses. If they don't like something, they do their best to change it, quickly.

Unfortunately, many entrepreneurs prefer to blame outside events and circumstances than take responsibility and to put things in place to achieve their goals.

When I got injured at the age 17 in the most important year of my tennis career, I could have settled for less and become bitter about everything in life. Why did I get injured? Why did life take away my dream of making it to the pros? Why did my sponsors and financial backers stop returning my calls from that point on? Why did tennis coaches stop spending time with me? Where would I be if I hadn't gotten injured?

I could have dwelled and complained for years and cursed the world for my injury. But I chose to do something about it and shift my attention to do something productive and proactive. You can't change the past, but you can change the way you view any event or situation.

I am a big fan of Jay Z, hip-hop legend turned entrepreneur who has a net worth of over 500 million dollars. He represents the perfect example of someone who created his own life in spite of starting out in an extremely tough place in life surrounded by extreme violence and poverty.

He was born in Brooklyn in New York and started selling drugs when he was only 15 years old. At age 25, he started making music and recorded his first album. The problem was, no major label wanted give him a record deal. Since everyone refused, he decided to create his own label and distribute his music himself.
He could have told himself that since record labels weren't interested, the public wouldn't be interested. That it was too difficult to start an independent label without any real experience in the industry and without any high-level college education.

Instead of that, he created his own label, Roc-A-Fella Records and released music himself. Since then, he's sold tens of millions of albums and downloads, performs at sold-out arenas and football stadiums, produced artists such as Rihanna and Kanye West, and even became a part-owner the Brooklyn Nets and founded his clothing company, restaurants, and much more.

The empire he built in the last 20 years was based on that initial decision of taking control of his situation to launch his own record label rather than accept the fact that labels at the time wanted nothing to do with him.

Where are you now? In a violent neighborhood? In an area where you can get shot anytime of the day? If Jay Z managed to build an empire that is now worth over half a billion dollars – without any formal education - why not YOU?

Another great example is Oprah Winfrey, who has a net worth of over two billion dollars. She created her own television channel and has built a rabid audience of millions of followers and fans who purchase pretty much anything she promotes. She is a master saleswoman; she's published dozens of books and is one of the most recognizable people in the world.

What few people know is that she went through extremely difficult times when she was young, including being repeatedly sexually abused and raped as a child. Despite all that, she managed to find the courage and the strength to change her life for the best and has since then impacted millions of people in the world with her TV shows.

Jay Z and Oprah are two examples that prove that no matter what your past is and no matter your background, it is possible to create the life you want, be the architect of your own life and achieve incredible amounts of success even when the odds are against you.

Your ideal lifestyle

Many entrepreneurs and business never "zoom out" of their daily lives and never have a clear idea of what they want to achieve and why they do the things they do. Here's an exercise I suggest you do now. Open a word document on your computer of grab a blank sheet of paper and a pen and answer the following questions with as much detail as possible. This will help you visualize your ideal daily and exactly know the lifestyle you want to reach.

Go through the following questions and describe the vision of a perfect, sustainable day could be lived every day of the year.

- What time would you wake up?
- What would you have for breakfast?
- Where would you have breakfast?
- What would you do in the morning? (Hike? Read? Meditate? Spend time with the family?)
- What would you do in the afternoon? (Sports? See friends? Go to the movies? Do charity work?)
- Where would you want to live? Which country, city? What type of house?
- How would you spend your days?
- How much time would you work?
- How much time would you spend with your loved ones?

Describe precisely what you would do, how you would feel, what exercise you would get, what hobbies you would take on, how much times you would spend with your loved ones, etc. Then, compare your ideal lifestyle with your current situation and see what areas you can immediately improve.

Many entrepreneurs I know love to work, love the daily grind and the hustle and wouldn't want to change a single thing. They love working late or waking up early to execute new ideas and grow their business.

But too many of them also live in complete denial and are not aware of their day-to-day habits and schedule and why they actually started their business in the first place. Years go by, and it usually takes a wake-up call such as deteriorating health or relationships to force them to look within and find out why they do the things they do.

2

FIRST, THE BAD NEWS

We live in interesting times, full of opportunity for some and disappointment for others.

When thousands of businesses are closing their doors and declaring bankruptcy, thousands of others are opening in the hope of finding their space in today's overcrowded marketplace.

And yet, the numbers are alarming. Here are some statistics you might find interesting for any entrepreneur or business owner:

- 96% of ALL businesses fail within 10 years of existence with 80% of those failing in their first 3 years.
- Nearly 60,000 businesses filed for bankruptcy last year alone in the United States.
- According to Dun & Bradstreet reports, "Businesses with fewer than 20 employees have only a 37% chance of surviving 4 years (of business) and only a 9% chance of surviving 10 years."
- In 2008, the U.S. Small Business Association reported that "an estimated 627,200 new employer firms began

operations in 2008, and 595,600 firms closed
that year."

Shocking? Merely.

Frightening? Pretty much, if you ask me.

Whether you're currently in business or you'd like to start your own business, the odds are clearly not in your favor. Regular business owners and
entrepreneurs often become overwhelmed by the day-to-day business
life filled with chaos, multitasking, long days, short sleepless nights, and
tough decisions to make.

How will you react when the pressure rises? Will you crumble or will you
stand strong?

Only time will tell.

My question to you is: are you sure going into business is what you really
want to do?

Are you ready to put up with the daily crises and putting out of fires?
As we're starting our journey to more profits in your business, let's address the age-old question that drives all businesses since the beginning
of time.

What is the goal of a business?

Many experts have deliberated about this and a fair share of them seems
to complicate things in such a way that makes it difficult to understand
the essence of it all.
To cut right to the chase, I believe you only have two main objectives as
an entrepreneur or a business owner:

> To serve your customers and fulfill their desires.
> To make a profit.

Let me add that there's absolutely no reason to shy away from point number 2. Unless you don't like making money, your priority should and must always be to make the maximum amount of profit while serving your customers the best you can. Everything else is just fluff.

As you get to know me, you'll discover that I make no apologies for being very straightforward and blunt. I tell it like it is. As a result, our clients and students have become incredibly successful and many have grown their businesses by 200% to 900% in a matter of weeks while decreasing their work hours.

At this point, I would also like to congratulate you for believing in yourself and your future business success enough to have gotten this book, whether you've purchased it or borrowed it from a friend. As a successful business owner, this book is the kind of book I wish I would have been lucky to read at the start of my entrepreneurial career.

This book will change the way you see things in your business and the way you operate tasks on a daily basis. It is not for the faint hearted. If you can't stomach change and are afraid of growing past your current business situation, this book is not for you.

But if you want a massive and dramatic boost in profits, increased sales, more repeat customers and a better life in general, then this book is written for you.

For the right person, it is the beginning of your way to massive profits in your business.

Let me caution you not to take the advice you find here lightly. It has the power to increase your business dramatically, improve your financial situation, and better the overall quality of your life. Don't just read the information you'll discover – use it and implement it in your business.

3

NOW, THE GOOD NEWS

Marketing.

A word so powerful it has made the happy days of businesses since the dawn of time and has destroyed the fortunes of many other ones.

You may have an idea you'd like to turn into a business, you may be running a start-up company or you may be running a successful business for a number of years. Whichever situation you're in, I guarantee you will find at least 5 profit-boosting strategies to increase your business in the next 60 days. Many of our clients have done so before you, and I hope you will too.

While companies fail every day and close their doors, you will discover little-known and practical strategies and tactics you can apply in your business immediately that will boost your profits more than you'd ever wished for.

And while some businesses struggle to attract new prospects, you will learn how to attract stampedes of qualified customers ready to do business with you over and over again.

As an aspiring entrepreneur or current business owner, you would certainly agree that no one has taken the time to teach you what you need to know to build a highly profitable business. The fact is that it just isn't your fault. No class or business school theories can prepare you for the harsh realities of running a real-world business.

In this book, I'll be sharing the very same techniques I've been using to build profitable multi-million dollar businesses during what has been described as "the worst financial crisis since the Great Depression of 1929".

In this book, you'll learn:

- Practical ways to attract tons of new buyers using little-known strategies you can implement today.
- How to craft irresistible offers that customers will fight for.
- Dirt-cheap techniques to create rabid fans and who will buy from you over and over again.
- Easy-to-implement ways to increase your sales and profits even during "bad" economic times and slow days of the week.
- How new tools can help you automate and system atize all your business tasks so you get to enjoy life and take time away from your business.
- The mindset shifts you'll need to adopt in order to prepare yourself for massive growth.
- And much, much more.

This book is all about helping you make more money and reduce your workload thanks to profit-producing strategies and tactics you can easily apply, no matter the size of your business.

You'll discover how the "new generation of entrepreneurs" are using renegade techniques to increase their bottom lines, offer top-quality customer service and support, live more fulfilling lives and make massive profit with minimum costs.

Let me ask you a question: why are some businesses generating 100 times more revenue than yours? Think about it.

Why is it that other human beings are currently generating revenues 50 to 100 times higher than you? Does that mean the owners and the management team is 50 to 100 times smarter than your team? Of course not.

It might actually be quite the contrary: bigger companies may be spending less time "working" than you.

Your competitors might be spending fewer hours actually running his business than you, but might be generating more revenue than you. I'm sure you'll agree that this needs to change.

Being actively involved with dozens of multi-million dollar companies over the last few years – many of which are run with minimal staff - I can positively say that many business owners are often very "simple" in the way they think and act. I remember meeting several billionaires over the last few years who run or have run billion-dollar businesses, and being almost disappointed by how simple their thoughts and processes were when it came to building and running their businesses. Einstein once said that:

"Any intelligent fool can make things bigger, more complex, and more violent. It takes a touch of genius -- and a lot of courage -- to move in the opposite direction."

It doesn't take a genius to build a money-generating machine. But it does take a stroke of genius to simplify processes without getting overwhelmed by the small daily tasks and fires that you must put out in your business on a day-to-day basis.

As you know, the cards have been reshuffled over the past recent years, and the world of business will never be the same again.

The reason why some entrepreneurs and business owners strive with their businesses is largely dependent on the quality of the systems they have put in motion that automate and increase productivity while decreasing the chances of inconsistent processes.

And thanks to all the new technology that is available (most of which is either free or dirt-cheap in comparison to the return on investment it will generate for you), any business now has the tools and the ability to compete with the massive Fortune 500 companies. And Fortune 500 companies now have the opportunity to drastically decrease their costs, even if most of them prefer flushing millions of dollars in unnecessary "brand-awareness" campaigns. More about that further in the book.

In writing this book, my goal was to assemble the best strategies and tactics for you to implement in your business. I have personally used the vast majority of the tools and strategies you will find in this book with a great level of success and tremendous results. I share here the good, the bad and the ugly, as well as a proven blueprint to increasing your profits starting today.

These strategies work and will grow your business, but only if you apply them to your organization. It doesn't matter whether you're running a small mom-and-pop type of operation, a local hair salon or a public company worth billions of dollars; I know that just ONE of the techniques you find in this book can have a dramatic increase in your bottom line in the next 60 days.

Let's dive right into this by looking one of the most common and DEADLY myths of entrepreneurship.

Deadly Myth
Good product = good sales

The business cemetery is paved with great ideas, great products and great services that simply weren't marketed in the way they should have. Some business owners think that just because they have the best product or service in the world, customers will automatically come flocking to their doorstep or website.

Nothing could be further from the truth. The reality is that you could have the best offer, the best service, and the best life-changing product; but if you fail to communicate that message to your prospective target audience, you will:

Lose money.
End up in bankruptcy court.

Business success is built on the efficiency of the marketing that is engineered by the entrepreneur: you or your marketing team. Businesses live by marketing, strive by marketing, and die by marketing. If you don't like the idea of marketing your business or your product, I frankly don't think you stand a good chance of survival in this economy.

If you follow my blog on MatthiasMazur.com, you know that I'm also involved in the entertainment business as a producer, and investor and an actor. I've had the good fortune of meeting and becoming close friends with some of the most powerful people within the industry and many of my friends are aspiring artists, actors and performers. Sadly enough, millions of talented artists fail to achieve the level of success they dream of because they think that creating "great" music and being a "great" actor is enough to achieve noticeable breakthroughs and gain popularity.

Although I firmly believe that the quality of the "product" is important – and the quality of your product must satisfy your target market – it is essential to understand that the product itself will rarely attract buyers. Hoping for positive "word-of-mouth" advertising as a means of generating new business has become highly risky and completely unpredictable.

Good marketing and advertising attracts prospective buyers while positioning your product and pre-sells them on your product or service. The "quality" of the product or service is what keeps the customer satisfied and increases the chances of him coming back for more frequent purchases.

It's a shame that so many entrepreneurs are forced to close shop because of lack of customers and sales when there are so many options and opportunities to attract hordes of hot buyers using the lead-generation strategies and conversion tactics I share in this book. In the end, it's all about increasing the number of sales, increasing the dollar amount of every transaction, and getting customers to buy more frequently.

It's time to act!

Whatever you do and wherever you might be in your entrepreneurial career - whether you own a business or professional practice, are a staff member in another's employ - you owe it to yourself, your company or practice, your employer, your career and your future to learn how to generate the maximum results from everything you do. Creating consistent breakthroughs is the answer you're after.

Whatever you're doing, however you're doing it and wherever you're doing it – you can and must find continually better ways to maximize your results. Maximizing results and creating breakthroughs means more than simply getting the most profit, highest performance, and the greatest productivity, opportunity or investment. It also means achieving maximum results with the minimum of time, effort, expense and risk - something few people practice or even think about.

Always seek the highest and best use of your time, money and effort.

In order to produce the highest number of breakthroughs possible, you should focus your thinking on the following fundamental objectives that will help you generate breakthroughs and drastic improvement in everything you do.

Implement at least one profit-generating idea for your business every 30 days. After a year, you will have 12 profit centers that will fuel your business on autopilot.

Never rely on a single source. Never rely on only one client, one way of driving sales, one sales person, one way of attracting customers. What happens when that resource disappears?

One of your goals is to always position yourself as the only viable option for your target customer. Make yourself and your product so desirable that he will not want to do business with anyone else than you.

Always take a step back and ask analyze what the hidden opportunity is in every situation you face.

The more value and satisfaction you can create for your client, the higher the chances of leveraging the benefits of lifetime customer value (referrals, more repeat sales, etc.)

A breakthrough's purpose is to help you achieve the highest results with the least amount of investment, effort and energy.

The best breakthroughs lower the perceived risk and make it easier for the other party (customer or joint venture partner) to say yes to your offer.

Breakthroughs occur when you take time to analyze what is going on in other markets and implement successful practices in your own industry.

The above concepts will be exposed in detail in the following pages and chapters.

4

GOING MENTAL

Every entrepreneur wants growth. More sales, more customers, more revenue and more profit. Oh, and less hassle too.

But what most business owners don't know or don't want to know is this: to achieve any kind of growth and improvement, it's essential to first take a step out of your daily activities and reflect on your current state of mind, and on the state of mind of your staff if you have people working for you in your organization.

I have no desire to make this yet another personal development book full of touchy-feely affirmations, but it is safe to say that the business you have built or will build is a very close reflection of your personality and your personal discipline.

After years of meeting and consulting with various business owners of small and large organizations, what I find most of the time is that the business is indeed a good indication of how the entrepreneur behind that business thinks, plans, and acts.

A slow, disorganized, late, and uninformed business owner usually doesn't perform anywhere as well as a fast-paced, disciplined, punctual and open-minded leader.

You must understand that in order to grow, change must be welcome. An unhealthy person will never become healthy by repeating the same habits they've always had. If improvement is wanted, change is inevitable, and must be accepted and expected.

Again, my intent is not to babble about self-improvement, but I will list several main personality traits you must develop in order to achieve maximum success and results in your business.

Long-term vision

If you want your business to thrive, it must have an impact on your customers' lives. Almost all the most successful entrepreneurs in the world who have built massive empires like Bill Gates from Microsoft, Steve Jobs from Apple, Jeff Bezos from Amazon.com, and Larry Page and Sergey Brin from Google all started with a long-term vision and are still following it during their everyday decisions and latest products.

For Bill Gates, the vision was to have a personal computer on every single desk at home across the world. For Larry Page and Sergey Brin, it was to build the best information finding tool ever built. It all started with one main long-term vision.

What is your long-term vision?
How do you plan on impacting people's lives with your business?
What do you have to offer and deliver to enrich the world?

Tough times don't last, tough people do. Many entrepreneurs hit a glass wall after a few years of building their business. Sales become slower, mis-hires become more common, product development is slower, and general management is not what you had hoped for when launching your business. Theory is nice, but life happens. And before you know it, a few years have passed, and you haven't reached your sales targets.

It's precisely during that period of time that most entrepreneurs hit the glass wall. At first, it just seems like a small slump, but months go by and things don't improve. This results in the entrepreneur becoming frustrated, and expectations are then lowered.

That's when businesses face a tough challenge: how to grow to the next level when you're facing adversity and resistance.

I've had the privilege to meet and spend some time with Lorenzo Neal, arguably one of the best blocking fullbacks in the history of American Football, and a wonderful and enriching human being. Having played in the NFL for over fifteen years, he knows what it takes to be at the top of his game for a decade and a half, while others come and go in a matter of months or a few short years. Where other athletes failed, Lorenzo stayed strong. His will and spirit were unquestioned and coaches have always had the most flattering things to say about what his mindset and the way he approaches life and sports.

Every human being faces adversity. Lance Armstrong got fired by his cycling team Cofidis when he was diagnosed from testicular cancer and came back to the Tour de France seven times in a row. Yes, he doped. But so did almost every other athlete in the peloton. I've always been a big fan of Lance even when the public turned against him in the face of his admissions. Donald Trump was $900 million in debt in the mid nineties and was back to being a billionaire less than a decade later.

Coming from a sporting background, more specifically from tennis, I can't recall the number of times where I've seen top players come back from two sets down to win a big game at a Grand Slam event. The point is that every single human being has faced or will face adversity and tougher times. The question is: how will you deal with it?

Continuous education

When it comes to growing a business and increasing sales, continuous education is vital. You need to know what's going on in your industry, what the recent developments are and what your competition is up to lately. Furthermore, you need to continually educate yourself about the ways you can increase your business. Attending seminars, conferences and other industry get-togethers are essential.

All the biggest athletes have had coaches since they started out and will continue to have coaches for as long as they wish to remain competitive. Michael Jordan was always accompanied by a personal coach during his years of domination in the NBA. Tiger Woods is also a great example of an athlete having reached incredible levels of success while being helped by a coach. Tennis legend Roger Federer - whom I have had the incredible fortune of meeting and practicing during my pro tennis years – also travels accompanied by his coach and physical trainer.

Many entrepreneurs have made the (very) costly mistake of trying to solve their own situations by doing everything themselves: acting as the doctor of the business, the curer, the outside consultant, all while trying to run the daily operations. This is unrealistic and non-productive. The point is that you need a fresh pair of eyes that can have a look at what you are currently doing. You may be spending so much time in your business that seeing the obvious becomes very difficult.

No excuses

It never ceases to amaze me how some entrepreneurs are tolerant to excuses. Excuses they use themselves and excuses they hear their staff use. If you want to achieve a higher level of success with your business, understand that the amount of excuses you make (or your employees make) is directly linked to the amount of success you have. Big and frequent excuses make your business stall and slow down.

As an entrepreneur, you want to remove every single excuse from your vocabulary, and be very firm with your staff as soon as you hear excuses for not meeting the level of success and the results you expect from them. Excuses like:

"The summer season is slower."
"Tuesdays are slow in business."
"People don't spend any more money on XYZ."
"Cold calling prospective clients is too hard and time-consuming."

"I was late because of the traffic."
And the list goes on.

Cut out excuses from your vocabulary, and start thinking in terms of solutions and possibilities. If sales are slower on a particular day of the week: the strategies you'll find in this book can literally double your business in the next 60 days. Keep on reading and taking notes. And get rid of excuses once and for all.

About details

In business, there is no such thing as a detail. I was brought up in the competitive tennis world and competed for years with and against the current cream of the crop of tennis players you see on television: Rafael Nadal, Novak Djokovic and Stan Wawrinka just to name a few. Tennis is such a fast-paced and tough sport that even the slightest detail can have a direct impact on a win or a loss. A win or a loss can mean winning or losing an entire championship. Winning or losing a championship can mean attracting or losing new sponsors who are willing write you a check for hundreds of thousands of dollars, if not millions. My coaches always told me to be maniacal and take control of every single detail I had control over: my rackets, my strings, my bag, my sleep, my food, my conditioning, etc. Tennis leaves no room for unprepared athletes. If you're average, you're out. If you're unprepared, you're out.

Why so detail-oriented, you ask? The answer is simple: when you arrive on a tennis court, you have no control over the level of form of your opponent, the crowd, the sun, the wind, or the referee giving bad calls because he had a bad day. The bottom-line is that there are so many things you don't have control over that you must be over-prepared for all the things that are actually in your control.

Maximum control = Maximum results

Smart and hard work pays off. That's what sports taught me. Remember, there's always someone who is more talented or more gifted than you. You can't control your competition's IQ, their plans or their talent. But one thing that you CAN control is the effort you put into YOU, your company, your business, your health and into anything you do.

I remember reading a book by Brad Gilbert (who coached Andre Agassi to success) called "Winning Ugly", which gets into the mindset of desiring control and mastery with anything controllable such as your preparation, equipment, sleep and training. There are so many things you can't control that it becomes vital to master everything you can control. You can't control the weather, the crowd, being sick, etc. This idea of work really stuck with me at a very early age. From then on, I always reminded myself: "the more prepared you are, the less you have to fear."

In business, the same rules apply. You have no power over the economy, your customers' health, their financial situation, the shipping company who ships out your stock and so on. That's why you absolutely must be perfect in all the areas you have control over:

- The efficiency of your marketing.
- How you attract new customers.
- The follow-up system you have in place when a prospect walks in the door.
- How you treat customers.
- Who you hire.
- The quality of the product you deliver.
- The referral system in place for getting new leads and recommendations.
- Etc.

When you collect the contact information of a prospect who has clearly mentioned his interest, don't leave things to luck and hope he buys. Create a process for following up in a systematic way to increase the likelihood of converting him into a buyer. Use different means of communication and delivery of your messages: email, direct mail, postcards, phone calls, etc. We'll get into the details of creating a killer follow-up sequence that will dramatically boost your conversions in the next few chapters.

My point for now is: life happens. Unexpected events come up. Being prepared and taking care of the small details will prevent you from bad surprises.

Think in solutions and possibilities

I strongly believe that there is (almost) always a way of going around things and solving issues. I was recently contacted by a business owner who had a very large email database (in the hundreds of thousands) of prospective prospects and customers who had been given 48 hours before getting his email software account shut down by his email marketing solution provider. His entire business model was based on contacting these prospects via email and offering them a range of products and services that could be instantly purchased online. The situation could have escalated into a bad blow for the entrepreneur. The main problem came from the fact that the email database was so large that many other email software providers could simply not offer any assistance in this case. Talk about not being able to contact your customer list!

A few days later, following my recommendation, everything was back into place, and the prospects were receiving the emails as if nothing had ever happened. What could have been a very big problem for the entrepreneur turned out to be a very small task that was managed and taken care of in less than a few days, without any hassle or long-term issues.
We live in a world of choice and possibility. Most likely, when you're facing a relatively big issue, it can be handled and taken care of if you shift your mind into thinking in possibilities instead of focusing on the problem itself.

Pilot procedures

When a pilot prepares for a flight, he always goes through preflight details making sure everything is ready and that the numbers are clear: weather conditions, recommended altitude, number of passengers, aircraft weight, fueling, distance to destination, crew condition, etc. All this gives him an accurate overview of the trip and helps him prepare for any potential issues he might encounter.

Every business owner needs to do the same. It is essential that you know your business numbers and metrics like the back of your hand. Here's an overview of some of the numbers you need to know and monitor on a daily/ weekly basis:

- How many people came to your store
- How many visitors came to your website
- How much time people spend on average in your store or on your website
- Daily/ weekly/ monthly gross revenue of the business
- Daily/ weekly/ monthly net profit of the business
- Average conversion rate from prospect into buyer
- Average revenue per customer
- Cost to acquire a new customer
- Average revenue per customer by time frame (30, 60, 90, 180, 365 days)
- Quality and quantity of the content published on your social media channels
- And so on.

You can have someone in your company keep track of all these numbers and submit them to you every week, or even every day. Specific software is available to track most of this, and you should make good use out of it. If you don't know the basic metrics of your business such as how much it costs you in advertising & marketing dollars to generate new customers and how much (and how soon) new customers spend with you buying your products and services, you're flying by the seat of your pants.

Speed of implementation

One of the key concepts I live by and try to communicate to our staff and people we do business with is what is called "the speed of implementation". Speed of implementation is a massive benefit that small businesses have in comparison to large multinational corporations that are relatively slow to implement new ideas because of the size and layers of management.

Businesses and entrepreneurs that execute faster and better than others and use the concept of speed of implementation often dominate their markets and gain enormous market share and competitive advantage. To benefit from it, the key is to bridge the gap between the moment you have an idea and the moment when you execute your idea.

One of my favorite entrepreneurs, Richard Branson, legendary founder of the Virgin empire (which includes brands such as Virgin Music, Virgin Airlines and Virgin America) shared a funny story at a conference I attended in Los Angeles which represents the essence of speed of implementation. One morning, British Airways (a direct competitor of Virgin Airlines) was having technical issues erecting the "London Eye" Ferris wheel, located along the Thames.

The world's press was waiting to see the Ferris wheel and Branson knew there was a huge opportunity to capitalize on the situation. He immediately scrambled a blimp and placed it just above the wheel bearing the slogan "BA can't get it up!!". This is what happens when marketing brilliance meets speed of implementation:

Source: Virgin.com

The press loved the event and Virgin got millions of dollars worth of free advertising all around the world. The beauty is that all this happened in a few hours morning. Branson could have found all the excuses in the world not to act quickly, but he seized the opportunity and generated free advertising as a result. Genius.

Speed of implementation is paramount, because movement always accomplishes more than meditation. The more we think and analyze things, the more it leads to self-doubt and to infamous "paralysis by analysis". Obviously, it is necessary to think and plan any project you'd like to execute, but don't make the mistake of perfecting your plan for years instead of executing TODAY and improving as you go.

I always advise entrepreneurs to execute quickly because that's when you see the results. Then, depending on the result, you can tweak your approach to improve the outcome. But being stuck in the "planning phase" is a scary thing. Put together a basic plan and execute on your ideas quickly to get some initial traction and improve as you go.

Imperfect action

Another concept that represents the essence of guerilla entrepreneurship 101 and that goes hand-in-hand with the speed of implementation concept which is so dear to my heart is what I call "imperfect action". Successful entrepreneurs usually act imperfectly and don't wait for months or years for the "perfect time" or the "perfect product" to launch a new business, a new offer or a new department within the company.

Nothing is perfect. The best-selling products are not perfect. Look at how many cars get recalled by major manufacturers like BMW or Toyota. Look at how many phones Apple recalled due to battery issues or when it knew that the iPhone 4 had antenna issues, yet launched the product and sold millions of units regardless.

Not a single product in the world is perfect. Perfection doesn't exist. If you're waiting to create the "perfect product" and launch it at the "perfect time", good luck. Call me when that works out for you.

Most wannabe entrepreneurs spend way too much time thinking, planning, ask thousands of questions to their relatives (who oftentimes have no clue and no experience in business) about the viability of a project without even launching it. And while those wannabe entrepreneurs wait for the perfect time and the perfect product, others are already selling in the marketplace and perfecting their execution. It's all about speed of implementation and speed to market.

When I launched my business at 17, I was lucky to implement the concept of imperfect action without even being aware of it. I guess that comes from my competitive background in pro sports: execution is key. And the day I launched my first business online, I remember that the site looked terrible, the marketing was very basic and the product was just "good". Not great, good. But the key was that I the product was in the marketplace and I could start seeing data about how the market would respond and tweak the offer and the business accordingly.

Instead of planning for months and months, we launched. Businesses that win are usually the ones who implement and execute quickly, even if things are not "perfect".

The concept also applies to health. People who are physically fit and healthy but who travel a lot can always come up with excuses like: "I'm jetlagged" or "there's no gym in my hotel". That's a loser mentality. Winners find solutions and workout in their rooms, go for a run outside or even in the hallway (yes, I've seen athletes run in the hallway to warm-up in the morning or after a long flight). There's always something that can be done, even if it's not "perfect" - but it's better than doing nothing at all.

To win in business, you must act MASSIVELY. The first project, product or offer might not be the best, but it will put you in the game. When you play tennis, nobody wins every game they play. I would estimate that during at least 50% of my games, I felt pain in my body: a sore back, a sore shoulder or tight calves from the previous game. The goal is just to show up and do the best you can. Not to wait for the body to feel perfect, because pro athletes rarely play without any pain.

The most successful entrepreneurs jump off cliffs and grow their wings on the way down. Ask any entrepreneur and they will have war stories about hectic times, but still pushed through and made things happen.

Success in business is often a reflection of the founder's personality and discipline. There is oftentimes a direct correlation between sometimes level of commitment, self-discipline and the results he gets in his business:

- Are you organized?
- Do you plan your projects and your business calendar?
- Do you have a clear vision to accomplish?
- Do you consistently execute on your vision?
- Can you sell and close deals?

Nothing moves without a sale

Whether you sell a tangible product or service or whether you're a politician looking to raise money for your next campaign, it is vital to understand that NOTHING moves without a sale. No sales means no revenue. No revenue means no cash flow. No cash flow means no way to pay your employees and a fast death in your business. To grow a business, you need to sell.

We live in a world that relies only and essentially through the exchange of value. You create an offer that provides value to the marketplace and the marketplace provides you with money. Selling is the exchange of money for a seller's product of service.

But it goes much deeper than that. Selling happens all the time, every day and everywhere in the world. Whether it's convincing your friends to buy you beers when they head to the supermarket before coming over to watch a game, convincing your spouse to go watch the movie YOU want to watch or getting your point across and motivating your employees on Monday morning, everything depends on sales.

If you're an entrepreneur and don't like marketing and sales, you need to get over that fear of selling and do everything you can to become a master salesman. If you don't know how to sell your products and services or sell your team into buying into your company culture and mission statement, you'll experience some pretty major disappointments sooner or later.

The notorious D.I.P.

One of the gifts of most entrepreneurs is usually being very creative and positive. Those are extremely useful and necessary traits, but they can also lead to unwanted surprises. In his book "The Dip", marketing guru Seth Godin details a very interesting concept that affects almost every person who starts any new venture.

When starting a new project, entrepreneurs are often filled with excitement and start pulling off all-nighters for their new project. At the beginning, progress and results usually come fast, but as time passes, they usually reach a "plateau", a period of stagnation. You might have experienced it in your business. Your revenue over the past 3 years might be pretty similar from year to year and you don't really know why the momentum seems gone and when you'll be able to reach the next level. As a result of the dip, you lose a bit of confidence and lower your expectations and your goals.

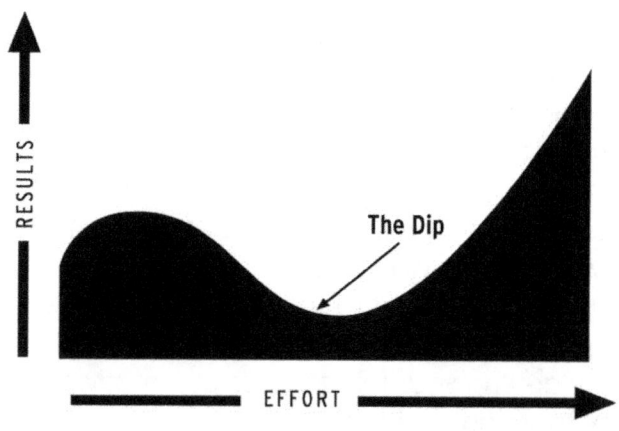

Source: « The Dip », Seth Godin, SethGodin.com

It's a phenomenon that happens to most entrepreneurs, but also to many athletes and people in other professions. And as they lower their goals and expectations, the business starts producing even less, because they've started accepting it and start settling into comfort.

Then comes the next "new" idea or project, and it's the same process all over again. Fast initial growth, stagnation and expectations lowered. And on goes the merry-go-round.

Don't make the mistake of looking for new "highs" and new excitement just because your current business isn't growing the way you want it too. Stay consistent, multiply your input and add new growth strategies and there's no reason why you can't increase your business by 50% to 500% in the next 12 months.

5

THE LITTLE-KNOWN SECRET OF EXPLODING PROFITS

Countless books have been written on the topic of business growth. Authors have presented ideas and theories about profit maximization and thousands of ways to develop and grow businesses. Unfortunately, many books leave out the absolute basic principles of true revenue enhancement and entrepreneurs are often left trying to figure out complex procedures.

Like in sports, it all boils down to mastering the basics. When things become too complex and out of hand, it is vital to come back to the basics of the game.

Have a look at tennis. When times get tough during a match, when the game is tied, the player who masters and executes the basics the best often ends up winning the game. What is the basic rule in tennis? Hitting the ball back in the court. That's it.

Not to hit winners, not to come up with an ingenious play that impresses the cameras and the fans, but simply to put the ball back into play. That's the basic rule of tennis: getting the ball back into play.

Yet so many players simply forget the basics when times become tough, when the pressure builds up, when the stakes are high and when the prize money comes into mind.

How does this relate to business? Well, the basic rule of business is to make more money than you are spending.

If you're spending $20 to acquire a new customer, you need to make more than $20 in lifetime customer value (and fast!) or your business won't last very long. Businesses become great businesses because they execute the basics better than the competition. In any situation you're facing in business, there are basically 3 ways to grow:

1. Increase the **number of customers.**
2. Increase the **size of each transaction**.
3. Increase the **number of repeat sales** from each customer.

The goal of this book is to give you strategies and tactics for each of these 3 ways. Even better: you'll quickly discover how to grow your business exponentially just by tweaking a few things in your current operation.

1. Increase the number of customers

Let's assume you're getting an average of 1000 new customers per year. One way to grow your income would be to increase your customers by 10%. That means you would be getting 1100 new customers per year.

For the sakes of the example, let's say you sell a product for $200.

1,000 customers/year X $200/sale = **$200,000 per year**

Now, let's assume you increase the number of customers by only 10%. This would give you:

$$1100 \text{ customers/year} \times \$200/\text{sale} = \textbf{\$220,000 per year}$$

You've just increased your annual income by $20,000 by just slightly increasing the number of new customers acquired. With all the new ways of customer acquisition you can implement, it is safe to say that you'll be capable of increasing your new customers by 10%-25%, especially by using the "new" ways of marketing and lead acquisition you'll be learning. Most of our clients do just that.

2. Increase the size of each first transaction

When a customer is buying a $200 product, he's in a buying state of mind and what I like to call "transaction mode". He just became a buyer, and has put his trust and commitment in your business. At that specific time, there's tremendous opportunity to increase the value and the size of the first transaction. This can be done by several ways that you'll be learning about further in this book. To make things short for now, let's say that you will be offering an additional product or service at the very moment when your customer is paying for the initial $50 transaction. This extra offer is known as an "upsell".

Some examples of upsells include:

- Selling an extended service contract as "maintenance"
- Suggesting a premium brand of alcohol when a brand is not specified by a customer.
- Suggesting that a customer purchase a larger hard drive when servicing his or her computer.
- Selling luxury options on a vehicle.
- Recommending that a customer purchase a more extensive car wash package.
- Asking the customer to "supersize" a meal at a fast food restaurant.
- Some sort of "premium" membership on a website.

After testing upsells in different markets and industries, we've found out that typically 10-25% of the customers who are offered a "better" alternative or an additional product as an upsell go ahead with the extra purchase. In some instances, we've managed to reach an 80% upsell rate, which means that 8 customers out of 10 took the higher (and most expensive) option when we offered it. We'll get more into depth about upsells and ways to increase the value of you customer's initial transaction later on in this book. To illustrate the power of upsells, let's continue with the same numbers we used earlier. Assuming you've increased your customer acquisition by 10% and you now have 1100 customers:

$$1100 \text{ customers/year} \times \$200/\text{sale} = \textbf{\$220,000 per year}$$

Let's see how this looks when you offer an upsell on a systematic basis. Let's say you're offering an "upsell" product/ service for $50, and only 10% of your customers take you up on the offer. That means 110 customers (10% of the initial 1100 customers) purchase the $50 upsell. This leaves you with an extra:

$$110 \text{ sales} \times \$50 = \textbf{\$5,500 per year}$$

Your business has just made $8,250 per year in what is literally "free money", with no additional customer acquisition or advertising costs. Keep in mind we used a very low number of conversion by using 15% for the above example. If the upsell is relevant to the product and is positioned as a good add-on benefit to the customer, your upsell numbers will likely be much higher. One of the keys to extreme business growth is to upsell the customer into some sort of monthly/ quarterly continuity program. It could be a monthly maintenance fee, a monthly added value service, some sort of "concierge" service, or a preferred "club" the customer can receive benefits from.

3. Increase the number of repeat sales

Once you've converted a prospect into a customer, you've converted a cold lead into a warm buyer, and that's when the buying relationship starts between your business and the buyer. As soon as that customer enters your database, you have all the information you need to offer him different buying opportunities in the upcoming weeks, months, and years. This will allow you to increase what is called the lifetime customer value of each customer, meaning how much money a customer will spend with you during the lifetime of his activity.

Being born and raised in Switzerland, skiing has always been a very popular sport. The lifetime value of a customer who likes to ski will easily be in the $3,000 to $10,000 range. He'll need to buy skis (which can cost up to a couple thousand dollars), boots (several hundred dollars), skiing outfits (several hundred dollars), gloves, etc. Furthermore, he'll probably refer a few of his friends or his family, who then will spend a few thousand dollars each.

You can quickly see that the lifetime customer value of a skier can be very interesting for the smart business owner, who can leverage different ways of getting referrals, upsells, and residual revenue programs.

Let's say you have a computer repair business. Once you've successfully repaired a customer's computer, you can then follow-up with him and offer him software at a discount, workshops to help him optimize the use of his computer, video games, and a yearly maintenance fee.

Let's go back to the example above and use the numbers for this example. Remember we now have 1,100 customers, and you have an upsell offer in place that upsells 15% of your customers to a premium offer.

Let's now assume you increase the number of repeat sales by only 10%.

$$\boxed{1100 \text{ transactions per year } X \ 1.1= \ \textbf{1,210 transactions per year}}$$

You've just made an extra 100 transactions simply by adding a decent follow-up system and keeping in touch with your customer base. Let's see how this matrix adds up when we add all 3 business-enhancing methods. Remember, they are:

1.   Increase the **number of customers.**
2.   Increase the **size of each transaction.**
3.   Increase the **number of repeat sales** from each customer.

Remember our original business figures:

1,000 customers/year X $200/sale = **$200,000 per year**

Here's how our business looks after a marketing face-lift...

10% increase in customers:

1100 customers/year X $200 = **$220,000 per year**

10% increase in size of transaction value with an upsell:

110 customers X $50 = **$5,500 extra per year**

10% increase in repeat sales at a $200 value per transaction:

110 new transactions X $200 = **$22,000 extra per year**

Our yearly business figures now look like this:

$220,000 + $5,500 + $22,000 = **$247,500**

A slight increase of 10% across the board increases your income by over 23.5 percent.

This is simple math and can be achieved time and time again if you create systems and automate processes in your current business. It doesn't matter what kind of product or service you sell. If you enhance just a little bit every aspect of what you do, the result will be exponential growth and there's no reason why any kind of business shouldn't be able to add at least 25% of revenue in a few short steps.

Let's go further and talk about prospects and clients, and what it takes to actually acquire a new customer. The process is simple at its very core.

It once again boils down to a 3-step plan:

1.   Lead generation
2.   Lead conversion
3.   Client fulfillment

Lead Generation

The primary goal of your business must be lead generation. With no leads, you have no prospects, no customers, no sales, and no income. And let me be blunt about something: if you "depend" on lead generation tactics that are out of your immediate control, your business is prone to unpredictable lows and you can't build a worthwhile business if you don't have an active lead generation system in place. Further in this book we'll talk in detail about the best lead generation techniques that will tremendously boost your business without costing you an arm and a leg.

You could use lead generation via direct mail, telemarketing, direct response advertising, joint ventures, referral marketing, internet marketing, and that's just to start with. There are literally thousands of ways to acquire new leads, but you absolutely need a structured and consistent way of attracting new prospects to your business.

Lead Conversion

Before you even have a good lead generation plan in place, it is crucial you have a solid lead conversion system in place. It could be your website, your staff who handles customers in your or your telephone staff. Either way, you need to have a system to turn leads into buyers. The internet offers several great ways of doing just that. One of the biggest mistakes business owners have made since the birth and the democratization of the internet is to think of their online presence as a mere display arcade with a simple contact information area. The internet is an incredible lead generation source, if and only if your website is properly optimized to act as a real lead conversion tool. When I work with a consulting client, one of the first things I look at is the client's website to see if the website is properly optimized for maximum efficiency. Most of the time - in 9 cases out of 10 - their website is a real mess and was designed by a company who had no idea of real life marketing, lead generation and lead conversion. When we talk about "lead conversion", we're talking about 3 different steps of conversions.

1. The first conversion is from "visitor" to "prospect". The goal of this step is to gather the contact information of the visitor in order to follow up with him by email, direct mail, or phone.
2. The second turns the "prospect" into a "customer".
3. The third state is to turn a "customer" into a "repeat customer".

The internet has made it possible to create a very systematic and accurate follow-up method, and this will allow you to turn your website visitors into customers all through the click of a button and via automated follow-up messages.

Client Fulfillment

Once you've converted a visitor into a customer, now comes the time of product fulfillment. You must deliver on your promise and satisfy the expectations of your new customer. We've talked about the importance and "lifetime customer value" earlier in this chapter and you now understand that repeat sales will dramatically improve your bottom line. Your goal in this third stage is to meet and exceed the customer's expectations. This will pay back ten-fold in the long-term and will result in you receiving referrals, repeat business, high customer loyalty, and enhances brand value.

If you don't like to personally interact with your buyers, that's not a problem.

You can have someone of your staff interact exclusively with new customers. Personally, I've always preferred focusing on creating systems in the businesses I'm involved in instead of directly interacting with customers. I always instruct my staff to personally call each and every new customer on the phone the very same day they purchased something from our site.

This did 4 things:

1.   Customer satisfaction went through the roof. Customers started writing blog posts online about my company and acting as a huge referral army without me having to ask them anything!

2.   It positioned us differently from the competition since we were giving each and every customer a call in the minutes or hours following their purchase.

3.   It reduced refunds dramatically by over 40%, by making customers feel less inclined to ask for a refund once they have personal contact with your business.

4.   It created a personal relationship with each buyer which increases the likelihood of repeat purchases in the future.

The business achieved all 4 things with a simple phone call. And I never made a single call myself. Don't underestimate the power of leveraging the relationship with each and every customer you have, as it can bring in more business than you can possibly handle.

The Bonus Factor

This is a great little technique that will considerably enhance the relationship between your business and your customers and will give you a powerful positioning spot in your marketplace. One of the goals in your business must be to satisfy your customers in a way that when they think of your business or your brand, the only thing they can say is "WOW". To achieve that, here's a neat tactic I've used in several of my businesses and that many of my clients have uses with great success. When selling a product/ service, list only the most decisive benefits and core elements of your offer.

The last time I bought a camera, the salesman used this very trick with great accuracy. The camera came with a small foam case to protect and store it which was part of the deal. After I paid over $400 for the camera, he came up to me and presented me with a small gift which was a small memory card that usually costs $40. This small complimentary gift probably cost the shop $5, which is something that almost all business owners can allow themselves to give away. That small gift earned my trust, and as a result I recommended that shop to several of my friends who were looking to buy cameras of their own. Each of my friends spent well over $300 each. From one small gift, they received thousands of dollars worth of referred customers. This is just a small example of a technique you can adapt in your own business to gain customers for life and massive referrals.

To understand why this works so efficiently, you must understand the psychology of a buyer. When a new prospect comes into your store and decides to purchase one of your products or services, he is taking a leap of faith in the unknown. He is parting from money he owns and is giving it to you in exchange for something he considers of value.

After the transaction takes place, the mind is in a state of euphoria, having achieved a high point during the whole process. At that moment, the new customer might start feeling remorse for his purchase. If you immediately follow-up with him and give him a coupon for future purchases, or even a free gift like I explained in the example above, you reassure the customers by showing and telling him it is perfectly "acceptable" and even "recommended" to do business with you.

Another element to consider is that when buying something, a customer has a set of expectations. When he buys a widget, he expects a widget or the benefit of the widget you are selling. If you raise his expectations by over-promising and under-delivering, you lose the trust customer's trust as well as his future business and referrals. When you over-promise and over-deliver, not only do you gain a customer for life but also endless referrals.

How the internet works

Now that you've seen the concept and the focus of geometric growth by simply increasing growth by 10% across the board, let's have a look at the internet basics and what it takes to bring in more prospects and customers using online methods.

Many books have been written about how the internet works and frankly, most of them are completely and utterly useless. They're written by people who have never actually used the internet in sales and marketing, much less started full-blown businesses. I'm here to tell you that all the internet jibber-jabber is not as complex as it seems, and should become a tremendous ally in the growth of your business if used the right way.

Let me start off by saying that establishing an online system for boosting your business boils down to 2 main elements:

1.   Traffic: the amount of visitors who come into contact with your business and enter your store, come to your web site, etc.
2.   Conversion: the systems you have in place to convert the visitors into leads and sales.

That's it.

Look at Amazon.com. They attract high amounts of traffic every single day and convert them into sales. That's their business model. That being said, in no way am I implying that the internet is easy for generating new leads and customers. Business owners have been hitting their heads against the wall for years, and many have simply let go of the idea that the internet is actually a viable source of lead generation and conversion.

6

ONCE UPON A TIME...

When a small business owner or entrepreneur reaches out to us for help, they often have a hard time expressing exactly what it is they need help with.

This is why it is important to understand that in order to reach new goals, you need to know what your current situation is. If an athlete wants to compete in an international high-level event, he has to know exactly where he stands in terms of physical fitness. Only then can he and his team come up with a realistic plan that can maximize his results.

Here are a set of questions you must be able to answer to assess your current strengths and weaknesses. This is a strategic analysis that is absolutely inevitable if you want your business to strive in the future.

Take the time to answer the following questions in detail as they will help you get a clear idea of where you presently are with your business. If you are unable to answer a particular question, you have a serious problem on your hands.

1. Why did I get into this business? (Motivation, goals, dreams, etc.)
2. When I started, how did I attract the first buyers? (Which processes, methods?)
3. Why did customers initially buy from me (or hire me)?
4. Why do customers buy from me (or hire me) now?
5. How did I generate the majority of customers who did business with me?
6. What sales or marketing efforts attracted the most customers?
7. Do I have a system to generate leads on a regular basis?
8. Do I test the marketing methods I use to get the best return on investment for my advertising dollars?
9. Where does the bulk of my customers come from? (City, state, country?)
10. Do I prefer to attract more new clients or get repeat business from my existing clients, and why?
11. How do I describe what my business does in less than 30 seconds? (What I sell, how I sell it, and who is my target market).
12. How efficient is my sales department? Am I closely monitoring each employee's results?
13. What is the lifetime value of the average customer who does business with me?
14. What is the biggest complaint customers have about my product/ service?
15. Who is my biggest competitor?
16. Do I have an advantage over him that I can use in my marketing and communication with prospects to convert them into buyers?
17. What do my customers really want? (be as specific as possible)
18. What is my Unique Selling Proposition ("USP")?
19. Is my image congruent with my marketing and my USP? If yes, how, and if no, why not?
20. Describe my marketing mix and what I use to generate sales and income in my business? (Postcard marketing,

direct mail, word of mouth, internet, newspaper ads, etc.)

21. What does it cost me to attract a new customer? (If I spend $500 and generate 5 customers, each customer would cost me $100)

22. What is my biggest source of new business and customers?

23. What is the biggest marketing challenge I'm currently facing in my business today? (be as specific as possible)

24. How could I increase conversions from prospect to customer by reducing the risk on the prospect's shoulders and make it easier for him to do business with me?

25. After generating a lead, do I have a system to follow-up with non-buyers and convert them into customers?

26. After the initial sale of a new customer, do I have a system in place to follow-up and increase the number of purchases of that new customer?

27. Do I have a system in place for capturing testimonials of satisfied clients?

28. Do I have a special area on my website where prospects can look at what past clients have to say about my product/ service?

29. Do I actively solicit referrals on a regular basis?

30. Have I ever tried to reactivate my former clients and un converted prospects? If not, why?

31. Does my business have a clear communication about what it is that we do?

32. Can I afford to break-even or even lose money on the first transaction with new customers?

33. Do I have any kind of guarantee to reassure prospects to do business with me? If not, why?

34. How do I capture the names and email addresses of people who come in contact with my business or who visit my website?

35. What is my average order, transaction value, and what can I do to increase it?

36. Do I know exactly what my staff is doing on a daily basis, and can I rearrange some workers to be more efficient at other jobs?

Take the time to answer all these questions, in writing if possible. It will give you a better understanding of where your business currently is.

The game plan

Once you have a clearer idea of where your business is currently standing, you need to assess the general strategy of your organization's activity. By this, I mean the overall plan, or the long-term strategy and goals for your business.

- What are the goals for the next few years?
- What are the revenue targets?
- What main lead generation and conversion strategies will you use?
- What difference do you want to make in the world?
- How do you want to grow your revenue and profits in the next 12-24 months?
- How many staff members do you need to accomplish those goals?
- Do you have an exit strategy?

Many entrepreneurs feel that they ended up in their business as a founder/ CEO by accident and have been treading water for years without having any clear sense of direction as to where they want their ship to head. Daily tasks become the main focus of the business and the entrepreneur can't focus on mapping out a plan to achieve the strategic growth he should be going after. It does take time to reflect on what it is exactly that you want from your business, how you want it to perform, what you want it to mean in the mind of your customers, what difference you want to make in the world, and what outcome you want to accomplish. Take a few minutes to ask yourself how you envision your business in the next few years, and what you plan to develop.

Strategies vs. Tactics

The word strategy derives from the Greek word "strategos", which translates to army leader. Essentially, strategy is the thinking aspect of planning a change, organizing something, or planning a war. Strategy lays out the goals that need to be accomplished and the ideas for achieving those goals. Strategy can be complex multi-layered plans for accomplishing objectives and may give consideration to tactics. Think of a strategy as being the "what" of your business.

Strategy is often confused with tactics, from the Greek "taktike". "Taktike" first Greek definition was "the military science that deals with the technique of deploying and directing troops, ships, and aircraft in effective maneuvers against an enemy". Think of a tactic as being the "how" in your business.

Example of a strategy: "Become the largest supplier of non-alcoholic beverages in our area by the next 24 months"

Tactics to reach that goal: "Market research to establish price points of our competition, and crafting offers that allow us to deliver more value and superior service to our clients and operate at higher margins, allowing us to increase profits at the same time."

The strategy is the final destination of your trip. The tactics consist in driving to the airport, booking a flight, and jumping in a taxi to reach your hotel room. Let's get back to your business. In order to achieve your goals in the next 2-5 years, what tactics will you use? What tools will you use to acquire new leads? What kind of website will you put up to attract new visitors? What internet marketing strategies will you implement to convert visitors into prospects?

What tactics will you use to accomplish the strategy?

If you haven't answered the questionnaire in this chapter, I urge you take a moment now to go through as many questions as possible. It will give you a much better understanding of your current situation, and will also help you focus on the rest of the main strategies and tactics in this book. Once you've gone through the questions, ask yourself how clear and defined your business strategy is, and what tactics you will be using to reach your strategic goals.

If you've had trouble answering one of the 36 questions in this chapter,

I recommend you apply for a 1-on-1 Business Breakthrough Session on MatthiasMazur.com/apply to discuss your situation and see how we can help you reach your goals.

7

YOUR CUSTOMER'S SHOE SIZE AND OTHER VITAL STATISTICS

In every industry, in every niche market, there is a customer waiting to be served by you. If you've been in business for any period of time, you've hopefully noticed that the customers you serve have several commonalities with each other. In this chapter, we're going to talk about one of the most important aspects of business and marketing, which is identifying the common traits of your current customer base in order to craft sales messages to attract new customers who share the same profile. We're going to talk about creating your customer avatar.

Let's have a look at what a detailed customer avatar sounds like if you're dealing in the sports equipment world. For the sakes of this example, we'll call our avatar Teddy. This is how you would describe a "Teddy":

> "My average customer is between 50 and 65 years old, he's retired or going into retirement. He earns an annual income of $40'000 - $70'000. He's married and is a family man. He's a sports lover and subscribes to at least 2 sports magazines that he gets every month at home. He likes to be outdoors and enjoys

trying new activities. He likes to workout at least twice a week. Generally, Teddy likes to play golf, tennis and likes to bike. He often hangs out with friends and colleagues and always likes to show his new moves and new equipment to the group. He likes to compete in regional championships every year. His biggest fears are to be unable to practice on a weekly basis, and he fears being left behind by his fellow colleagues and not being competitive. He spends between $3,000 - $5,000 per year on new sports gear and equipment. He's afraid that his family might think he's letting them down by being so passionately involved in sports. He sometimes gets upset at home when he discusses purchasing new sports equipment with his wife and feels that she doesn't support and understand his passion. His goal is to win the club championship to prove to himself and to others that he's competitive even though he's over 50 years old. Deep down, he wants to feel recognized and rewarded for all the effort he's put in his sports over the last 20 years."

That's a detailed customer avatar. You absolutely must be able to describe in detail about who your average customer is, not only in terms of where he's located geographically, but what he does in life, what his circle of influence is, what his biggest goals and deepest fears are. In every message you create, every time you communicate with Teddy, you must always connect with him and speak to Teddy's fears, goals, needs and wants. Answer the following questions in order to have a better understanding of how your average customer thinks, acts and behaves:

- What do your customers have in common?
- How old is your ideal customer?
- What is his annual income?
- What is his biggest objective in life?
- What is his biggest frustration?
- What is your customer embarrassed to admit, even to himself?
- What is the conversation going on in their head?
- Where does he feel misunderstood?

- What service can you provide to him to make his life easier and alleviate his frustrations?
- What other details can you gather about your ideal customer?

The reason why it's so important for you to have an extremely clear vision of who your ideal customer is because it's one of the biggest mistakes business owners make is to think that "everybody" is their customer.
It's like renting a big hot air balloon and posting it above your city. Yes, you'll be the talk of the town, but you haven't selected your target market at all. I call this the "shotgun approach".

This step alone is often the reason entrepreneurs see a 10% to 50% increase in revenue since they now know exactly which segment of the market to target.

Once you've created your customer avatar, the next step is to reflect on the type of relationship you currently have with your customers, as well as the relationship you ideally wish to have with them. Your goal is to create a deep relationship with your customers, or at least a relationship that is perceived to be deep.

Sometimes, clients tell me they attract 100-200 customers each and every day, and it can indeed become difficult to interact with hundreds of new customers on a daily basis. And this is where technology comes into play. You want your customers to perceive you as being the only real available option in the marketplace. You don't want to be seen as a commodity.

Even if you're selling a product that is not unique at all and that thousands of other businesses are selling, you still have to think about a way to position yourself differently from the competition. We'll get into positioning and finding your unique selling proposition in a later chapter.

For now, keep in mind that you MUST develop a strong relationship with every customer, and the way to do that is either by having your customer support team (or just do it yourself if you're a one-man shop) contact your new buyers, or by setting up automated systems using software tools that are readily available and that will take all the workload off your customer relationship people.

One of the best ways to create a deeper relationship with your customers is to have an active follow-up sequence once they've actually done their first transaction with you. You can use a tool called an autoresponder that will act as a personalized follow-up system and will help you bond with your customers at a much deeper level, giving you the ability to position yourself in the mind of your buyers as their only viable option, hence increasing the likelihood of getting repeat sales in the future and referrals.

The ultimate goal is to create a dialog between your avatar and your business. One of ways to do that is to demonstrate compassion towards your prospects and customers, and making them understand that you "get" what they are feeling, that you understand their emotions and actions. In every piece of communication you publish, be it on your website, in your follow-up series, on the phone, or in person, you have to make them understand that you experience the same emotion as them.

Whether you're selling to John Doe or a Fortune 500 CEO, you always need to connect with the customer on a deep emotional level. I'm not talking about dancing together and having drinks until 5 in the morning. I'm talking about putting yourself in their shoes and seeing life through their eyes. How does it feel to wake up every day in your customer's shoes?

Once you start thinking with their view of the world, you'll be able to craft sales messages that perfectly suit their desires. Something magic happens when a person feels understood. They "open" up. They trust you. And finally, they buy more often from you.

So ask yourself...

- What would make my prospect feel understood?
- How can I build trust with my prospects to increase the conversions into customers?

- What can I add to my current communication to make my customers feel more appreciated?

In any given market, you can almost always sum up your customers' frustrations in less than 20 seconds. What you'll find most of the time that there are only a few key frustrations that your target market may be experiencing. In the diet and weight-loss market, common frustrations that come up time and time again in market research data are one of the following:

- Can't fit into their clothes anymore.
- Scared of what family and friends think of them.
- Feel tired and exhausted when they use the stairs.
- Feel a certain level of shame when they look at themselves in the mirror.
- Are afraid to not attract people from the opposite sex.

Those are a few of the main frustrations that trigger customers to buy into diet programs. In every market, no matter what industry you're in and what product or service you sell, prospects and customers have common frustrations, either rational or irrational. It's your job to map out all the frustrations, dreams and desires of the people in your target market. Then and only then can you create appropriate ways of communicating with them on a deeper and more emotional level. Another question you must have a clear answer to by the end of this book is the following: why do people really buy from you?

People don't buy a drill for the sakes of having a power tool that they can hang in their living room. People buy a drill because they need a hole.

Why do some people buy Ferraris and others buy than Fiats? Both represent the same physical object, don't they? Of course they do, but they appeal to different segments of the automobile industry and use different emotional triggers in order to hook prospects and turn them into customers and repeat customers. Fiats will take you from place A to place B, the same way that Ferraris will. Why do people some people stay at the Four Seasons Hotel and others stay in Comfort Inns? Access to money is, of course, an element to the answer, but the decision is mainly triggered by an emotional response. Why do some people fly coach and others charter private jets? Again, owning or renting a jet appeals to another segment of the travel industry, a much smaller but more elite group of people.

From all the choices and options they have in the marketplace, why do your customers buy from you? Is it because they feel they're getting a better guarantee? Is it because they feel respected when they speak with your customer service team?

One of the keys to dramatically increasing your business in sales is to figure out what the top 3 frustrations of your marketplace are and create marketing materials that appeal to that segment of the market exclusively.

Don't make the costly mistake of thinking that everybody is a potential customer. If you appeal to everyone, you really appeal to no one. It's vital to understand that by casting a smaller net and targeting smaller niche markets, you'll eventually end up with more customers and profits than if you try to appeal to the mainstream market.

8

ONLINE DOMINATION

You've probably heard all the hype that surrounds the internet. The "Dot Com bubble", the thousands of venture capital funded startup companies that went bust in just a few short days at the beginning of the new millennium, and all sorts of other hyped up numbers are figures.

So the question is: can the internet really bring in more business to your current activities? Yes, it absolutely can, but only if you do it the right way. Let me be clear about something right from the start: putting up a simple website online is not nearly enough to generate any kind of return. Having a simple display website that isn't sales and marketing oriented and optimized will do you more harm than good.

A website simply isn't enough. Not when competitors are pouring in tens or even hundreds of thousands of dollars in advertising and brand awareness on Facebook and other social media platforms. What you need is an online marketing and sales system: a system that can generate traffic, leads, and customers online without you having to do any of the work yourself.

Having an internet sales and marketing system in place is absolutely vital to the survival of your business. With more and more people using the internet to find information about their future purchases, having an internet marketing sales system in place is a must if you want your business to survive and thrive in any economy.

Consider this: despite the economic climate, the average growth of e-commerce is around 25 % per year, and 81% of small businesses that have an online presence during last year's holiday season reached new customers, leading to an increase in sales and profitability according to a survey conducted by Harris Interactive. If this does not convince you to take your business online, here are 10 reasons why you need an internet marketing and sales presence:

1. Rise of the "New Economy"

The internet has created a new economy, which by its explosive growth and sheer size has already changed our perception of the traditional way of doing business. Companies like Amazon.com and eBay.com generate billions of dollars in sales and have successfully created new segments of old marketplaces using the internet, where just a few years ago traditional brick-and-mortar companies were kings. The good thing is that in order to be successful on the internet, you don't need to pour tens of millions of dollars to boost your sales. Many clients I've worked with who own small and mid-size businesses have managed to use the web to add tremendous growth in their daily operations. I predict that small and mid-size companies will be the main growth force of e-commerce in coming years.

2. The internet is a PERFECT place for business

In order to make a sale, you need visitors to come to your shop. On the internet, your shop could be only a click away from your prospective customers. With a good marketing system in place, your online store can have more buyers than you'll ever be able to attract in a regular brick-and-mortar shop

3. People surf the web before buying, especially locally

Whether you sell products or services, having an internet presence is more than a necessity, it's a means of survival. A recent study by Kelsey Group indicates that 97% of consumers use the internet to research products or services in their local area. And 90% of those people use search engines as a way of finding information before buying a product or service. The study also shows that people are starting the buying process online, which underlines the importance of having a well-optimized online system that can convert those visitors into customers in a matter of minutes. In fact, according to the study, consumers use 7.9 different media sources for research when looking for products and services. That speaks to the importance of being visible on a number of channels — your site, your blog, Google Maps, important industry sites, and so forth. That is why you need a high-converting sales-oriented website.

4. Better customer support

Customer retention is one of the key factors in growing your business. Going after new customers is great for future business, but having current customers increase the frequency of their purchases will make a dramatic boost in your profits. Having a good customer support system in place will lower your customer-acquisition costs too.

5. Information more easily available to customers

Just a few years ago, updating information about a product used to take days, if not weeks. And educating prospects about your products and services is a terrific way to convert leads into buyers. One of our agency clients is a watch brand based in Switzerland, and one of the strategies we started using is publishing regular articles and interviews online explaining the process of creating a watch. These watches are priced between $1,000 and $10,000 a piece, which makes it affordable for everyday people who are browsing online for Swiss watches.

By educating and providing in-depth information about your products and services to potential customers on your site as well as publishing those same articles on dozens of online article directories, you'll be able to establish the credibility of your brand and increase your reach and position in the search engines.

6. Cutting costs

New technologies allow you to take virtually any part of your business online, including product management, billing, shipping, and customer support. Streamlining these business processes through online systems will allow you to cut costs significantly in almost every aspect of your business.

7. Doing business 24/7

One of the biggest benefits of having an online marketing and sales system is that you'll be able to take orders 24 hours a day, 7 days a week. When your competition closes shop, you'll be able to attract hot leads to your website even during "down" peaks and slow times.

8. Traffic and exposure will grow over time

When you start publishing and marketing online, your website traffic and rankings in the search engines will grow over time. Although you will make immediate sales and gather highly targeted leads in the very first days and weeks following the implementation of your online presence, the number of visitors you'll attract will increase as time goes by, increasing your sales and bottom line for months and years to come, without having to "work" to maintain the flood of new business.

9. A global marketplace and more freedom for you

This is probably the single most extraordinary turning point in the history of business. Think about it: a small local shop in India can now sell products and ship to Paris. If a customer purchases one of your physical products, he can have it at home in a matter of days, if not hours. And if he's buying a digital product, he can download it within seconds following his purchase. Small local businesses can compete with huge established brands, and become leaders in tight niche markets, which was practically impossible even a few years ago. The internet presence will allow you to do business from anywhere in the world. This will open completely new avenues and give you tremendous freedom to explore new opportunities, new markets and new demographics to market to. Having a solid internet presence will also allow you to take more time away from the business, yet still be connected as much as needed.

10. Cheaper lead acquisition

Having an online marketing and sales system in place will allow you to cut costs, be open for business every day of the year, and attract more customers than you'll be able to handle. Plus, generating new customers using online methods will often be much cheaper than generating leads in the offline world.

To clear things up, let's have a look at the following questions...

- Can the internet help cut costs, generate new leads and customers, help develop new business opportunities and streamline operations? Undoubtedly, yes.

- Can an online marketing and sales system educate customers about your products and services, offer them practical information and support, extend trading hours, expand my markets, increase revenue and convert leads into customers using advanced follow-up methods? Right on.

Many entrepreneurs I meet and who have always been skeptical or late to adopt the internet as one their MAIN ways of generating new business are rushing to launch their online presence because they understand that having even an online presence is a necessity today. Many people who arrive in a new city and want to eat good food search for places on the internet. If a restaurant is not listed online, it just doesn't exist in the prospect's mind.

Another great benefit of the internet for the use of business is the un-limited space you can use to communicate your entire message for an unlimited period of time. It's way more affordable and economical than the Yellow Pages and allows you to personalize every aspect of it.

Lead conversion

Remember what we mentioned in an earlier chapter, online success is based upon 2 elements:

1. Traffic
2. Conversion

We'll get into traffic in a further chapter. Right now, let's talk about conversion. In the online world, "conversion" relates to the fact of converting a website visitor into (A) a sign-up to your mailing list, or (B) a customer. And one of the keys in marketing your business on the internet is to have an autoresponder system with which you can gather the contact information of visitors who come to your website. One of the keys to making your internet presence insanely profitable is to build your own database of email leads, or email "opt-ins", as we also refer to them.

If you haven't heard of the power of email lists, know that an email list will become one of the most important assets in your business.

Your email list will be worth far more than your staff, your offices, your machines and your products combined. Why? Simply because this email list will allow you to reach all your prospects and customers via email by the push of a button.

Launching a new product or service? Send an email, watch the sales come in.

Making a discounted offer for Valentines' day? Send an email, watch the sales come in.

Doing a joint venture with a strategic partner? Send an email, watch the sales come in.

You get the point. An email list is worth gold.

The power of an autoresponder

An autoresponder is a piece of software that allows you to do basically 3 main things:

1. Gather the contact information of people who visit your website.
2. Create a sequence of follow-up messages that are pre defined to be sent X number of days after a new person signs up.
3. Send out broadcast emails to the entire email list. Whether you have 10 or 10,000 subscribers, all subscribers receive your email within minutes of sending the message out.

To give you an example, one of my first businesses was selling online training courses to small business owners who wanted to generate more leads. We had approximately 100,000 people subscribed to the mailing list, meaning 100,000 people had submitted their email contact information one of my websites to sign up to my newsletter. Every time I created a new training program, I simply wrote an email (which took me about 10 minutes), loaded it into the autoresponder (which took about 2 minutes), and pressed the "send" button. In the next few minutes, all 100,000 subscribers received my email, and I started seeing sales coming in literally minutes after sending out the email. It's as simple as that, and it proves case and point the power of an autoresponder. We'll talk more in detail about autoresponders in a later chapter.

So you need steady lead flow. You need to be able to generate sustainable and steady leads. If you can't generate leads on a steady and on-going basis, you're going to have a lot of trouble creating a sustainable business because you can't rely on word-of-mouth, otherwise you're always at the mercy of the outside world and what other people say – or don't say – about you.

And the second thing you need is to have a means of converting leads into customers, which is what I call having a "Conversion Engine". You need to have a conversion engine that converts leads into buyers. This must be a predictable and scalable system and if you don't know how to convert leads into sales, you MUST have a system that does all the heavy lifting for you, otherwise you will lose your best prospects to your competitors.

The worst number

One of the keys to grow your business is the fact of never depend on only one source of customer acquisition, one source of income or one key employee. What happens when that source dries up or if that key person quits?

That kind of situation happened a few years ago when thousands of advertisers got banned by Google, lost their Google advertising account and were literally unable to advertise on the platform.

Literally overnight, hundreds of thousands of stores and websites that used to pay Google to display advertising to generate leads and sales were wiped out without any chance of coming back. This caused many businesses to go bankrupt because most of them only relied on ONE source of lead-generation. The lesson is that you should always have several sources of traffic. Always have several sourced of income. Always have several ways to convert prospects into customers. Always have several employees you can rely on if someone quits.

The worst number in business is "1". If you rely on one source of traffic, one big customer, one product to sell, a single sales process or a single technology, it's like relying on a one-legged table. What happens when it breaks?

9

BUILDING YOUR OWN TRIBE

In this chapter, we'll talk about one of the best ways to capture your prospects information and convert more prospects into lifelong and loyal customers.

This technique consists in building your own database – your own tribe – of prospects that interact with your business. Before going into detail, here's why it is very important to begin to build a list of prospects and customers.

Your list is your livelihood

Having your own list of prospects and customers you can contact by phone, email, social media or physical mail gives you enormous leverage and allows you to promote anything you want, anytime you want to.

This will allow you to generate windfalls of new sales at the push of a button by emailing them educational information, special offers and interesting content to start building a relationship with people who are interested in your solutions.

If you're not currently collecting the contact information of ALL prospects and customers who come into your store or your website, you're leaving insane amounts of money on the table. Numerous marketing studies have shown time and time again that it usually takes 5 to 10 touches for a prospect to even consider buying from you. These touches can be email contacts, direct mail, phone conversations or webinar presentations. The bottom line is: you MUST have a way to contact your prospects directly to start the nurturing and sales process.

The money is in the list

When you collect the contact information of your prospects and customers, you start building one of the most important assets in your business: your prospect and customer list.

Business owners wrongfully believe that the most important asset in their business is their location, the quality of their product or their employees, but by experience building multi-million dollar businesses over the last 10 years and helping clients generate tens of millions of dollars in extra revenue, I can safely say that the most important asset is your database: your list of prospects and customers.

If your office burns down, your staff quits overnight or your sites get hacked, you can still survive and generate revenue by emailing your database with an offer and generate sales within minutes. That's the power of having a list.

Every business must have a list

Whether you have a restaurant, a hair salon, a clothing or pastry store, a car dealership or an online business, it is essential to build your list leads and customers.If you don't have one yet, the beauty is that you can start building it today. You don't need to have any special expertise or experience other than a pen and paper.

In a later chapter, I'll share some of the tools and the technology we use to automate the entire process. For now, keep in mind that each passing day where you don't compile the contact information people who reach out to your business or your website is a lost day.

10

MONEY LOVES SPEED

As you now know, the rise of new technology and the internet makes it easier for smaller companies to be able to compete with Fortune 500 companies who spend millions on branding and advertising. Another key factor small businesses can benefit from hugely is speed. Most large corporate businesses have layers upon layers of management staff and resources, making it very difficult for fast decision-making. New strategies and tactics are often put aside and can't be used effectively simply because implementing changes takes weeks, if not months. And this is one of the most vital advantages small businesses have and would be foolish not to use.

In your organization, if you want to be able to challenge the big dogs and be on the forefront of sales and profits in your market, you absolutely make speed of implementation one of your main ways of acting and doing business on a daily basis. If you're slow to implement a new strategy or tactic, you can be sure that one of your competitors soon will. In order to use speed of implementation effectively, you need to bridge the gap between the moment you have an idea and the time at which you implement it in your business. The less time you leave between idea generation and idea implantation, the faster you'll gather results and be able to judge if a new tactic or strategy is worth implementing on a bigger scale in your business.

I travel quite a lot to speak and deliver keynotes at events and I sometimes run into the same people from conference to conference. Over the course of the year, you could clearly distinguish two groups of people.

The first group is filled with people who think, plan, think, plan, and think, without implementing a single bit of strategy in their businesses. I would meet someone at some point and run into the same person a few months later, and he'd always come up with a new excuse for not having achieved his desired level of growth. Unfortunately, I estimate that over 90% of the people and entrepreneurs never get around to implementing what they learn and the strategies or tactics they discover.

On the other hand, there is a small percentage of people who are speedy implementers. As soon as they learn about a new way of increasing their business, they immediately put it to action. It could be as simple as mapping out a plan to systemize the way of getting referrals from current happy customers. Remember the numbers we analyzed at the beginning of the book and remember that growth is always geometric when you implement changes in several different areas of your business. If you implement a quick plan to attract 10 or 20 percent of new leads in your funnel and another plan to add an upsell to your current transactions, you can increase your business geometrically in a short amount of time. It all depends on how fast you implement the arsenal of strategies and tactics we lay out for you.

When I ran my seminar business in the French market teaching people how to build an online business to fuel their passion and get their message out to the world, I estimate that approximately 5 percent of the attendees went home and actually implemented the strategies we taught. And those people were the ones who generated enough money to be able to quit their full-time job and make money from home. The other 95% of the people also took notes, were excited, but never implemented the plan in its entirety, and unfortunately always came up with excuses for not taking action on what they'd learnt during the workshop or seminar.

Speed of implementation is one of the underground shortcuts to transforming your business and dominating your competition.

Remove the time between idea and action, and you win.

It's the magic sauce that makes small business be able to compete with massive organizations who can't act fast since they have too many people to go through to simply have an idea or new plan accepted.

Jack Welch, the legendary CEO of General Electric, was a fanatic and big advocate of the need for speed in business. When he took over GE, he took over a huge, slow-moving organization that couldn't perform quickly and couldn't shift strategies fast enough to meet the market's demands. He talked a lot about the "penalty for hesitation in the marketplace", and the reality is that things have seriously changed in the last 10-20 years since he brought speed as being a vital component in business.

The truth is that in today's day and age, things have gotten even more competitive than when Mr. Welch was running GE. Everybody I meet in the business world often has dozens of fascinating and great ideas. Many of them are bright executives, business owners, entrepreneurs, managers, writers, speakers, freelancers, marketers or publishers. Having an idea is great, but nothing will be useful if you don't make a commitment and get things done.

Every minute of every day, your competition is thinking of ways to increase the market reach and their profits. They might be better funded than you, have a better network of contacts than you or have a bigger sales force they can make use of. The main question you have to ask yourself is: will somebody else get to completion first or will I be the one to roll out a new product, market to a new segment or use a new lead generation mechanism before them?

Another element to consider is that ideas and realizations often lose their power over time. Ideas generate excitement and enthusiasm once they emerge but dissipate over time. That's why it's vitally important to execute and put plans in motion as soon as they surface rather than over-thinking them and letting them sleep in your notebook. My attitude is that you can always stop a project once it's started, but completing a project not started is pretty much impossible.

Napoleon Hill, author of "Think and Grow Rich", once said that "thoughts are things". I disagree. Most thoughts are clouds, they come and go, and before long, you can't remember how exactly they came up and how they can help you improve your business. The truth is that most projects never exit the mind, and never even get started. Thoughts and ideas have the POTENTIAL to be great and to change the world IF they are implemented decisively. I'm happy to say that after some time of pounding this concept in our client's minds', even the most stubborn have started to understand and implement it. I'm very critical of the value of ideas and usually very weary of people who come up to me with "new ideas"... but who haven't implemented or executed the previous 10 ideas they had. Pardon my French, but to put it bluntly:

Ideas are s***. Execution is key.

Ultimately, the most driven entrepreneurs understand the importance of speed of implementation. Like the late Jack Welch obsessively hammered it to his entire workforce that "Speed is EVERYTHING. It is THE indispensable ingredient in competitiveness."

He was also an advocate of simplicity in communication, and would often blow up at meetings when things got slower and colleagues couldn't get to the point fast enough or in a clear way for everyone to understand. He would routinely terminate 10 to 20 percent of the workforce, and only keep the most productive and fast-working elements of his organization. Furthermore, he never hesitated to launch several projects at the same time rather than waiting for results and implementing strategies one by one. This is one of the key things we bring to the attention of our consulting clients. Implementing 5 new ideas will bring you tremendous geometric growth immediately rather than waiting for one strategy to show its results. Remember: businesses don't achieve remarkable growth by doing regular things in a step-by-step way.

When Steve Jobs came back to Apple in 1996, he immediately took decisive and simultaneous steps of getting rid of unproductive work teams, as well as trimming the total number of projects, firing lazy workers, and revamping the product line and general strategy for the next few years. Had he taken a step-by-step approach, Apple would have crashed into the ground since the company was losing money every day and was just months away from a declaring bankruptcy. Both Jack Welch and Steve Jobs tried to infuse the "small-business soul" into their massive organizations, so it could be run like a corner grocery store. Fewer unproductive workers and layers of management combined with lower costs and useless bureaucracy can do wonders for any company.

Shortcuts are Essential

Another skill you need to develop as a business owner is to always recognize and take the shortest path possible between A and B. Shortcuts will allow you to accelerate the growth in your daily tasks and allow your revenue and profits to grow faster than if you use the concept of doing everything alone and trying to figure out everything by yourself. Michael Gerber, author of "The E-Myth", underlines the importance of spending time working ON your business rather than IN your business.

The concept can be quite difficult to grasp and implement even for established entrepreneurs and business owners, but it's the only way to achieve tremendous exponential growth. So, what's the difference between working on your business rather than in your business? Well, consider the activities that you encounter on a daily basis.

Do you spend more time answering to daily tasks or on creating systems so your business can run by itself in the near future? What would happen if you took a step out of your business for a week or two – would your business be able to run and grow even when you're not present and actively working?

Stepping out of your business and reflecting on what the general strategy is, what the tactics are, what your daily operations look like are something you absolutely need to do if you want to make your business run more efficiently. Sometimes, working with someone who is outside of your business can give you tremendous insights that you may never have thought of by yourself. Taking a shortcut in business is the reason why sharp business owners are able to build big profit-producing companies in a very short amount of time: they don't mind making use of someone with an outside perspective, knowing that a fresh pair eyes always sees things in a different way.

Multi-front Motion

I mentioned the importance of taking multiple simultaneous actions in your business in order to achieve geometric growth in the shortest amount of time possible. Remember what Steve Jobs when Apple brought him back as interim CEO in 1996: multiple changes at multiple levels. Not only in product development, but also in management, staffing, planning, execution, and team organization.

When ZuraMedia takes on a new client, there are often several areas that need to be taken care of at the same time. The first thing we do is find out where the holes are in his business, and put together a plan to plug in those holes so all the waste is removed and the business can stop treading water. Simultaneously (and depending on the scope of the project and our availability), we might spend time improving their social media presence (or even totally creating it from scratch depending on how bad it is) to observe what changes can be brought to the workforce to make it perform at a higher level. If the client needs leads and sales, we'll implement a heavy-hitting online lead generation strategy.

But most of the time, clients come to us asking for "more visibility, customers and profits", because that's where our past clients have had a tremendous amount of success after implementing just a few of our recommendations.

And while we're doing that, we push the client to maximize the revenue from all sources possible, which altogether adds substantial increases in profits at very little – if any – cost.

Always be active

I'm always amazed by the number of business owners who work less than their own employees. Take the example of a restaurant owner. When I see an empty restaurant, I always see a lazy business owner who's afraid of getting out in the world and making things happen. There are a ton of things that business owner can do to attract new business: giving out flyers, creating partnerships with strategic joint venture partners, implementing a referral system to gather referrals from past customers, or giving a discount coupon to past customers to reactivate and attract new business.

There, I just mentioned several ways a restaurant owner can attract business in a matter of days, not years. Restaurant owners often rely on word of mouth to get new customers in the door. That's all fine and well until you realize that very few customers actually recommend a business or a restaurant from their own good will. In the majority of cases, you have to actively solicit referrals and word of mouth advertising.

Relying on past customers to promote your restaurant just because they ate a good dish is foolish and careless. If you use just half of the strategies and tactics you'll discover in this book, you'll never have to worry about getting new customers again, and you'll be flooded with new business coming your way.

But once again: you have to actively market your business. Expecting people outside your organization to market your business for you without any incentive is just naïve and will quickly land you in bankruptcy court. I hear business owners talking about the bad economy and complain that times are hard. And they almost use the economy as an excuse for not being active and spending at least a few hours every day setting up systems to attract new customers.

Perfecting your Priorities

In 1906, Italian economist Vilfredo Pareto created a mathematical formula to describe the unequal distribution of wealth in his country, noticing that 20% of the people owned 80% of the wealth. After Pareto made his observation and created his formula, many others observed similar phe nomena in their own areas of expertise. A Quality Management pioneer, Juran, working at the time in the United States in the 1930s and 1940s recognized a universal principle he called the "vital few and trivial many" and started writing about it in his works. As a result, Juran's observation of the "vital few and trivial many", the principle that 20 percent of something always are responsible for 80 percent of the results, became known as "Pareto's Principle" or the "80/20 Rule".

The 80/20 Rule means that in any given situation, a few (20%) are vital and many (80%) are trivial. In Pareto's case it meant 20% of the people owned 80% of the wealth. In Juran's initial work, he identified 20% of the defects causing 80% of the problems. Project managers know that 20% of the work (the first 10% and the last 10%) consume 80% of your time and resources. You can apply the 80/20 Rule to almost anything, from the science of management to business.

For example, 80% of your sales will come from 20% of your sales staff, and 20% of your staff will cause 80% of your problems, but another 20% of your staff will provide 80% of your production. It works both ways.

From my experience, I actually think it's more 95/5. Meaning that 5% of your daily activities generate 95% of the results you get.

The value of the theory for you is to focus on the 5% that bring in 95% of the results. Of the things you do during your business on a day-to-day basis, only 5% really matter and will generate additional sales and new customers. Those 5% produce 95% of your results. Take a moment and ask yourself what processes generate the bulk of your revenue, and think about how you can increase and leverage the effort you put in to attract new business.

It's not enough to just "work smart". You need to work smart on the RIGHT things. To take matters even further, I have noticed instances where the "95/5" principle was even more relevant, meaning that 95% of the results and sales come from only 5% of the work done.

11

POWER POSITIONING

I want to start this chapter by asking you a very powerful question:

How UNIQUE are you?

In business, standing out more favorably in the prospect's or client's eyes is a big reason why customers will choose YOU over your competitor. The more clearly you communicate what makes you the better choice, the more often they'll choose you over your competition. You need to create maximum real and perceived advantage in your customers' mind at all times. In this chapter, you'll learn to develop a "Unique Selling Proposition" that sets your business apart from your competition and attracts customers by offering them a powerful (and or perceived) and unique benefit.

Let's try to answer this honest question: how can you elevate yourself or your business to a position of remarkable superiority over your competition, and why should people decide to do business with you rather than your competition?

In order to stand above the crowded marketplace, your company must offer your prospect or customers one or more unique and distinctive benefits that are clearly different and more attractive than what your competitors are doing. If you don't, people have no motivation to do business with you instead of your competition.

Identify and understand what your company can do or can start doing for your customers that will provide them with a greater benefit than your competition. When Wal-Mart labels itself as "THE Low Price Leader," it's made a powerful USP that takes a strong position in the customer's mind.

This is called the Unique Selling Proposition (USP). Your Unique Selling Proposition is that distinct, appealing idea that sets your business apart from the rest of the competition out there.

When you identify what that distinct advantage is, you must integrate it into all your promotional, marketing, advertising and selling operations. This includes for example what you or your salespeople do and say, plus all the collateral material you use, the brochures, the sales letters, advertising and what not. Stating your USP over and over again is not enough – you need to constantly demonstrate it. You need to live it, and live up to it. That means that whatever your USP stands for, you have to do at all times.

A USP is different depending on each company and each market it operates in. Before creating your own USP, I recommend you have a look at what your competitors are using as part of their USP in their marketing and sales communication.

Be warned: developing, identifying, and incorporating a strong and personal USP into everything you do in your business can be challenging. But the rewards will be well worth the time. It will give you the differentiation, the distinction and the advantage against everyone in your marketplace. So, don't rush it.

Here's a tip to put you on the path to finding your own USP: think of what you do, and think about what your competitors do, or don't do, and how you could do it differently or better.

When we work with clients, we often find that most entrepreneurs have a hard time coming up with a distinctive USP. When you ask an entrepreneur to articulate his USP clearly and concisely in one paragraph or less, most have no answer. Most of them have no USP, only a "me too" ordinary and nondescript business that counts upon hope and luck to attract new customers. They promise no great value, benefit, or service – just "buy from us" for no justifiable reason.

Your USP may express the "theme" of your business, product, or service.

Think: Which coffee is "mountain grown"? Which water is "untouched by man"?

Here's a list of more USPs to get your mind buzzing with ideas:

"You get fresh, hot pizza delivered to your door in 30 minutes or less - or it's free."
- Domino's Pizza

"When your package absolutely, positively has to get there overnight"
- FedEx

"The King of Pop"
- Michael Jackson

"The World's Favorite Airline"
- British Airways

"It's the real thing"
- Coca-Cola

"Diamonds are forever"
- DeBeers

"The ultimate driving machine"
- BMW

"The best a man can get"
- Gillette

"We're Number Two. We Try Harder."
- Avis

These examples show that a USP can be based on just about anything: price, product ingredient, positioning. Some USPs based on size, scent, celebrity endorsement, location, hours of operation, and so on. As you focus on creating a new USP for your business, you'll start thinking of the USPs used by other businesses and will start getting more and more ideas for yourself.

To sharpen your marketing mind, you need to become USP-sensitive and ask these questions about every business, product, and service you encounter in your daily life:

- Does this business have a USP?
- If not, can I think of one for it?
- If so, is there a way I can think of to improve it?
- Is there any idea here I can swipe for my own use?

Your entire marketing and operational success should be built upon your Unique Selling Proposition.

It's no surprise that most businesses lacking a USP merely get by, and most of them fail quickly and miserably. What's even stranger is that business owners couldn't care less and consequently only get a small share of potential business.

It's foolish to operate any business without carefully crafting a clear, strong and compelling USP into the personality of your business's daily existence. The good news is that you'll be among the elite of all business professionals who enjoy much more success than those without one.

They have a profound advantage over all their competitors. How do you pick a great USP? The first thing you must do is identify which needs are going unfulfilled within your marketplace. It could be any of the following:

- A broad selection.
- Big discounts.
- Advice and assistance.
- Convenience (i.e. location, fully stocked shelves, immediate delivery).
- Top-of-the-line products or services.
- Speedy service.
- Services above and beyond the basics
- A longer and more comprehensive warranty or guarantee than the norm.

The Domino's effect

A brilliant USP was one created by Tom Monaghan, founder of Domino's Pizza. At the time Domino's came to market in the 1960s, not only were there already dominant pizza brands in existence, but pizza delivery was not a novelty. The ultimate question to answer was once again: how can you make your potential customers understand why you are different, both logically and emotionally?

Domino's Pizza's came up with this now legendary USP: "You get fresh, hot pizza delivered to your door in 30 minutes or less -- or it's free." The concept of a fast delivery service may be commonplace in the pizza business now, but when it was first introduced by Domino's Pizza, it was a mark of genius.

Let's have a deeper look at powerful these few words are, and how they built a billion-dollar business simply by positioning Domino's as the leader in the pizza delivery market.

"Fresh": feature. "I don't want old, stale pizza, but I want it fresh."

"Hot": feature. It can be eaten and enjoyed immediately. It arrives warm and doesn't need to be warmed up in the oven.

"Pizza": what you are getting, it's not a vague "meal" or "hunger satisfied."

"Delivered to your door": benefit. The convenience of the service which appeals to anyone who doesn't want to make any effort, offering a hands-free solution.

"In 30 minutes or less": a specific promise. Domino's doesn't say "delivered as soon as we can" but within 30 minutes so within 31 minutes you can be eating pizza.

"Or it's free": the guarantee. A lot of messages packed into a very short sentence, but it powered Domino's to the number 1 position in the pizza market in the US.

You can see how the entire sentence makes sense logically and emotionally. You can also see what the Domino's USP doesn't say. The USP does not say "the best pizza money can buy". It doesn't even claim to be delicious - just hot and fresh. It doesn't claim to be healthy or low in calories and carbohydrates. But for someone who is hungry, wants to eat but can't be bothered to cook or go out, it is compelling.

How a strange USP boosted beer sales
In 1919, a business consultant was hired by Schlitz beer to create an ad that would save the company. The company was nearly bankrupt: beer sales were miserable and their market share was sinking to frightening depths.

The consultant insisted on making the trip to Wisconsin to visit the brewery. He started looking for the company's hidden assets: he wanted to know what could make their beer appear remarkable and stand out from others. It was impossible to tell an engaging story in advertisements without knowing every detail of how the product was made. The consultant was looking for an inspiring 'hook' which would transform the market's perception of the brand.

He was amazed at what he found. The beer executives saw nothing exceptional in their brewing methods since they'd lived with them every day for as long as they could remember.

They saw nothing different in how their deep drilled wells gave the purest water; nothing different in how their glass-enclosed rooms stopped contaminants; nothing different in how their bottles were cleaned, re-cleaned, and sanitized a dozen times; and nothing different in the kind of yeast they used the make the product.

"That's amazing!" the consultant said. "Why haven't your advertising people told the world about this truly remarkable brewing process?"

The Schlitz executives shrugged and said "Our competitors use virtually the same process for their beer too"

"Maybe..." replied the consultant "but no-one has told the market. We'll be the first ones. The beer drinking public will see Schlitz beer's offering as something truly remarkable!"

Just 6 months later, Schlitz became the #1 selling beer brand in the country.

With a fresh pair of eyes, the consultant was able to see something that the company executives thought mundane and unremarkable. Not even its own marketing department had picked up on it. Despite all the time and effort that went into the creation of the product, nothing was as powerful as the story and the offer stated by telling the entire process to the consumer market. That's an example of how you can position a product's perception without having to change anything in the actual product.

The Secret Power of Storytelling
The company was able to engage the market with a wonderful story explaining how Schlitz cared about the process of product creation and the market reciprocated immediately. They understood Schlitz's value proposition and uniqueness. This example should give you a major insight as to how you can integrate storytelling into your marketing, and how

powerful it can be to educate the marketplace about your company's uniqueness (or perceived uniqueness).

Be clear and concise

Before you can integrate and communicate your chosen USP through various marketing channels, you need to concentrate and articulate it clearly, concisely and with impact. Brainstorm until you can articulate it in one crystal-clear, compelling, appealing paragraph or less.

Your USP is the core around which you build your company and brand's success, fame, and wealth. That is why it's crucial that you be able to state it clearly. If you can't state it, your prospects won't understand it. Whenever a prospect needs the type of product or service you provide, your USP should bring you and your company immediately to mind as their number one and only alternative. Clearly conveying the USP through your marketing and business will increase your chances of getting to the top of the customer's mind and will give you a competitive edge over the rest of the market. You must boil down your USP to its bare essence and communicate the main benefit(s) to the prospective customer.

Take a few moments to write down a few ideas for your new USP. At the beginning, you may have some trouble expressing it tightly and specifically. It may take a few paragraphs or more, but it will get your creative juices flowing. Then, edit away the generalities and focus on a concise and clear declaration that is the most compelling statement a prospect could hear from you. Delete the excess wording until you have a clearly defined Unique Selling Proposition that a client or prospect can immediately grasp.

By now you should have a good idea about how to craft a powerful USP, and you should obsessively integrate it into the headline and message of every ad and marketing piece you run or send out. But integrating your USP into just your ads and mailing pieces is not enough. You must integrate it into every form of your marketing, and live it day by day.

When you or your salespeople are in direct contact with prospects or customers, everything you say should reinforce your USP. You should explain the USP to the client in a clear and concise way. Throughout the sales pitch, your sales team should refer to the USP benefits to the end buyer. Be clear and passionate about your USP. Be sure you and everyone on your team can clearly express your USP and explain to a prospect what sets you apart from your competition.

Citing examples of how past customers have benefited from your USP is also a powerful way of demonstrating your USP at work. One of the many benefits of a USP is that it can rejuvenate old companies and products and create a brand new image of your business, product or service in a matter of weeks, all while boosting your sales and profits.

Marketing by Values

There's a famous quote in marketing that goes:

"If you stand for nothing, you'll fall for anything."

Just about anything – bad economic times, increased competition — can bring down a business that doesn't incorporate and communicate strong values. Although I rarely (if ever) eat in fast food restaurants, the fast food industry uses marketing brilliantly and McDonald's is without doubt one of the best examples. The McDonald's empire was built on Ray Kroc's fanatical commitment to consistency — the idea that a product in a Los Angeles branch should be identical to one on the other side of the country or even in a separate continent. The result is that every time you go to McDonald's, you know what to expect and you'll get. Other franchises have since then adopted a similar way of doing things in order to emulate the Golden Arch company's success.

Another perfect example of a company literally tearing through the competition through a commitment to values is FedEx. Federal Express invented, built, and dominated an industry because of a commitment to on-time, as promised delivery.

The key when developing your USP is to remember this: you will not appeal to everybody. In fact, most USPs are designed to appeal only to spe cific segments of a market. If you like competition and a good challenge, you can actually compete against yourself by adopting different USPs and developing different divisions of your business which complement each one another. For example, you could develop an exclusive and high-end sales operation that caters to the affluent and wealthy and go after the low-volume, high-profit end of your market, while developing a high-volume sales department to go after your mass market. In that way, you serve all the parts of the market, without diminishing the value of your high-end brand. The bottom-line is: develop a USP and integrate it to all parts of your business and communication. It can help you dominate an entire industry for decades.

Power Positioning

In their 1981 book, "Positioning: The Battle for your Mind", Al Ries and Jack Trout brought to light the importance of positioning and how it is used as a communication tool to reach target customers in a crowded marketplace. Once the concept became more familiar among marketers and sales people, advertising agencies began to develop positioning slogans for their clients and positioning became a key aspect of marketing and communicating the benefit to the prospective buyer.

Here are a few key concepts that will help you understand how to power position your business to become the main choice in your prospects' and customers' mind.

While positioning begins with a product, the concept is about positioning that product in the mind of the prospective customer. Given the current state of noise in the marketplace your prospects are facing in this day and age, and because we're all getting bombarded with a continuous stream of advertising, prospects have become numb to "me-too" marketing, and it's your responsibility to find something to break through the noise and capture the attention of your target market.

It is difficult to change a prospect's impression once it is formed. Prospects cope with information overload by oversimplifying and are likely to shut out anything inconsistent with their knowledge and experience. In an over-crowded advertising environment, you should present a simpli fied message and make that message consistent with what the consumer already believes by focusing on his perceptions rather than on the reality of the product. This is absolutely vital if your goal is to increase your share in the market.

Getting into the Customer's Mind

The easiest way of getting into a prospect's mind is to be FIRST in a category. It is very easy to remember who is first, more difficult to remember who is second, and even harder to remember who are third or fourth in a market space. Even if the second entrant offers a better product, the first mover has a large advantage that is difficult to overcome.

However, you can still thrive even if you're not number 1 in your market. By using the same storytelling concept we discussed earlier that was used by Schlitz and being the first to claim a unique position in the mind the consumer, you can achieve tremendous results and even overcome the market leader. For example, Miller Lite was not the first light beer, but it was the first to be positioned as a light beer, with a name to support that position. Similarly, Lowenbrau was the most popular German beer sold in America, but Beck's Beer successfully carved a unique position using the advertising slogan:

> "You've tasted the German beer that's the most popular in America.
> Now taste the German beer that's the most popular in Germany."

Consumers rank brands and companies in their minds using a ladder system. If a brand is not number one, you must relate in some way to the number one brand. A campaign that pretends that the market leader does not exist is likely to fail. A great example of positioning a number 2 brand in a very competitive industry was used by Avis in the rent-a-car market. Avis tried unsuccessfully for years to win customers, pretending that the number one Hertz did not exist. Finally, it began using the line, "Avis is only No. 2 in rent-a-cars, so why go with us? We try harder." After launching the campaign, Avis quickly became hugely profitable. Whether Avis actually tried harder was not particularly relevant to their success. Rather, consumers finally were able to relate Avis to Hertz, which was number one in their minds.

If you're competing against a bigger player in your industry, you'll most likely have a hard time displacing the leader, especially in the short-term. On the other hand, you can much easily find a way to position yourself in relation to that market leader to so consumers have a frame of reference you can benefit from.

Positioning of a Leader

Generally, the top three brands in a product category occupy market share in a ratio of 4:2:1. That is, the number one brand has twice the market share of number two, which has twice the market share of number three. If a company was the first to introduce a product, then the advertising campaign should reinforce that fact. Coca-Cola's "the real thing" does just that, and implies that other colas are just imitations.

Another element to be noted is that change is inevitable and a leader must be willing to embrace change rather than resist it. When new technology opens the possibility of new markets, a company should enter the new market as fast as possible in order to have first-mover advantage in it. In that way, the internet will give you a double benefit: as you'll discover further in this book, it's a great way to attract unlimited quantities of targeted prospects and customers, and it can also serve as an automated sales system that does all the marketing and sales heavy-lifting for your business.

Repositioning the Competition

If you've spent countless hours going through the Yellow Pages and researching the internet to see what your competitors are doing in terms of marketing and positioning, one action that has been responsible for making and breaking entire brands is the concept repositioning a competitor. This works by suggesting to prospects and customers to view your competition in a different way. Many big brands have used this concept very tactfully with great results. For example, Tylenol successfully repositioned aspirin by running advertisements explaining the negative side effects of aspirin.

Another example of repositioning was done in the alcoholic beverage industry. Although most Vodkas in the U.S. carried Russian names, very few were actually made in Russia. Stolichnaya vodka successfully repositioned its Russian-sounding competitors by exposing the fact that they all actually were made in the U.S., and that Stolichnaya was made in Leningrad, Russia.

When Pringle's new potato chips were introduced, they quickly gained market share. However, Wise Potato Chips successfully repositioned Pringle's in the mind of consumers by listing some of Pringle's non-natural ingredients that sounded like harsh chemicals, even though they were not. Wise Potato Chips marketed itself as containing only "Potatoes. Vegetable oil. Salt." As a resulting of this advertising, Pringle's quickly lost market share, with consumers complaining that Pringle's tasted like cardboard, most likely as a consequence of their thinking about all the chemical ingredients.

Powerful Names

Your brand's name is perhaps the most important factor affecting perceptions of it. In the past, before there was a wide range of brands available, a company could name a product just about anything. Today however, it is vital to have a memorable name that evokes images that help position the product in your prospect's mind.

Names like "Energizer" for a battery, "Head & Shoulders" for a shampoo, "Red Bull" for an energy drink, and "People" for a gossip magazine are well-chosen names. A brilliant example that I always use to explain the power of a good name is the name of a coffee place franchise in the Netherlands called "Coffee Company". In two words, the brand communicates instantly what it does and its first two letters are identical in both words, making the brand sound very good when you say it out loud.

A problem that some companies face is confusion with another company that has a similar name. Consumers frequently confused the tire manufacturer B.F. Goodrich with Goodyear. The Goodyear blimp had made Goodyear tires well-known, and Goodyear frequently received credit by consumers for tire products that B.F. Goodrich has pioneered.

A USP and positioning go hand in hand together. Your USP has to be suited and must support your positioning. Your positioning must be summarized and understood as quickly as possible in your USP.

To help you with the thinking process of coming up with a good positioning angle and a powerful USP, here are a few questions you can ask yourself to get your mental juices flowing. Take a few moments to think about your answers.

1.   What position do you currently own?

Positioning is largely thinking in reverse. Start with the prospect's mind and ask yourself what position you already own in the mind of your prospect and customer. Changing the mind of your brand and your business is a very difficult task. You have to ask yourself the question "what position does my business, product or service currently own in the mind of own prospects and customers?".

It's vital you come up with a very accurate answer, because it will then guide you to implement the actions to move to the position you want to reach. Spending some time and even money on this research will allow you to be more aware of what you're up against.

2.   What position do you eventually want to own?

Think about which position you want to own in the long-term, say 18 from 36 months from now. How do you want prospects and customers to perceive your business, product or service? You need to have a very clear idea of what you want your business to represent, what edge you want to have over the rest of the market, and why you want your customers to come back for and recommend you to their friends, family, and colleagues. Think about how you can progressively add this new positioning angle to everything your business does, and what you want to stand for. Just remember the cardinal rule of USP and positioning: if you try to be all things to all people, you end up with nothing. You will be far better off narrowing the focus of your target to establish a unique position as a specialist, not as a jack-of-all-trades generalist.

3.   Who do you have to beat?

If the positioning you want to achieve requires a direct fight against a leader in your market, it's best not to use full force. It's much easier to go around a closed gate than to try to destroy it. The key would be to try to select a position that no one else currently owns. I recommend that you spend time thinking and researching everything you can from the point

of view of your customers and your competition. Analyze what they're doing well, and where they're falling short. How can you improve your communication about you deliver to the customer and what benefits he'll get by doing business with you.

4.   Do you have enough resources?

A major mistake many businesses do very frequently is trying to achieve the impossible when implementing a new strategy to reach a new positioning objective. It takes time, money and resources to build a share of mind. It takes time, money and resources to establish a position. It takes money, resources and incredible focus to hold a position once you've established it. The noise level today is fierce, and consumer attention is more deficient than ever before in the history of marketing and advertising. There are so many me-too products and me-too companies fighting for the mind of the prospect. Getting noticed is getting tougher.

According to a study done by the New York Times Magazine, the average consumer is exposed to anywhere from 3,000 to 5,000 advertising messages every single day, averaging over 10 to 18 million ads per year. This includes the logo on your watch, the logo on your phone, the logo on your fridge, the logo on my knife and fork, product placements on TV and radio shows, banner ads count you see on the internet, and Spam you receive in your email inbox just to cite a few.

In 2011, the average cost of a 30-second commercial during the NFL Super Bowl was approximately US $3 million. This excludes costs and fees for actors, equipment, ad agencies, directors, crew and other personnel. When you remember that a 30 second $3 million Super Bowl commercial can make only one of those 10 million impressions, the odds against an advertiser today are enormous.

This is why a company like Procter & Gamble can dominate dozens of markets in a very short amount of time. When it launches a new product, the company can afford to invest millions of dollars to position itself in the consumer's mind. The best way to compete with such big competitors is to reduce the geographical or demographical scope of your target, and appeal to certain segments of your market.

5.   Can you integrate it into everything you do?

Brainstorm how you can integrate your new USP into everything you do: marketing messages, advertisements, sales letters, customer support, online advertising, website design and communication, etc. This will require you to think and plan for everything your company does. From the way you greet someone who calls your hotline to the slogan on your website, it's crucial that you integrate your new positioning and USP in everything you do, and live up to the promises you make to your prospects and customers. Consistency is the key to carving out a space in the mind of the prospect, and you must be ready to target a defined segment of the market that you can then dominate if you want to achieve one main strategic objective.

It must also be said that most successful companies rarely change a winning formula.

How many years have you seen those Marlboro cowboys riding into the sunset?

Domino's has delivered "fresh, hot pizza delivered to your door in 30 minutes or less -- or it's free" for decades. Creativity is great for artists, but when it comes to sales and marketing, it's best to stick with what works once you've found a winning formula.

Become famous

We live in a celebrity-obsessed culture and do business in a celebrity-driven marketplace. Look at how many glossy celebrity magazines are on display at your local supermarket. Celebrities are more than ever present in our everyday life, maybe not physically, but with the products they endorse, the clothes they wear, and the power of the message they carry.

Not so long ago, the general public had more respect for degree and certification-driven individuals, but society has faced interesting changes over the last two decades. People who have appeared on national television or in a TV reality show become instant celebrities and draw much more attention than in the past. Although I must say that I am not pleased with this instant celebrity rush, there is an upside for you: anyone can now become a celebrity (or perceived celebrity) in their marketplace simply by tweaking a few key elements in their marketing and positioning.

You may not want to appear on Oprah or Ellen, but achieving celebrity status in your marketplace is something that must be on your top priority list if you want to increase sales and profits. You and your business have to be known for something.

Many of my close friends in the business world as well as our clients have achieved a celebrity status in their industries, and it is not rare for them to be stopped by people at conventions and other industry-related events to have their picture taken. At a local or niche industry level, it's quite simple to reach celebrity status simply by making yourself and your business the talk of the town or industry.

Local celebrity status can land you on national television and bring you national and even international exposure.

Becoming a celebrity with your own customer base can be very easily done and will increase customer satisfaction, repeat sales, customer spending, help reduce refunds, and allow you to generate more referrals from your current loyal buyers. To position yourself as a celebrity in your marketplace, you work on self-aggrandizement, self-promotion, and associating yourself and your business with celebrities and people who are respected by your target market. Any relationship or name-dropping you can use in your communication that features you and a celebrity is worth using.

Imagine this situation: you'd like to lose a few extra pounds and you decide to hire a personal trainer. If money was no issue, would you rather hire a local trainer who just got out of a personal trainer school, or a personal trainer who works with world-class athletes and celebrities and gets them ripped for blockbuster movies? Easy answer if you're honest with yourself. The celebrity trainer, even though he himself isn't famous, is perceived as a bigger celebrity than your local trainer, simply because he has contact with actors and famous individuals. This allows him to charge higher fees than a no-name trainer simply because he has a higher perceived social status. Ask yourself: do I know anyone in my area, city, or network of contacts who is perceived as famous and from which I can benefit from just be assimilating myself with?

Can you have a celebrity endorse your business, product, or service, even without being financially compensated? You'd be amazed of the number of people out there who can help vitalize your business's perceived image without costing you any money. A lot of local celebrities are willing and available to help you out, you just have to get out there and ask around.

Crafting your new image

Achieving expert status can fortunately be self-created and self-manufactured. You have everything in your power and reach to turn yourself and your business into highly-respected entities benefiting from celebrity status. You can appoint yourself a world-class expert in most fields just by studying every material available for an hour a day for just a year.

This allowed me to build a highly profitable internet business in just a few years and become a highly paid business consultant. I spoke on stage in front of thousands of business owners and entrepreneurs, and hundreds of thousands of people have subscribed to my online newsletter to receive my advice on business-building, marketing, and internet marketing. I've also managed to build a huge network of highly-successful and powerful contacts in the world, attracting plenty of new business venture deals and securing several cash plus equity deals in established businesses in Europe and the United States, in exchange for my business and marketing consulting advice.

Desiderius Erasmus, a Dutch Renaissance humanist who lived in the 16th Century once said: "in the land of blind, the one-eyed man is king". If you know more about your topic and your industry and are perceived higher than your competition, you'll become the obvious choice for your prospects and customers. Specialization, even if it's self-declared, raises your expert status and the notoriety of your business. People want to do business with experts and businesses that are perceived as being more "famous". This in turn will allow you to convert more prospects into customers with less price resistance.

How to become famous in your industry
Let's have a look at a few ways to achieve relative fame in your industry.

1. Publish a book or a report
Once you have your name on a publication, or better yet, several publications, you are considered an obvious authority on your subject. Today, publishing is easier than ever before and it won't cost you a fortune and won't take you months of your time. You can either write a short industry report like some kind of "consumer report", or a full-blown book of 100-150 pages. You can hire a ghostwriter for a few thousand dollars or use voice recognition software on a simple laptop to get most of the top written without needing to write a single word. This will give you instant authority in your marketplace.

2. Speak at seminars and conventions
Speaking, even only in your local community, will establish you as a go-to person in your field and will help you get plenty of referral opportunities. Even if you have no previous public speaking experience, you can simply come up with a short 15 to 30 minute speech about the "10 things people can do to improve X, Y or Z" a specific area in their life.

3. Master Social Media
Facebook, Twitter, Instagram, Medium, Vine, YouTube, Snapchat, Pinterest... and the list goes on. Hundreds of millions of customers are spending more and more time (several HOURS every day) on those platforms. If you're not telling your story and publishing relevant content on social

media in a strategic way (not just blasting your promotions and special offers every day), you're losing the game and you need help. Reach out to us fast. I'm serious.

4. Publish Your Own Newsletter

Publishing your own electronic or hardcopy newsletter will boost your respect and power in the marketplace, as well as allow you to build a great relationship using email marketing, a strategy we'll get into detail further in this book. This will allow you to constantly communicate with your target market and prospective customers, building brand loyalty and increasing future repeat transaction.

5. Get published in magazines and trade journals

Writing articles increases your name recognition while boosting your credibility as a source of expert information. This is true no cost marketing, plus you can funnel readers back to your website and collect their email address and add them to your email follow-up sequence.

6. Use the media effectively

Once you understand how your business is newsworthy, you should use frequent press releases to gain positive publicity and attention from your local radio, newspaper and what not. Traditional media outlets still carry a lot of weight and their message is read and listened to by thousands if not millions of readers.

7. Be known for something

An interactive and educational online presence will allow you to gain a lot of credibility by publishing free information and materials that your prospective customers can consult anytime they wish. With the power of the internet, your potential market expands instantly from "around the neighborhood" to "around the globe". The key to dominating the internet and attracting floods of leads and customers is to have a platform that is optimized for internet marketing and selling, not only as another "nice but useless" website.

Look at the example of Disney. Personally, I'm a big Disney fan, and like visiting their parks and amenities because I think they're fun, but also because Disney breathes sales and marketing in everything it does. I believe anyone interested in sales and marketing should frequently visit their parks and amenities to see how well a business can be run with incredible

values and remain highly profitable for decades. From the start, it's been a characteristic of Disney to keep the parks clean for the guests. Jack Lindquist, a former Disney president and marketing executive, recalled the story of a journalist telling Walt Disney he believed that the park was beautiful that day—but would rapidly become dirty when the crowds continued to flow through. Walt disagreed strongly and answered, "we're going to make it so clean that people are going to be embarrassed to throw anything on the ground."

Lindquist recalled: "I saw that happen continuously. I'd see people carry cigarette butts until they could find a trash container to put them in. On Fifth Avenue or Regent Street, London, they'd never think twice about throwing a cigarette on the ground. At Disneyland, they thought about it. Because there wasn't any litter or dirt on the ground."

Since then, Disneyland has become renowned for being clean, friendly and fun. And people keep coming back. I've yet to meet someone who can say something negative about what Disney stands for: family fun, entertainment and a clean environment. The first rule of Disney's famous employee orientation is: "We create happiness". But the second is right behind it: "Everyone picks up trash."

Of course, there are wonderful cast members assigned to emptying trash receptacles, handling sweeper pans and brooms, and carrying out specific maintenance duties, like changing out light bulbs. But no cast member, whether a waste removal person or an executive vice president should walk by a leftover napkin or an empty water bottle and not pick it up.

Every time you go to Disney, you know that to expect: a good time in a safe and clean environment. It's become their operating standard, and whether you go to the Disney parks in Paris, Orlando, or Los Angeles (I've been to all three), you'll notice they're always on top of their game. If a massive company like Disney - that employs 150,000 people and attracts close to 120 million visitors to its parks every year - can achieve such a high customer satisfaction level and repeat business from past customers and visitors, you can without doubt achieve at least the same kind of customer retention and satisfaction in your current business.

The most powerful force for good or evil in your business is word-of-mouth. And unfortunately, bad word of mouth spreads much faster than good word of mouth. You must refuse to tolerate any kind of injustice practiced by your employees when addressing customer needs. Don't tolerate anything less than excellence from your staff. Some time ago, running a mediocre business with mediocre practices and mediocre customer satisfaction was enough to make a good income. Today, you simply can't afford to. You should strive to deliver not only the best quality products and services, but also unexpected extras and experiences to surprise and WOW your customers.

First point of contact

The internet has become an inevitable media in our everyday life, and whether you like it or not, it has the power to make or severely hinder any business you can think of. From the power of social networking leading to opportunities of brilliant referral marketing to the power of paid online advertising to generate new leads non-stop, the internet has grown into a full-blown platform that you absolutely must integrate in your business and marketing plan. If you're not using the internet, it is safe to say that you are far from maximizing your profits on top of leaving insane amounts of money on the table. And if you already are using the internet and currently have a website up, I would confidently say that you currently are not using the web to its full extent and that you could be generating considerably more profits on a daily basis.

Having a simple website will do you no good at all if your web presence is not properly optimized. And in most cases, it can even do more harm than good. If you really want to get the most results out of your business, it's crucial for you to have a highly optimized internet marketing sales system in place. It will blow your competition out of the water, and it's like shooting fish in a barrel. More about that later in this book.

The first impression, whether it's in person, over the phone, or when someone visits the internet, is probably the most important moment in the timeline of the business/customer relationship. First impressions are very, very hard to change. Think about what kind of first impression your business is currently making. How does your staff answer the phone?

How do they greet customers in your store? How fast does your website load? Is your online presence optimized to its full potential? Can your prospects easily find you when they type in your business or company name in the search engines?

Millions of people nowadays rely almost exclusively on internet commu-nication and search engine results to decide where they go to eat, to shop, what hotel they stay in, what coat they want to buy, and so on. You need to make it a priority to leverage the incredible power of internet marketing in your business.

12

THE BILLIONAIRE'S SECRET WEAPON

As an entrepreneur and business owner, your goal is to create the maximum return for your dollar investment.

Mass branding is great for companies that like flushing millions of dollars down the drain because they need to spend their budgets, but if you want results and fast money, you need to stay far away from traditional "billboard and branding advertising". To achieve the best ROI for your business, the most efficient way of communicating is using "direct response" advertising and marketing.

Basically, direct response marketing is a form of marketing designed to solicit a response which is specific and measurable. The delivery of the response is direct between the target market and the advertiser, which means the customer responds directly to the company advertising the product.

The response can be filling out a form and sending it back, completing an application online, picking up the phone and dialing a specific number, or making a purchase. Direct response marketing seeks to elicit action. If you want to attract new prospects and customers at minimal cost, you won't find a more affordable and faster way direct-response advertising and marketing.

The benefits of direct response advertising are too big to ignore:

- It's affordable.
- It's measurable.
- It allows you to target very specific demographics and areas.
- You can test different parts of your ad, your package or your list to determine what works best for your situation.
- You can see results of a campaign in a matter of days, and even hours in some cases.

To maximize the results of any direct response advertising campaign, you will need to create a compelling message (or offer) that specifically matches the market you wish to cater to. Furthermore, you need to use right media in order to reach yous prospective customers.

In summary, the key to making a direct-response marketing campaign work is to create the right message that matches to the right market by using the right media.

Think of this as fishing: in order to attract a specific kind of fish, you need to use specific bait (the message) using a specific tool (the media).

With direct response marketing, customers respond directly to you. Customers make a conscious effort to get hold of you by phone, on the internet or visit your shop in person. And when they do so, they are ready to part with money for your product or service because they are perfectly pre-qualified.

When you use direct response marketing, you employ an advertising medium like the internet, the radio, TV, direct mail, or printed media to invite people to raise their hands and contact you for more information about your product or service.

Your advertising piece makes it clear what people have to do to get hold of you. You give a phone number, an email address, or a physical address. People contact you because they want to and have qualified themselves from the marketplace.

Direct response on the internet

The internet is a perfect place to use direct response marketing and attract leads at a fraction of what it would cost you if you were using TV or radio ads. Online, you can target very specifically what segments of the market you want to advertise to.

Using paid advertising like Facebook Ads, Twitter Ads, LinkedIn Ads, Google AdWords, Yahoo Search Marketing and other paid media enables you to target people who live in your local area or are interested in your specific industry and the kind of solutions you provide. Furthermore, you can choose display ads only during times of the day, show up on sites that you choose, and you can even choose to pay only once a prospect has clicked on of your advertisement and arrived on your site.

The most frequent model of paid advertising used online is called "pay per click" advertising.

In essence, the internet allows for very deep and accurate market research, know where your target market hangs out and spends the most of their time. More than that, you can go through the forums the interact on and see exactly what is going through in their minds, helping you craft the best advertising material to trigger the highest response possible.

In the past, direct response marketing was largely used by businesses that sent out direct mail to lists of potential prospects. Every letter or postcard had to be printed, stamped, and sent. And it would take weeks to find out the results of how successful a campaign was. Not to mention the cost of having staff take care of preparing all the envelopes. The internet now makes it possible to post millions of advertisements right in front of your target market's eyes in less than a few hours and attract prospects to your business.

Whether you deal locally or internationally, the internet will help you explode the amount of leads you generate in your business, and test advertising campaigns on the fly, gathering results in just a few days. Once you gather the results of how a campaign has performed, you can tweak the various elements in the process. By increasing the efficiency of each step (the percentage of clicks on your ads, the conversion rate of your website, the conversion efficiency of your follow-up sequence, etc.), your business can achieve exponential growth in a few weeks.

My agency, ZuraMedia, helps clients in dozens of industries leverage direct-response advertising and marketing on the internet in a way that brings you an ROI. Go to **MatthiasMazur.com/agency** or visit **ZuraMedia.com** for more details.

How to write a great performing advertisement
First of all, you need to understand that an efficient advertisement, whether it's online or offline is not any of the following:

- It's not designed to satisfy art directors, agency executives, or even clients. It's made to attract a prospect to take a decisive action: raise his hand and ask for more information, call a toll-free number, or go to a shop to buy something.
- It's not made for entertainment purposes, win awards. It's made to sell.
- It's not cute or funny.
- In other words, it's everything but what you could learn as an academic student in any basic advertising class. An ad's primary focus must be to generate leads and make sales. That's it.

Here are some characteristics of successful direct-response ads:

1. They get **ATTENTION**! The ad should stop the reader dead in his tracks with an intriguing headline.

2.   They stress a **BENEFIT** to the end user. The unique sell-
       ing proposition is not cleverly hidden – it's made
       immediately clear.

3.   They create DESIRE in the customer's mind by triggering
       elements the prospect wants and desires.

4.   They arouse **CURIOSITY**. The key is not to be outra
       geous but to address the strongest interests and
       concerns of your target audience. Example: "How a strange
       discovery helped me lost 12 pounds of fat in 20 days"
       appeals to the reader's desire to lose weight in a finite
       amount of time.

5.   They provide **INFORMATION**. The headline "How to
       Stop Emission Problems—at Half the Cost of Conventional
       Air Pollution Control Devices" lures the reader because it
       promises information. Prospects today seek specific,
       usable information on highly specialized topics. Ads that
       provide information the reader wants get higher reader-
       ship and better response.

6.   They are **INSIGHTFUL**. Successful ad copy reflects a
       high level of knowledge and understanding of the product
       and the problem it solves. An effective technique is to tell
       the reader something he's currently experiencing and that
       he wants to get away from.

7.   They have a strong **CALL TO ACTION.** Good
       ads contain a strong and appealing offer. They tell the
       reader the next step in the buying process and encourage
       him to take it now. All ads should have an offer, because it
       generates immediate response and business from pros-
       pects that are in a "buy mode". Without an offer, "urgent"
       prospects are not encouraged to take action, making you
       lose many potential customers. Additionally, strong offers
       increase readership and attract more eyeballs to your ad,
       because people like ads that offer them something—
       especially if it is free and has high perceived value. For
       example, offering a printed kit sent by mail on your
       website increases your chances of converting a prospect
       into a customer because you're taking the time and effor

to educate him too.

8.   They emphasize the **OFFER.** Everything must be done to emphasize the offer. Graphic elements such as bold headlines, frequent use of subheads, bullet points, coupons, toll-free numbers set in large type, pictures of response booklets and brochures, dashed coupon areas, asterisks, and marginal notes make your ads more eye-catching and response-oriented, increasing reader-ship.Try to emulate the font as graphic style newspapers and magazines use.

9.   When illustrated, they use **CLEAR** pictures. Good advertising does not use abstract art or concepts that force the reader to over-think what's being advertised. Ideally, someone who sees your ad should be able to understand exactly what the main benefit is in less than five seconds. People just don't have the time to dig into your ad if they can't understand the essence of "what's in it for them" in the first few seconds. Consumer attention is so scarce in our day and age that it's crucial you get your point across as fast and clear as possible.

If you're currently using general advertising, you would be foolish not to start using direct response techniques like the use of coupons, direct mail, direct email, internet marketing, inbound and outbound telemarketing, as well as a strong call to action, toll-free numbers, free booklets, benefit-headlines, etc. Everything a business should do with its advertising should be direct-response oriented. I guarantee you'll get a better bang for your buck, and attract much more prospective customers than with broad general advertising featuring an average "image" advertisement.

Test and track everything

When helping entrepreneurs and business owners in their businesses, I'm always astounded as to how much money they're leaving on the table by failing to test and track what they do. The people who deserve the most in business are mostly the ones who always get the maximum result from the minimum effort, in other terms, the ones who maximize what they do. If you understand that one approach to getting clients may produce five times the results of another and you stick with the approach that yields the best results, you're on your way to building a tremendously successful business.

The legend says that John Wanamaker – who is considered to be the father of modern advertising – once stated: "Half the money I spend on advertising is wasted; the trouble is I don't know which half". What is worth mentioning is that Wanamaker was active as an entrepreneur in the late 19th century, until the 1920s, and yet many business owners in our day and age are still experiencing the same issue. It arrives time and time again: a business makes money for a few months, saves that money, and then goes out on an advertising shopping spree using dumb branding methods. A few months later, unable to see the return on investment because nothing was tracked and tested, and as sales start slowing down, the business finds itself in a critical situation. If this sounds familiar, don't worry.

Almost all clients and business owners we consult with have been in that situation in the past. I think it is insane in today's economic climate to leave anything up to luck when there are so many great tools and testing and tracking techniques available for free or at a very low cost. It's crucial you start implementing tracking methods to be able to see exactly how many new prospects and customers you attract using the different means of advertising you're incorporating in your strategy. Let's have a closer look at how you can implement a tracking method to know where your prospects and customers are coming from.

First, let's talk about print ads. If you are not the one answering the phone, have you instructed your staff to ask everyone who calls how they heard about you? If not, you're missing a step. An incentive you can add to your advertisement pieces is a line like "mention this ad and get a free gift worth $20." This provides an incentive for your leads to tell you how they heard about you.

It's also important to realize that even if your ad appears in print media, many people will not call you when they see your ad; they will go to your website instead. This hasn't always been the case, but now that people are spending more and more time online and are getting used to checking out websites and buying online, you need to·track your website traffic in order to effectively track response to print ads.

Here's another example: let's say you purchase an ad in a magazine that displays a link to your website. If you are not tracking your website traffic, how can you know which advertisement worked the best and sent the highest number of leads and sales?

If you find out that you're attracting a high number of leads clicking over to your site but notice that sales numbers are low, you can tweak the message and call to action in your ad to attract higher quality prospects that are better qualified to buy.

If you're not tracking the incoming leads and sales you're generating, you'll never be able to optimize your sales and marketing success, and you'll constantly spend more money than needed.

Testing applies not only to outside sales efforts but to every aspect of marketing and advertising. If you run ads in newspapers or magazines, test different approaches, different headlines, different calls to action, different packages, different offers, different pricing, and different bonuses. Test where your commercials run – what media you use and what time of day.

If you don't run ads, you can still apply the testing and tracking concept and to your sales presentations. You can test different headlines and grabbers against whatever it is you or your sales staff currently use. You'll quickly notice that one presentation gets a better result than the others. Make specific offers and analyze the number of responses, traffic to your website, prospects, and resulting sales for each specific ad piece you put out. Then, analyze the data to find out the cost-per-prospect, cost-per-sale, the average sale-per-prospect, average conversion-per-prospect, and the average profit-per-sale. Remember, your staff gets paid monthly, whether they make one sale a day or five sales a day. Likewise, an ad costs you the same amount of space and production time, whether it produces 100 prospects, 1,000 prospects, or 10,000 prospects.

The purpose of testing is to achieve the highest performance from every marketing and advertising effort you come up with.

If your salespeople each make 100 calls a day, it makes sense to find one main sales presentation or offer that increases your sales conversion rate across the board.

Many highly successful business owners we help have become obsessed with testing the minute we showed them how much money they'd been leaving on the table for years by being lazy. That is the reason why I recommend you try different approaches, different sales triggers, different offers, different prices, different upsells, different follow-up sequences, and different guarantee approaches. Keep testing to come up with even better approaches that beat your current "control." Your control is the concept, approach, offer, or sales presentation which has consistently proven to be the best performer you've been using. By constantly testing and improving your control, you'll be able to generate far more inquiries, clients and sales for the same money just by testing alternatives against each other.

Here's a short list of a few things you can start testing immediately:

- Different headlines.
- Different sales copy.
- Different ad placements.
- Different mailing lists.
- Different radio time slots.
- Different offers.
- Different prices.
- Different guarantees.
- Different sales presentations.
- Different direct mail packages.

A rule of testing is never to test big if you can test small.

A good way to test two approaches simultaneously is by running what is called an "A/B split test". This allows you to create two different ads, the "A" ad and the "B" ad. These two ads are then presented to a similar target market, putting each ad in fairly similar conditions.

A/B testing allows you to test different versions of a marketing piece without sacrificing your returns, but still gives you very specific results you can then analyze and implement into the rest of your marketing and advertising.

It takes a certain level of humility to be able to come back to business basics and consider that we know nothing about nothing, and that the only way of winning is by letting the market give us the answers. That's why you have to test and perpetually track results. Gather all your data, such as:

- Which advertisement brings in the most sales and profits.
- How many orders an ad produces.
- How much money a given ad generates or loses.
- How much the average order is worth.
- How much a new customer costs.
- How much or how many times the client re-orders.
- How well your upsells are performing.

When we were selling an online training program as a means of generating leads, we tested different prices: $9.95, $17, $47, $97. The results were interesting to say the least.

With no other change than the price, this is what we discovered:

- $9.95 didn't generate as many sales as expected
- $17 made the biggest number of sales
- $47 was breaking even but not generating profits
- $97 was making the least amount of sales but was the most profitable price point

Ultimately, we stuck with the $97 price point, which generated more profits than all the other prices we tested, and we noticed that people who paid the highest price were much higher quality customers than people who paid the lowest $9.95 price because they ended up buying more products and services on the back-end, hence increasing the Lifetime Customer Value (LCV).

Sometimes the best price is higher. Sometimes the lowest price is better. It depends on what your goals are: mass volume with repeat low-end sales, or high-end exclusive offers. This shows again that guessing can be misleading, and can cost you a lot of money.

You'll be shocked by how fast your profits can soar with just a few changes in your ads and marketing pieces.

Word needs to be said about pricing. I am a big believer in raising prices in your marketplace, and use your marketing to attract high-quality buyers who will buy from you no matter what price you adopt.

Freebie seekers and tire-kickers are the worst crowd to attract as they will ultimately leave you the minute your competition lowers their prices. On top of that, operating at low margins disables from you from offering extra value and treatment to your customers, hence lowering the quality of what you deliver. We'll talk about the value of raising your fees in a later chapter.

13

HOW TO BECOME A CUSTOMER MACHINE

One of the ways to achieve massive growth in your business is by constantly attracting new prospects to your funnel. In this chapter, we will discuss in depth and look at the most effective ways to attract new customers with the least amount of time and effort. We'll focus essentially on offline strategies and tactics you can implement immediately to grow your customer base.

The goal of your advertising campaign is to attract highly targeted leads you can convert into sales, increased profits and a healthier bottom line. There are three important questions you need to ask yourself before choosing how you want to advertise:

Market: Where are your target buyers?
Media: What is the best media to reach them with?
Message: What compelling message can you create to hook prospects?

Market, media, message. You need to target the right market using the right media and a compelling message. Without one of those 3 elements, you are doomed to fail. For example, if you're selling to high-level corporate executives, you could put together the best advertising that appeals to their needs and desires, but if you fail to use the right media and use blogs for example (which aren't a media that high-level corporate executives are used to), your campaign will fall short. There are no hard-and-fast rules as to which media is better. The right media for one business may be wrong for another. Let's have a look at the pros and cons of different offline advertising methods that are known to be the most effective for attracting new business.

Newspapers

Newspapers are one of the traditional mediums used by businesses, both big and small alike, to advertise their businesses.

Benefits
- Allows you to reach a large number of people in a given geographic area.
- You have the flexibility in deciding the ad size and placement within the newspaper.
- Use of direct-response advertising is perfectly suited.
- Free help in creating and producing ad copy is usually available.
- Quick turn-around helps your ad reflect the changing market conditions. The ad you create today can be published in a matter of days.
- Results of testing and tracking are relatively fast and easy to implement.

Challenges
- Ad space can be expensive. The key is to use remnant space.
- You're competing against hundreds of different ads in the very same newspaper, including the giant ads run by supermarkets well as the ads of your competitors.
- Your ad is bound to have a short life as newspapers are usually read once and then discarded the next day.
- You may be paying to send your message to a lot

of people who will probably never be in the market to buy from you since you're not targeting a specific segment of the market.

- Newspapers are a highly visible medium, so your competitors can quickly react to your prices and strategies.
- With the increasing popularity of the internet, newspapers face declining readership and market penetration. A growing number of readers now skip the print version of the newspaper (and hence the print ads) and instead read the online version of the publication.

The power of remnant advertising

Remnant advertising (also known as remainder advertising) refers to the advertising space that a media company has been unable to sell in advance. Depending on the medium, it could be ad space or time (on television). The beauty about this for you is that it can be bought at a big discount. If it is not sold, it is lost, used for a "house ad", or given away for public service announcements or some other non-revenue producing filler. So instead of taking a loss for unsold airtime or ad space, media outlets will often accept cheap advertising fees to unload their remnant space, giving you the opportunity of buying what would typically be expensive media at a great discounted price. When I first started advertising I made the mistake of taking the most coveted and expensive slots in the newspapers. The outcome was rather painful and, with the benefit of hindsight, somewhat predictable. I got great coverage and a good response but the return on investment was negligible because of the high premium I paid. So be on the lookout for remnant advertising at all times!

Magazines

Magazines are a more focused but also more expensive alternative way to newspaper advertising. This allows you much to reach much higher targeted audiences than using general circulation newspapers.

Benefits
- Allows you to better target your audience as you can

choose magazine publications that cater to your specific target market

- High reader involvement means that more attention will be paid to your advertisement.
- Better quality paper permits better color reproduction and full-color ads.

Challenges

- Since magazines appear only once or twice a month, it will take you longer to gather results and tracking from the ad you're placing.
- Limited flexibility in terms of ad placement and format, less flexibility in terms of the content of your ad.
- Space and ad layout costs are higher.

Radio

Radio is a universal medium enjoyed by people at one time or another during the day, mostly while driving in the car or commuting in heavy traffic.

Benefits

- Being able to select a specific target market given the vast range of radio shows airing worldwide.
- Gives your business personality through the creation of campaigns using sounds and voices.
- Rates can generally be negotiated.
- Often a lot of remnant time available for the taking.

Challenges

- Because radio listeners are spread over many stations, you may need to advertise simultaneously on several stations to reach your target audience.
- Listeners cannot go back to your ads to go over important points.
- Ads are an interruption in the entertainment schedule. Listeners don't actively follow what is being said during radio ads.

- Radio is a background medium. Most listeners are doing something else while listening, which means that your ad has to work hard to get their attention.
- Can be difficult to track different response rates across different ads/ stations/ shows.

Television

The vast majority of television advertisements today consist of brief advertising spots, ranging from a few seconds to hours in the case of infomercials. TV advertisements have been used to sell every product imaginable over the years, from goods and services to political campaigns. The effect of commercial advertisements upon the viewing public has been so successful that in some countries like the United States, it is considered impossible for a politician to create a successful campaign without making heavy use of television advertising.

Benefits
- Television allows you to reach large numbers of people on a national or regional level in a short period of time.
- Independent stations and cable offer new opportunities to target local audiences.
- Television being an image-building and visual medium, it offers the ability to convey your message using different senses such as sight, sound and motion.

Challenges
- The message is temporary, and may require multiple exposures to rise above the clutter, which means high costs.
- Preferred ad times are often sold out far in advance.
- Limited length of exposure, as most ads are only thirty seconds long or less, which limits the amount of information you can communicate.
- Relatively expensive in terms of creative, production and airtime costs.
- "Shotgun approach" means that you're wasting 80% of your advertising dollars because it's impossible to

laser-target your audience.

Direct Mail

Direct mail is a marketing tool that communicates directly with the buyer. It includes catalogs, sales letters, brochures, and postcards.

Benefits

- Targeting can be extremely specific: you can deliver your advertising message to those most likely to buy your product or service.
- Marketing message can be personalized, thus helping increase positive response
- Your message can be as long as is necessary to fully tell your story.
- Easy to measure the ROI of any campaign through testing and tracking.
- You have total control over the presentation of your advertising message.
- Your ad campaign is hidden from your competitors until it's too late for them to react
- Active involvement - the act of opening the mail and reading it -- can be elicited from the target market.
- You can test small by mailing just a few thousand pieces before rolling out a big promotion.

Challenges

- If you don't do a good job with your packaging, some people will consider your envelope as junk mail and throw without even opening it.
- You need to have a high-quality list or a good list broker because 90% of the success of a direct mail campaign depends on the quality of your mailing list.
- Producing direct mail materials entail the expense of using various professionals - copywriter, artists, photographers, printers, etc.
- Can be expensive if you don't test and track everything you do

Some business owners who hear about using direct mail as part of their marketing arsenal run to the hills in blind panic. Just because it is different to other forms of marketing doesn't mean it is something entirely new or unique. There are many reassuring commonalities between tackling a direct mail campaign and tackling a purely online campaign. Ultimately, however you decide to communicate with your target audience you are using the concept of "salesmanship in print", that is, getting your spoken message across using the written word.

As you would communicate your business' message to a prospect in person, you must apply the same principles to this in the printed form. Creating desire, excitement, credibility, using proof, building trust, etc. applies to direct mail as it does to internet marketing.

Telemarketing

Much has been written about telemarketing and many marketers have called it a dead technique. The truth is that telemarketing is far from dead. The key is to have prospective customers pick up the phone and call you instead of spending hours trying to get through to someone who doesn't know you. This is one of the core strategies we implement and take care of for our agency clients. Offering your products and services on the phone to people who have actively reached out to YOU is one of the best ways to generate a windfall of sales.

Benefits
- Gives you direct contact and communication with the prospect, answering any questions or concerns they ,may have about your product or service.
- It can be outsourced, is very cost-effective, and set-up cost is minimal.
- Results are highly measurable.
- You can get a lot of information across if your script is properly structured.
- Great tool to improve customer relationship and maintain contact with existing customers, as well as to introduce new products and services.
- Great way to prelaunch a new product to a target

audience.
- Makes it easy to expand sales territory as the phone allows you to call local, national and global prospects.

Challenges
- More people are using technology to screen out unwanted callers, particularly telemarketers.
- If hiring an outside firm to do telemarketing, there is lesser control in the process given that the people doing the calls are not your employees.
- If you do in-house sales, you need to hire and train a sales team.
- You need a proven high-converting sales script that fits into your sales process.
- You need a system in place to be able to scale effectively.
- It can be extremely expensive, particularly if the telemarketing is outsourced or not well monitored.

We've helped numerous clients integrate a phone sales operation in their business and even take on sales for our clients in some rare cases where our in-house team of telephone sales experts contacts your leads and close sales on your behalf. There is an application process for this service and we are selective of who we take on as a client. If you're interested in outsourcing your sales efforts, you can contact us by going to Matthias-Mazur.com/apply.

I personally started experimenting with phone sales in my own business in 2008 selling training packages at prices between $3,000 and $25,000. In just a few days, I filled up one our seminars with 15 attendees and generated over $50,000 in revenue that first week. Since then, I've scaled our telephone operations in other ventures, hired over 150 sales reps over the years, built sales teams of up to 30 in-house phone agents and trained hundreds of salespeople for our clients and at sales seminars I have spoken at.

Like all the other marketing methods listed here, this is yet another way for you to communicate your message but it must be done in such a way as to engender trust, build rapport with the prospect, create interest and desire in the prospect and ultimately deliver sufficient value, emotional weight and logical reasoning to compel the prospect to become a customer.

Active prospecting

How much time do you spend weekly on lead generation? How much time do spend on creating new direct response ads, setting up new customer-getting strategies, analyzing the results of your online presence, creating referral systems, etc.? Sadly, many business owners don't spend enough time growing their business. They only spend time managing daily operations and putting out daily fires.

Managing a business is totally different from growing a business. If you're not spending time every single day improving your sales system or implementing at least one new strategy to attract new customers, you are cheating yourself. Here's a list of different activities you should be doing every single day to attract new business:

- Creating solid follow-up sequences for your new prospect.
- Planning new launches and relaunches of your products or services to your current prospect and customer base.
- Creating effective phone scripts so your telemarketers can gather appointments and sales.
- Following up personally with hot prospects and customer.
- Contacting newspapers to find out how much advertising space costs, and trying to negotiate a better price.
- Approaching joint venture partners who share a similar customer base but are not in direct competition with you to set up strategic long-term deals.
- Creating systems and operational guidelines to automate the tasks of your staff
- Implementing a new internet marketing lead generation campaign to gather new leads.
- Writing articles or reports to position yourself as the obvious expert in your field.

That's just a short list of things you can do every day to attract new business. As a rule of thumb, commit yourself to spending at least two hours per day for five days per week actively prospecting or creating advertising materials to generate responses and leads on a regular basis.

The "New" Customer

In the last few years, businesses have seen the rise of what we refer to as the "new customer". The new customer is an evolved version of his former self, much smarter, sometimes more skeptical, and who spends his money more wisely than a decade or two ago. Since the recession started hitting hard, many "old customers" have become "new customers". This is what it really means to you as a business owner:

1. The new customer has all the power, and he knows it.

He spends money with more caution than ever before. He can find information about the product or service he's interested in simply by spending a few minutes on the internet. He can compare what different businesses offer, and he'll spend his money with the business that provides him with the best-perceived value and customer care, or that offers him something extra. He can book last-minute travel deals for a few hundred dollars that used to cost thousands just a few years ago. He can compare restaurant prices and pictures in a matter of seconds. He'll base his opinion of your entire business on what he finds out on your website. If you don't have a stellar online presence, you are losing customers. That is an indisputable fact.

He's become sometimes slightly arrogant, and doesn't tolerate anything less than premium quality. He knows his rights, and if you're currently doing something "ordinary" that doesn't offer him something "extra", you're on the path to business hell. He has zero tolerance for mediocre products and services.

2. The new customer has so much choice that he's overwhelmed.

Chances are that he can find something similar just by asking and looking around or shopping online. It's up to you to earn your prospects' and customers' business by doing the right things, never being satisfied by the way things are going, and always trying to over deliver to every customer that walks in your store.

3. The new customer wants to deal with experts.
He will do business with you only if you are positioned in the marketplace as a perceived leader and if you offer something, different, more or better than your competition.

I've seen so many businesses fail simply because they never thought of adding something extra to sweeten the pot when prospects were in their shop or on their site. There will always be new buyers, but they will be much more picky with whom they do business with. That's why having a highly efficient internet presence has become an absolute necessity if you want to attract more customers.

Here are a few interesting numbers that prove how powerful the internet has become, how it influences daily sales and decisions, and how it will continue to influence sales in the upcoming years. Forrester Research Inc. releases reports and statistics on a regular basis about web trends, and here's what you have to know about the trends in the next few years.

- 70% of online consumers already have researched products online and then bought them offline.
- By 2017, online sales will total $370 billion.
- The web accounted for or influenced 42% of retail sales in the last 18 months.
- 48% of all retail sales (excluding autos, travel and prescription drugs) are already being influenced by the web.
- Sales influenced by the web that year will reach $1.8 trillion, and that the direct web sales and those influenced by the internet will account for 53% of retail sales in 2017.
- 154 million U.S. consumers made online purchases in 2014, representing 67% of those who use the internet. That means two people out of three who use the internet have already bought something.
- The European Commission states that nearly 64% of the population in Europe has researched products and

services online within the last 3 months.

As you can see, the internet is not the future anymore. It is the present, and it is an absolute must for any business no matter what market you may be in. Let's have a deeper look at how to attract unlimited amounts of customers using the strategies used by my businesses and by my clients.

14

HOW TO ATTRACT THE NEW BREED OF "E-CUSTOMERS"

The internet is a fabulous way to drive thousands of visitors and prospects to your offers, allowing you to gather their contact information, follow-up with them, convert them into buyers and then into repeat buyers on a 100% automated process.

On top of that, it will give tremendous freedom, allowing you to spend more time off from the daily tasks in your business. If the internet is something that you still fear in terms of advertising and marketing, this chapter will remove all doubts possible and show you exactly how you can generate tons of new business using systemized marketing processes that run on autopilot.

On the internet, there are basically two ways of generating visitors to your traffic: using free methods, and paid methods. This means that you can either buy advertising and placements on other websites to send visitors to your site or publish free optimized content, press releases and use social media tools to get the word out about your existence at no cost. To be more accurate, the cost of using "free" or "organic" methods such as social media or search engine optimization is time. This means that if you're running a one-man operation and YOU are the business, you might not wish to pay for exposure through paid ads (although I *highly* recommend you do) in which case you would rather be investing your time.

My objective is not to fill this book with gibberish words that only techno-geeks can understand, but rather to give a solid and practical understanding about how the internet can help you to attract new business.

Organic Methods

The top online search engines are currently Google (approximately 70% market share) and Yahoo/ Bing (approximately 27% market share) account for close 97% of all searches made on the internet, with the main player being Google by far.

Search Engine Optimization

Search engine optimization (also known as "SEO") is the process of improving the visibility of a website or a web page in search engines via the "natural" and free (also known as "organic") search results. Other forms of "Search Engine Marketing" (SEM) target paid listings. In general, the higher a page appears in the search engines, the more visitors it will attract. Know that it is possible to optimize not only your static web pages, but also your videos and the pictures you publish. As an internet marketing strategy, SEO considers how search engines work and what people search for.

Optimizing a website may involve editing its content and HTML code (the backbone structure of how a website is created) to both increase its relevance to specific keywords when someone searches for a specific keyword in a search engine like Google.

Promoting a site to increase the number of links pointing to it is another SEO tactic that allows websites to rise in the search engine rankings.

Your website should be optimized for local search, as well as worldwide search. If you own a kitchen supply business, your site must show up in the top 3 results of Google when someone types in "kitchen supply + your city". If your company is based in Austin, Texas, your site must show up when someone types in "kitchen supply Austin Texas". If you don't appear in the top 10 results of Google, I can tell you that you're losing hundreds of hot prospects every single month who are actively looking for your product or service.

I'm always surprised to see how many incompetent web designers get away by creating utterly useless websites that don't benefit the business owner one bit and won't help him attract new business.

The goal of your web presence is to attract prospects and customers and educate them about why you are the best solution to their problem. If you currently have a website that doesn't show up in the search engine results when you type in "your product + city", you have a major problem: you are invisible to people looking for you!

Press releases

Press releases are a very effective way to attract media attention, on-line traffic and visitors, and high search engine rankings in a very short amount of time. One of the benefits is that press releases have a very high esteem in Google's eyes and algorithm, which means your press release will generally stay in a high position for weeks and months (and even years in some instances). The internet makes it now possible to publish press releases very easily and cheaply too. There are free services you can use, as well as paid offerings done by professional press release companies. You can instantly reach thousands of media outlets by posting your press release online, all while attracting tons of highly-targeted visitors and gaining credibility in your market. For example, you can inform the public of your new products or services or any relevant information about your business that is likely to be considered as news.

Your press release has to answer the following questions: Who, what, when, where, why, and how.

- Who is involved in your story?
- What is the topic of your news?

- When is this new event taking place?
- Where is it based?
- Why is this news newsworthy?
- How is your news useful to your industry or to the world?

Press releases generally contain a few paragraphs, approximately 20 to 25 lines of text. When you submit a press release online, you are providing valuable traffic to your website. With the exposure of the release you submitted to press release sites, you will find yourself getting new hits each day, and with the right press release distribution partner, your site can gain popularity in a matter of weeks. Do a search for "press release services" in Google, and you'll find dozens of websites that allow you to submit a free press release and paid services for less than $200. If you have a budget available, you can also choose to submit it to paid press release sites which will give you even more exposure and in most cases a direct access to journalists and media platforms.

Blogging

Blogging is another excellent technique to build an authoritative online presence for your business. Blogs have become very popular online and have gone from being the small internet diaries they once were less than a decade ago to being full-blown customer-generating platforms that allow businesses to connect and interact with their audience. Many smart businesses communicate essentially using their blog when they have an important update or announcement to make to the world. Here are some of the benefits of using blogging as part of your online strategy to get the word out about your business and attract new customers:

Sense of community: blogs provide your business with a chance to share your expertise and knowledge with a larger audience, helping you connect with a wider audience and build a community of readers and followers that can easily enter your sales funnel.

Very easy to use and update: blogs are easy to use: you can simply write your thoughts, link to resources, or publish new pictures and videos all at the push of a few buttons.

High search engine rankings: now that you know how search engines work, keep in mind that they absolutely love fresh new content and websites that are updated on a regular basis.

Better communication at minimal cost: blogging will give you several ways to communicate with your audience at minimal cost. You can publish articles, audio files, videos and pictures all the click of a button. It's also a great way to collect prospects' contact information to follow-up the day they join your mailing list.

Online video
Online video has become a major tool that smart businesses have started using with great efficiency in the last recent years. With YouTube and Facebook attracting billions of video views every single day, exposure coming from video sites is something you need to seize immediately. There has never been a better time for small businesses to jump on the incredible opportunity of online video. Here are a few reasons why.

Low production cost: videos can be produced and look professional for a few hundred dollars, especially with the rise of high-quality pocket cameras and small camcorders.

Easy hosting: there are literally dozens if not hundreds of places you can broadcast your videos online like YouTube or directly on Facebook.

Infinite possibilities: with online video, you can entertain, inspire, sell, add personality, and even have a show related to your market or your expertise. Everything is possible nowadays with technology becoming cheaper by the minute.

Personality: people like doing business with other people, not with faceless corporations. If you work in a big Fortune 500 company, you can still add a voice and a face to your company and give it a human identity. Google and Zappos do it with their blogs and online videos, so there's no reason you shouldn't be doing it. The second best thing to face-to-face contact is video, as it creates a much more personal connections with your prospects and customers.

Viral effect: video nowadays can easily go viral and get picked up by traditional media like network television. You can post your video links to Twitter, Facebook, and on your blog to increase search engine rankings and attract new visitors and prospects.

How to lose $180 million in 4 days

Here's an example of how a YouTube video went completely viral, attracted millions of views, got national media coverage, and blew the whistle on the malpractice of a major company. "United Breaks Guitars" is a song by Canadian musician David Carroll and his band, Sons of Maxwell, which chronicles a real-life experience of how his guitar was broken during a trip on United Airlines in 2008, and the subsequent reaction from the airline. Mr. Carroll said that he and fellow passengers on board a flight plane had witnessed baggage-handling crew throwing guitars on the tarmac in Chicago Airport on his flight to Omaha, Nebraska. He then discovered that his $3,500 guitar had suffered a broken neck. After nine months of fruitless negotiations with the airline for compensation, Carroll wrote a song and created a music video about his experience. The song became an immediate hit on YouTube.com upon its release in July 2009, attracting more than 10 million in a matter of weeks. The media reported the story of the song's instant success and the public relations humiliation for United Airlines. Later on, The Times newspaper reported that within 4 days of the video being posted online, United Airline's stock price fell 10%, costing stockholders about $180 million in value. That proves the power and reach of what a single video posted on the internet can have on a huge billion-dollar company like United Airlines.

Old Spice Guy

In the summer of 2010, Old Spice, an American brand of male grooming products manufactured by Procter & Gamble launched the fastest growing online viral video campaign ever, attracting 6.7 million views in the first 24 hours, and reaching over 23 million views after 36 hours. After a raving first day of online buzz followed by millions of viewers and attracting national media attention, the campaign's TV commercial star, Isaiah Mustafa, personally replied to 186 online comments and questions from websites like Twitter, Facebook and YouTube by shooting personalized 30-60 second videos that also generated tens of millions of views.

During the four weeks following the viral video campaign that lasted 3 days, sales of the product increased by 107% and the campaign ended up attracting over 40 million unique views.

Online video will allow you to add personality to your business, giving you the ability to show various aspects of your company hence increasing trust with your target market and building a stronger relationship. Your site should feature videos explaining website visitors who you are, what you do, and show the viewer around in your business. For example, you could do a video walk-through in your companies' offices, introduce key staff people, and show different funny and casual things you may have in your office: a cat, a foosball area, and use a casual and humorous tone.

Paid lead-generation methods

If you have a marketing budget, this is where things get very interesting. Buying internet advertising will allow you to speed up considerably your lead and customer generation process. Let's discuss the most effective methods you can use to drive as many highly-targeted visitors to your website with the most cost-effective tactics.

Common pricing models

Before we dive into the various online paid advertising methods, you need to know that there are basically three types of pricing models.

CPM – stands for "Cost per Thousand impressions", the 'M' being the Roman numeral "thousand". It is a predetermined cost of how much you will pay after your advertisement message has been displayed one thousand times.

CPC or **PPC** – stands for "Cost per Click" or "Pay per Click". You only pay each time a viewer clicks on an online ad that sends him to your website.

CPA – stands for "Cost per Acquisition". You only pay for customers who complete an action you desire (make a purchase, sign-up to a newsletter, download information, etc). This model can be effective if your campaign has a very specific and measurable goal.

Pay-per-Click (PPC)

Pay-per-click (PPC) is an internet advertising model where advertisers pay only when their ad is clicked. In search engines, advertisers typically bid on keyword phrases relevant to their target market. Cost per click (CPC) is the amount of money an advertiser pays the advertising platform for a single click on its ad that brings one visitor to its website.

There are dozens of PPC networks, but the biggest ones are Google AdWords, Facebook Ads and Bing and all three operate on a bid-based basis. Cost per click (CPC) varies depending on many different variables too long to list here. Mainly, it depends on the ad platform, the level of competition for a particular keyword, as well as the geographical area you would like to be targeting.

Facebook Ads

Facebook has become one of the world's best-known websites with around 1.5 billion members who share information with their circle of friends online. Of those 1.5 billion members, 1 billion are active and log into their account every single day. As impressive as the numbers are, the site's true power lies in its database of demographics. When a user creates a new personal account, he is asked questions about his scholarship, friend circle, music and movie influences, hobbies, marital status, favorite books, etc. This is all under the pretext of helping you connect with other Facebook users - and yes, it's very effective at doing that. But the demographic information that Facebook has accumulated in the process is a goldmine for advertisers and marketers.

There has never been a more complete and accurate collection of demographic information for such a large group of people worldwide readily accessible to advertisers. And you can take advantage of it today using Facebook's pay per click advertising platform. Here are some of the ways you can target Facebook users:

- Location (Country, state, city, etc.)
- Gender
- Age
- Education (College grad, in college, high school, etc.)

- Workplace
- Relationship (Single, in a relationship, engaged, married, etc.)
- Language
- Interests (this is where things really get interesting – think book titles, TV shows, political causes, etc.)
- Pages liked
- Etc.

The true power of Facebook Ads is in combining different demographic data to drill down and run ads to a highly targeted group of individuals who are your ideal prospects. Here are a few examples:

Let's say you have a pet shop in Chicago and you're running a two-week clearance campaign. You can select to display your advertisement only to Facebook users who have liked dog pages and who live in the Chicago area. You can choose to not target anyone else than people in the Chicago area, so users in New York won't see the ad.

If you sell an online program teaching people how to improve relationships and live a better life with their loved one, you can target people who have selected "Married" as their relationship status.

Never before in the history of advertising has it been possible to target specific niche markets so specifically. The possibilities are mind-blowing. With a powerful combination of 1 billion active users, unparalleled demographic targeting capabilities and a relatively low level of competition, Facebook PPC is the perfect place to advertise your products and services.

We run and manage Facebook advertising campaigns for our own businesses as well as for our clients and event several celebrities. If you'd like to find out how we can help you generate a flow of laser-targeted prospects who are interested in your product or service, reach out to us on MatthiasMazur.com/apply and let's chat.

Google AdWords

Many people know that Google is the world's biggest search engine. What they don't know is that Google is also the world's biggest advertising agency. Its advertising platform is called Google AdWords, and offers pay-per-click advertising, and site-targeted advertising for text, banner, and rich-media (animated) ads. The AdWords program includes local, national, and international advertising reach. Google's text advertisements are short, consisting of one headline and two additional text lines. Image ads can be one of several different standard sizes.

To advertise, you select the keywords that should trigger your ads and the maximum amount you're willing to pay per click. When a user searches on Google's search engine on www.google.com or the relevant local/national Google server (e.g. www.google.co.uk for the United Kingdom), ads for relevant keywords are shown as "sponsored links" on the right side of the screen, and sometimes above the main search results.

Without getting caught up in all the technicalities, just know that Google has a complex way of ranking the relevance of which ad should be displayed in which order. Over the years, internet marketing experts have figured out ways to understand how Google works, but every few months, the search engine comes out with a new set of rules and advertisers must follow the guidelines or risk getting kicked from the advertising program. Google is very protective of which ads are displayed on their search engine and it only wants the most relevant ads to be shown to people who use their search engine. I've seen many instances where people who were spending millions of dollars every year with Google got their account shut down because they didn't follow the new guidelines. So make sure you follow the rules if you want Google to show your ads to the world.

The "Google Display Network" (also known as the "content network") shows AdWords ads on sites that are not search engines, such as blogs, forums, and other content-rich websites. These content network sites are those that use AdSense, the other side of the Google advertising model. AdSense is used by website owners who wish to make money by displaying ads on their websites. Google robots (known as "spiders") crawl through millions of web pages online and automatically determine the topic of pages and display relevant ads based on the advertisers' needs. Most online advertising platforms allow you to run ads across Google's network, including text ads (that look like small newspaper classified ads), image ads (also known as "banner ads"), local business ads, mobile text ads, and in-page video ads.

Bing Ads

Bing Ads (previously MSN AdCenter) combines with its inventory with Yahoo's inventory and has its own PPC network that works in the same way as Google AdWords. Keep in mind that even though Yahoo owns a smaller share of the search engine market, it can still be extremely beneficial to your business and help you attract more leads than you can handle.

Benefits of advertising on PPC networks

There are many benefits to advertising your business using PPC networks. Here's why you should start using Pay per Click advertising to generate leads and customers:

- **Low risk**. You can start with a minimal investment, and you only pay when someone clicks on your ad and visits your site, so you have absolute control over the cost per visitor.
- **Flexible.** No long-term contracts or commitments. You can change your bids nearly instantly and can increase, decrease, or stop your spending at any time. You can also easily add new keywords and launch new campaigns literally every single day.
- **Immediate results.** Paid advertising can deliver prospects to your website in a matter of hours.
- **Easy and fast to implement**. A campaign can be up and running in less than 30 minutes. Even large pay per click campaigns running across many search sites take only a few days to launch.
- **Can fit any budget.** If your budget is limited and you can't afford to advertise in newspapers or on television,

you can still attract highly targeted prospects by selecting keywords that are less popular and less expensive but still relevant to your business.

- **Easily trackable.** With PPC campaigns, you're able to track exactly how many people visited your site as a result of a specific ad, for a specific keyword, on a specific site and you know exactly how much you paid to get them there. You can also follow their path once they're on your website, and see exactly where they go, and what percentage of leads complete the actions you create (fill out a form, buy a product, book and appointment, etc.)

Direct Response Magic

Most business owners have never heard of a direct response website. They spend thousands of dollars on a beautiful but useless website, only to find that it does not generate any leads and customers on an automatic and regular basis. If your website is not turning your prospects into paying customers, you're wasting your money, and you could be doing much better.

We previously outlined the importance of direct response advertising and marketing when creating ads and marketing pieces, now let's talk about the importance of having a direct response website.

As I mentioned earlier, the purpose of a direct response website is very simple: to get some form of response from someone visiting your website. Your website should either prompt the visitor to give you his contact information, call your office for more information or make a sale.

Once the prospect has signed up on your site and has given you permission to contact him, you can then follow-up and build a relationship. If your website is not moving the prospect forward in the sales process, you are leaving money on the table every single day. Here are the major differences between image based websites and direct response websites.

"Image based websites" are designed to impress, they focus on your business, and tell visitors how great your business is. The truth is that customers don't care about you. They only care about themselves and what's in it for them.

Direct response websites focus on the customer. They tell the customer what's in it for them and focus on their benefits. The customer wants to know how his life will be improved by using your product or service. He doesn't care about how great your organization is.

Direct response websites enable you to capture your visitors' contact information and receive permission from them to communicate with them. You can (and absolutely should) send him a series of follow-up emails that shows him step-by-step how to use your product, and how it will benefit him. This can be fully automated.

Direct response websites allow you to build a relationship with your prospect over time. On average, you'll need to communicate between 5 and 15 times with your prospect before he pays attention to your message and decides to buy. This turns a cold prospect into a warm paying customer.

Direct response websites allow you to automatically follow up with your customers after they buy something on your website. By servicing your customer after the sale, you make sure your customer is satisfied. This allows you to continue to market to him over weeks, months and years. Shift the focus from shouting how great your organization is to educating your prospects and customers what benefits they will get by using your products and services and your business will soar.

What information should you collect?

One of the main components of your website that must be displayed on every page is a form where visitors can enter their email address to be added to your mailing list. This will give you an incredible asset: an email list that you can use to communicate directly with your prospect and customer base on a very personal level. The higher the opt-in rate on your website, the bigger the list of prospect you'll build. Having a responsive list is an incredible asset in your business, giving you the ability to reach out to your customers at any time.

The bare minimum you need to collect is the visitor's email address. With his email address, you can then ask him to fill in a bigger form, providing you with more data like his full name, his phone number, his physical address, etc. Request only the visitor's email address on your website on the first page, and once he's entered his email address, you can then send him to a page to have him fill in a longer form with full contact information. That way, you already have his email address added to your auto-responder and you can start following-up with him and start building a long-term relationship via email to educate him about your products and services.

The Ethical Bribe

A very effective tactic to increase the amount of opt-ins on your site is to offer what we like call an "ethical bribe". Don't worry, it's not shady, and it won't put you in jail. But it will put a lot of money in your pocket. Since the goal is to build the best relationship possible with everyone who joins your list, it's best you offer something of value to a new prospect that joins your email list. In other words, you need to bribe him with something valuable enough to compel him to sign up to your email list.

One of the most popular ethical bribes is a free report your prospect can download online after opting in. If you run a hair salon, it could be a report about the "10 tips choose a perfect hair cut". If you own a software company that sells to high-level executives, it could be a whitepaper about the "7 ways to increase customer management". In essence, you have to create a special gift to incentivize people of joining your list. Your gift could be a downloadable tip sheet, a special report, an audio interview, a video recording, a great resource list, etc., or anything else that can appeal to the visitor's interest in your product or service. The free gift can also be something you ship through the mail.

Make sure you format your ethical bribe professionally. It will show your subscribers that you offer them professional quality even in the free information you give away. That lets them know what they can expect from you in the products and services you market. If they are impressed with the free gift they receive simply by signing up, it increases the chances of positioning you as the go-to company in your marketplace.

Your Automated Sales Force

Not so long ago, following up with leads and customers was probably the most difficult thing to do in business. Using physical mail meant paying for copywriting efforts, printing, buying envelopes, and shipping and handling among other things. Nowadays, you can use software called an autoresponder, which is a tool that enables you to collect and store the information of people who opt-in to your list, send emails as part of a follow-up sequence, and it doesn't involve spam or sending unsolicited email.

What it means is that once a prospect subscribes to your mailing list, you can set up a sequence of prewritten emails that are sent to prospects at regular intervals that you choose. The most incredible asset you can have in your online presence is a big list of people on you mailing list that are interested in your products or services, and whom you can contact frequently at the touch of a button.

You can use an autoresponder to essentially send emails out to your prospect list even when you're not at your computer by using either the follow-up or broadcast method.

This is how a follow-up sequence works. For example, you can create a 7-part email course that educates your prospects about the benefits of your products and services. You can then set the intervals of your choice for the emails to be sent out every two days. You write the emails once and then anyone who subscribes to your list will automatically be sent those emails for as long as you create the sequence for. Using an autoresponder in your business has the power to double your sales over the next 90 days. We've seen it happen with many of our clients and members. It takes a few hours (or few days at most) to get up and running, and will bring in money for months and even years to come.

And it doesn't matter if you're online or if you're away from the computer. The emails will get sent automatically at the intervals you choose, and new prospects that sign up to your list will be added to the same follow-up sequence and receive the emails you created in a sequential manner. If they choose to unsubscribe (which happens over time), all of that is taken care of without you having to lift a finger.

Keep in mind that this is not spamming. This is permission-based email marketing, as you're only contacting people who have requested more information from your company.

The main benefit of using an autoresponder is the fact that the majority of people need to be exposed to a solution several times before they make a buying decision.

Most visitors who are landing on your website are looking around at what you're offering, and then end up leaving the site because you have no means of capturing their information and following-up with them. So unless you can get them onto your email list (also known as an opt-in list), the chances are you've lost those visitors forever.

What you'll find is that people get to know and trust you over time as you send them more and more valuable information. The longer you can maintain a relationship with them, the more likely they are to do business with you.

The beauty of using an autoresponder is it saves you printing, posting and packaging costs and enables you to contact all your prospects and customers around the clock, anytime you like.

The second type of email messages you can use is called a broadcast email. A broadcast email is a message you can set up in your autoresponder that will be sent to your entire email list. Whereas email follow-up message get sent in a sequential manner, broadcasts can be sent at a specific time and date and reach every all your email subscribers. This is very useful if you want to inform your prospects about a special sale you're doing next week or for an upcoming launch of your next product.

Let's imagine you have an auto repair shop, and you're looking to attract a new wave of customers. You could type an email, upload it to you autoresponder, and reach all your subscribers in a matter of minutes telling them that you're offering a free oil change for anyone who comes in your shop and buys something for over $50.

I know a small restaurant in the Netherlands that achieves incredible results by doing very basic email marketing. The restaurant has approximately 15 tables, prices aren't cheap, and the menu isn't very long. But the owner does something very smart: at the end of every dinner, he asks customers for their email address, and asks them if he can add them to his mailing list. He adds them manually to a basic autoresponder and sends a broadcast email to the whole list once every month. His list has approximately 800 email contacts and every time he emails the list, his restaurant gets packed for an entire week. Keep in mind that he does many things wrong by using bad subject lines and bad email copy, but it still gets the job done. This is an excellent example of how any local business can increase its business by using effective email marketing.

Recommended tools

There are hundreds of email marketing software solutions on the market. Some are great, some are terrible. Here are the ones I recommend and use in our businesses every single day. All three work well and are can be setup in less than an hour:

GetResponse.com

This company based in Europe works extremely well and is affordable even for someone with a limited budget. The service is available in several languages and the interface is extremely easy to use. We've used their service for over 10 years and the results and ease of use of the platform are always satisfying. For more information, check them out at GetResponse.com.

Aweber.com

One of the best-known email autoresponder services on the market. It is very similar to GetResponse, and everything is hosted on the Aweber platform – so there's nothing to download on your side. Check them out at aWeber.com.

ConstantContact.com

Although the interface and writing emails is a bit more complex and clunky than GetResponse and aWeber, the benefit with ConstantContact is that it allows you to upload your own list of prospects and customers without having to request an audit. AWeber and GetResponse usually require manual approval for each user you upload to their platform, which can be damaging to your business because you will lose between 30% and 80% of your prospects – who will not understand why they need to "activate" their email address. If you currently have a database or a customer list and want to upload them to an autoresponder service, I would recommend using ConstantContact.com. Check them out at Constant-Contact.com.

15

SELLING MORE WITH SOCIAL MEDIA

If you started out in business only to make money, perceive your customers as numbers and don't want to provide any substantial value to the marketplace, I can already predict - even before we dig into this chapter - that the use of social media probably will not help you at all.

But if you believe your company's mission, your products and your services enrich and improve the lives of your customers, using social media to promote your business will bring you not only growth in revenue but also tremendous positive response and "social love and admiration" from your market.

Personalized Marketing

I firmly believe that in the coming years, personalized marketing will be one of the most valuable methods to grow a company's revenue and break through plateaus. The good news is that very few companies really understand this, and if you understand that every prospect is in a different situation than others, you can really crush it using free online tools and platforms.

The fact is that small to medium-sized businesses currently have a tremendous opportunity to capitalize on the use of social media, while competitors still ask themselves if "this whole social media thing is here to stay".

Like I said in a previous chapter, the future belongs to companies that execute and implement quickly and decisively. In this chapter, I'll share several concepts from what I call "relationship marketing" that allow you to create incredible trust with your target market and growth in sales and exposure. I am convinced that one-on-one marketing is the best way for small businesses to take off quickly, even if they don't have the same budgets or brand recognition than some of the largest companies in their industry.

Today, with different social networks and social sharing platforms such as Facebook, Twitter, LinkedIn, Instagram, Google+, Snapchat, Vine, You-Tube, it is possible to establish a precise profile of each person in your target market.

With the emergence of these new platforms that give the ability to everyone to express themselves, share pictures and interesting links or simply connect with friends - it is possible for any entrepreneur to know precisely any prospect's preferences, tastes, desires, and the things that make your target market "tick". On top of that, social media gives you the power to create an incredible culture for your brand and free word-of-mouth and viral advertising. Imagine having hundreds or even thousands of your fans sharing and recommending your products and services to their friends. Wouldn't that be a dream? In today's connected world, it happens literally every single day for businesses that know how to play the game. If you're new to this and don't know what to start with, relax. Learn how to play the social media game and you'll win customers for life.

Be first: Speed to market

Currently, it baffles me when I see how many businesses are still lazy and skeptical about the benefits of social media. I really believe there isn't any downside in using social media to promote your brand. Very few understand and really care about connecting on a personal basis with their customers. I'm not saying you need to spend months coming with a perfect social media campaign, but you need to get going and start somewhere.

If you want to multiply your revenue, you MUST use social media because you need to be everywhere. Be everywhere.

Sharing pictures, videos and interesting and fun content about your brand on social media will force you to raise your game and perform at a higher level. That's a massive benefit I've found to be true for almost every single client we work with. Once their presence starts becoming known on social media, their customer service starts improving, their sales increase and their brand recognition and even their work ethic improves. It's quite phenomenal.

Creating value

Offering and creating value is the first step to making social media work for you, which is why it's crucial to publish interesting and rich content (blog posts, videos, cool pictures, infographics, articles, free reports and whitepapers, etc.). You MUST come up with interesting and useful content, not with pitch upon pitch upon pitch. Nobody cares about your "special offers" and "50% discounts" if you haven't been providing interesting and cool stuff online and interacted with your audience and followers.

If you don't provide any value to your market on social media, you don't deserve to make a single sale because you haven't played the game right.

If you have good products and are open and willing to provide cool stuff to your audience on Facebook, Twitter, LinkedIn, Instagram or any other social network where your audience spends the most time in, you win. If your customer service or your products suck and your customers hate your guts, social media will destroy you, as it rightfully should.

The myth of word of mouth

Wannabe entrepreneurs who start a new venture still believe that word-of-mouth will make their business successful and still believe that if they have a good product, people will talk about it. The truth is that you need to market your offers. You need to spread the word. You need to be on the offense. You need to play to WIN. And being aggressive on social media in providing as much VALUE as possible is the way to win. Don't be aggressive by pitching your offers all over the place. The truth is that many businesses are afraid of the power of social media and what it can do to a brand when all your stuff is publicly available online. The truth is, you don't have a choice anymore. Society has decided that "this internet thing" is here to stay and that people love sharing links and pictures and content online and the more you delay your use of social media, the more ground you lose against your competition.

How to play the social media game

Many books have been written about social media and to be honest, most of them are way too theoretical and don't drive sales. The bottom line is that your social media strategy needs to support your business strategy. It makes no sense at all to start using Facebook and Twitter to-day without having a clear vision of what you want to accomplish online. Using Twitter and Facebook is not in itself a marketing strategy. There are many ways to make social media work, but I firmly believe it should not be the only thing you do. Social media must complement your overall strategy and work hand-in-hand with your marketing and sales strategy.

My philosophy is that social media is a MUST for any business in today's economy. Whether you sell peanuts, boots, airplanes or roofing supplies, there is always a way to make social media work to your advantage. And it all starts by being clear on the strategy you're going after:

- Are you looking to build a massive audience of raving fans?
- Are you looking to raise awareness for your brand?
- Are you looking for more traffic to your website?
- Are you looking to acquire a new segment of the market?
- Are you looking to gain intelligence and data from your

market?
- Are you looking to increase sales in the next quarter?

Social media is an amazing vehicle, but you just need to be clear on the goal(s) you want to reach. You can't reach all goals at the same time and energy, and some will take longer than others. First, you have to understand HOW social media networks work. You need to understand the specific use each of them has and how each platform differs from the other.

Facebook

Facebook is obviously the 800-pound gorilla. If your business isn't on Facebook, you've missed out on hundreds of thousands and even millions of dollars in the past few years. Love it or hate it, it's here to stay. With over 1.5 billion users, you can pretty much find any target market that you can think of. Facebook allows you to create incredibly deep connections with your market and share content without any limits in size or frequency. You can post articles, links, videos, lectures, documentaries, pictures, infographics and anything you can dream of.

The lifetime of a Facebook post can last days and even weeks, which enables you to benefit from social proof since thousands of people can view your content, click "like", comment and share it with their own network of friends. The big secret to get the most out of Facebook is to use the Facebook Advertising platform and promote your content. Yes, it will cost you money, but I firmly believe it is THE number 1 way to put your content in front of the right people at the right time. For this, you definitely want to experiment and start using what is known as "Facebook Dark Posts", which allow you to promote any piece of content to specific segments of your market with a budget that you control and with statistics you can track at any given time.

Remember rule number 1 of marketing: it's all about putting the right MESSAGE in front of the right MARKET using the right MEDIA. Facebook advertising allows you to laser-target who you want your content to be seen by. It's a marketer's dream come true.

Follow me on Facebook.com/Matthias Mazur

Twitter

Twitter allows users to share small tidbits of content such as quotes, links, pictures or videos with messages of up to 140 characters at most. One of the main features of Twitter is that it's the closest to "real time" that exists.

It's ideal for sharing news-worthy content and links to pieces of content to build your brand recognition. Think of Twitter as the world's biggest cocktail party where you can pretty much interact with anyone who has a Twitter account. I've personally tweeted and gotten the attention and responses from numerous celebrities and people who were previously impossible to reach 10 or 20 years ago. It's a giant networking platform that enables you to reach out personally to your customers and send them cool and relevant content and build deeper connections thanks to real interactions.

Long gone are the days of one-way street communication where cor-porations would publish press releases and could get away without ever hearing their customers voices or complaints. Now you can tweet pretty much any company and voice your appreciation or frustration with a product or service. This is a GIANT opportunity for businesses to build more meaningful and long-term relationships with their audiences.

The shelf life of a tweet is a few minutes to a few hours at the very most because of the abundance of content shared by the people you follow. Because of this, I genuinely believe there is nothing wrong with sharing the same piece of content multiple times and at different times of the day. Your fans won't mind and the people who haven't seen your content yet will have the opportunity to see it more than if you just post it once.

Follow me on Twitter: @MattMazur

LinkedIn

LinkedIn boasts over 350 million users, which is 4 times less than Face-book. But it has a massive feature that makes it a very serious platform, especially for business owners. It's the main hub for professionals and usage is high among the educated (bachelor's degree holders and up), and high earners who make over $75,000 per year. It's a great platform to create connections if you're in B2B (business-to-business) world because it's very easy to find people in key positions in companies you might be targeting as prospective customers.

LinkedIn also has a very solid self-publishing platform called Linked Pulse, which allows you to share content in a blog style. Most publishing is related to finance, marketing, business, personal growth and technology, which makes it an ideal way to share valuable content with other professionals and interact with your audience. The bottom line is, if you're in B2B, you MUST treat LinkedIn as the number 1 tool to share content, connect with decision-makers and get new business.

Let's connect on LinkedIn: **LinkedIn.com/in/MatthiasMazur**

Google+

Google+ is Google's attempt at taking on the big dogs of social media such as Facebook and Twitter. Despite a massive budget and brand notoriety (Google, duh), it never really happened. Less than 10% of the users actually use the platform and (at the time of this writing) it really doesn't seem to be getting any traction or attention by users. Yes, small businesses can still benefit by the free exposure and publicity by just adding their content to the platform. It's free and can add another page 1 result in Google for your company name and brand. Although I wouldn't focus on it – simply because people aren't really paying attention to it – we still use it to get more free exposure. If you're targeting B2B and small businesses, I'd go with LinkedIn and Facebook as a priority. If you want to be everywhere – like my companies and clients are – it's an extra free vehicle for your content.

Pinterest

Pinterest is basically a giant online pinboard where you can like and share, which makes it a very interesting platform if you're involved in anything visual. The platform currently has over 80 million users and is growing rapidly. The premise is that you can't share anything on the platform unless there's an image involved. If you run a brick and mortar operation and sell physical products, you need to be on it. Here are 3 fascinating facts about Pinterest:

- 71% of users are women
- 65% of users make over $50,000 in yearly income
- 93% of users shopped online in the past 6 months

This means that if your target market predominantly consists of women and you're not actively involved on Pinterest in sharing your content, you are missing the game. It's not too late to get in, but you need to move fast.

Follow me on Pinterest: **Pinterest.com/MatthiasMazur86**

Vine

Vine is a very fun and interesting video platform that allows you to share content in pieces of 6-second videos that loop over and over again. That's it: 6 seconds. That means you need to be able to tell your story and capture people's attention very quickly. With video being so easily available on mobile devices and computers, it's become indispensable to start creating video-based content, and Vine is a great way to do just that.

Twitter acquired Vine for $30 million in 2012, and the platform now integrates hand-in-hand with Twitter.

Big brands such as Dunkin' Donuts, Samsung, Target, Oreos and Trident jumped on Vine and started putting out fun and share-worthy videos. In 6 seconds, it's not about selling. It's about making a mark in the customer's mind and creating content that is share-worthy on Twitter.

Follow me on Vine: **Vine.co/MatthiasMazur**

Instagram

Instagram is a picture and video (up to 15 seconds only) sharing platform. Facebook acquired it for $1 billion dollars (yes, with a "B"), and it currently boasts over 300 million users.

Instagram allows you to upload and edit pictures and videos and tag them with hashtags (#). Instagram is a massive opportunity for marketers in today's social media space: Piper Jaffray's teen survey concluded that it has become the most important and most-used social network for teens in the United States, well ahead of Facebook.

The platform isn't filled up with links like some of its competitors – the only place that allows you to display a clickable link URL is on your profile page. Generally, I recommend linking directly to your website, your blog, a product page or a lead capture page (where you can get the visitor's email and contact information).

Because Instagram allows you to upload and edit pictures and videos through its multiple filters and lenses, you can pretty much make any mediocre picture really attractive. If you're selling a physical product, it's an ideal place to showcase them and give a human touch to your brand.

If you're selling a service, share videos of your staff, testimonials from happy customers, interactions with your clients and behind-the-scenes footage of your offices and day-to-day operations.

I really recommend posting different types of pictures: some really polished and professional ones (if you're showcasing your products), but also make sure you publish "TMZ-style" footage and amateur pictures that aren't perfectly assembled. People LOVE watching amateur pictures and videos rather than just looking at stock photo footage. Remember: people want to connect with real human beings, not with robots that look too perfect or airbrushed.

Follow me on Instagram: **Instagram.com/MatthiasMazur**

Snapchat

You might have heard of Snapchat from conventional big media outlets saying that teenagers are using Snapchat more than they are using Facebook. And that's correct. That's why Facebook acquired Snapchat for $1 billion (again – yes, billion with a "b") and currently has over 100 million daily active users. Business Insider reports that Snapchat's top demographic is 15 to 25-year-olds (45%) and 25 to 34-year-olds (26%). It's the numbers 1 social network for the young generation (45%), ahead of Vine (28%) and Instagram (23%).

Remember that we mentioned that marketing and selling is all about attention and getting attention? Snapchat allows senders to share content (pictures and videos) that is only available for a few seconds (the sender decides how many seconds he wants the content visible by the receiver. Think of it as "this message will self-destruct in 1-10 seconds".

This is a HUGE deal because it means that the user receiving the content can only see it for a few seconds. Consequently, the receiver needs to pay attention to the content and actually consume it... because once it's gone after a few seconds, it disappears forever. That's where Snapchat is a beast: receivers MUST absorb and consume your content because they will never have another chance to see it again. The disappearing aspect is the key to the platform and there is a very personal feeling to receiving a Snapchat message because of its short shelf life.

If you're marketing to teenagers or young adults, you definitely need to start playing around with Snapchat to understand the dynamic and the environment of it. A word of warning: don't use airbrushed pictures and perfect-looking models in your content – Snapchat is not the place for that. Think of Snapchat as a secret whisper or a note you sent to classmates sitting at the other end of the classroom without the teacher seeing it: keep it real and amateurish.

Follow me on Snapchat: **@MatthiasMazur**

Periscope

Periscope is a live-streaming video platform that got acquired for $100 million by Twitter and launched in the spring of 2015. It allows you to broadcast in real-time to the internet and integrates with your Twitter followers, by letting them know you're about the go "live" when you start a new broadcast. Even though services like Ustream and Livestream have been around for years and numerous brands, Periscope and Meerkat (covered in the next section) took video live-streaming to a whole new level. You can broadcast videos from your office, on a hike, from a concert, your house, your car, or anywhere else just by downloading the free application. Everyone can now broadcast, for free.

It's a revolutionary tool for any brand and business and gives the opportunity to create incredible social proof, authenticity and proximity with your fans and customers and lets viewers ask you questions during the live broadcast. I'm a big advocate of using as many tools as possible to connect with your audience and being EVERYWHERE: on Facebook, Twitter, Periscope, LinkedIn, Meerkat, Google+, your blog, in your customers' homes (books, posters, CDs, USB cards, physical samples, etc.).

What to share on Periscope? Simple: just share cool and fun content. Don't overthink it, just the application, give it a simple and attractive title and press "Broadcast now". Commit to creating live broadcasts every single week or even every single day. This could be when you're driving to the office, walking to meetings, going for a hike, showing your employees, giving motivational tips, doing live Q&A, sharing "7 techniques to live healthier", "3 ways to save money", "5 techniques to do XYZ", behind the scenes content and so on. Even if you only have 3 viewers during your first few broadcasts, commit to broadcasting regularly and have fun with it. Your customers will love you for it.

Follow me on Periscope: @MattMazur

Meerkat

Meerkat is Periscope's big competitor and actually launched before Periscope. Both applications offer pretty much the same service - live-streaming video – but also have a few differences. Since Periscope is owned by Twitter, we can expect it to keep having more impact in the long-term because of Twitter weight and user base. At the time of this writing, there isn't a clear winner between both platforms, although I do believe Periscope might get the advantage due to Twitter's support. Given the speed at which the social media and app space work, I might be proven wrong. That's why I recommend using both services: Periscope and Meerkat.

Both have growing audiences and it would be silly to discard one at this stage.

Follow me on Meerkat: @MattMazur

Not sure about using social media? Read this

The social media game is about understanding where your audience is and committing to spending as much time on the relevant platforms.

If you're selling to women over 40 years old, you need to be on Facebook, Twitter and Pinterest. If you're selling to teens and people in their twenties, you need to be on Snapchat and Instagram too. If you're selling B2B, you need to be on LinkedIn.

So many business owners get caught up in their ego thinking that they "don't have time for social media" or they "don't understand such and such new platform". That's ludicrous. Here's the thing: it's all about your target market. Your target market doesn't care ONE BIT if you believe or not in these new platforms. Do your research and look at the data about each platform and where your audience spends its time, then go there and start creating value, start interacting and building your presence. If you don't... 12, 24 or 48 months from now, you might be wondering why your numbers are down and asking yourself what happened. If you want to dominate and win, you need to adapt. If you don't do it, someone else will.

Supreme Transparency

One of the reasons why many entrepreneurs are slow to have a presence on social networks is their fear of negative comment, criticism, "trolls" and "haters". The truth is that negativity is part daily business life. You can offer the best product or service in the world, there will always be people who find something to criticize.

You need to make the decision of fully committing to your brand, your business and your product. There's no way around it with social media. You will get criticized, you will get people who take pleasure in posting ridiculous and hurtful comments. That's the world we live in. But the more you post on social media, the more you'll protect yourself because if you do a good job, the positive comments and support will outgrow the negative comments. Plus, you'll have a lot of fun interacting with your hardcore fans and followers.

Kill the monster when it's small

If you're not open to the idea of interaction and transparency with your fans and followers, social networks will hurt you. The benefit of being omnipresent online is that it gives you a chance to know exactly what's going on in the market and to handle any criticism or complaint as soon as they appear – before it becomes a massive P.R. crisis like it did for United Airlines (remember the "United breaks Guitars" viral video on YouTube that got picked up by CNN, NBC and major news outlets?). Being a good listener on social media enables you to tackle issues when they're still small.

Let your fans talk about you

One of the benefits of having a solid social media game is that your customers and followers can become your very own advertising department, for free. If you publish an article on your blog, on Facebook, Tumblr or Medium, your members can share your content with their friends.

Be careful not to fall into the trap of "one-way" communication. It's crucial to interact with your audience, ask questions, reply when possible (or at least to the first 10 or 20 replies) and give them the feeling of a genuine human interaction.

Complimenting your internet strategy

Social media should complement what you're already doing. It's not an "all or nothing" game, and I see social media as indispensable yet complementary. Having a good internet marketing and sales strategy is critical for cash flow and revenue purposes, but playing the social media game is a long-term investment in brand equity.

Another benefit of social media is that search engines have started to pay more and more attention to brands that have good social media presence, rewarding them with multiple page 1 results.

Use calls to action to spread your message

Make sure you have a call to action on your key pieces of content (blog posts, videos, etc.) to direct viewers towards the action you want them to take. Having a Twitter or Facebook share button at the end of an article doesn't mean that readers will share it. That's why it is important to clearly encourage viewers to share your content and to give them a reason why they should. It could be as simple as "share this article with a colleague by tagging them" or "share this article and I'll send you my latest white paper about XYZ topic". Don't just assume that people – even your most loyal fans – will share what you publish.

The deadly trap of social networks

You know it: social networks are a goldmine of information. But they can also be a deadly trap for entrepreneurs in terms of time management. Unfortunately, many entrepreneurs think that they need to live on social media to actually build a business. The truth is, Bill Gates, Mark Cuban, Howard Schulz and Madonna haven't built their careers on social media, and they just use it to complement what they are already doing. And even though you can be posting all day long on social media, the truth is that you need to focus on what brings revenue in your business. Having a good marketing strategy and a really effective sales system will actually do more for your business than spending your life on Twitter or Facebook if you're not selling anything at the moment. The bottom line is to use social media as a complement to what you're doing.

At the end of your life, you probably won't tell yourself "oh, I wish I had spent more time on Instagram". Make sure you have your priorities straight and even though I love the power of social media and use it every day, make sure that you actually living a real life and not getting too addicted by life on social networks.

Social proof

You probably noticed it in the past, having someone else talk about you is infinitely more powerful than tooting your own horn. In that respect, it makes even more sense to have testimonials on your website and on your social media profiles. Social proof is absolutely essential to your business. That means that if you can publish behind-the-scenes footage like amateur pictures or videos about your business or even day-to-day shots of life in your company, your audience will finally be able to get a sense of what it really means to be involved with your brand. The more customer testimonials you, the more trust you put out in the marketplace and the more long-term success you create for yourself.

Pride

As a business leader, you need to be really proud of the products or the service you're delivering to the marketplace. Obviously, I assume that you're trying to promote something that has a value and that really satisfies people who are buying it. One of the great benefits of being proud of what you do is that it will inevitably push you to be more creative with your marketing and promotional efforts.

A friend of mine who runs an 8-figure cosmetic company selling high-priced products uses a technique that creates tremendous social proof. In the package his company sends to customers after they purchase, he includes a small video camera that costs less than $20 and a letter that says something like this:

> "Thank you for your order. I would be grateful if you could record a short 30-second video after having tried the product that you just ordered. I also included an envelope with our company address and $20 to cover shipping to send us the camera back. Please only do it if you are satisfied with your order and the experience we have provided. Thank you."

His company goes very deep into the customer relationship and gets amazing testimonials that look extremely authentic and he currently has hundreds of videos on his website that he also shares on Facebook, Instagram and other platforms. That means he doesn't even need to sell his product as "hard" as his competitors because his customers are doing the selling for him. Imagine having hundred the videos from happy customers all over the Internet, wouldn't that be immensely persuasive to people who are thinking of doing business with you?

Send a different email to your customers after purchase

Many companies email their customers after purchase with a very simple (and often stale and lame) template email thanking them for the business. But this is a tremendous opportunity to do more and to stand out from your competition. After someone has purchased something, they perceive your brand as superior to others because they have just given you money. A neat trick that one of our clients uses is to email every customer after the purchase and ask them for a quick webcam testimonial. Obviously not everyone agrees, but it's the ideal moment to ask for something more than just money. For legal purposes, just make sure we have the consent of your customer to use the testimonial in your marketing material.

A note about asking for social proof

I highly recommend giving something in exchange for someone's time and I'm always baffled by companies to ask for testimonials without giving anything in return. I recently received a letter from the car dealership where I bought my last car, asking me to rate their services and answer a 3-page survey. I looked at the package they sent, and they didn't include any benefits for me. If you expect your customers to give 10 or 15 minutes of their time to answer a survey and to give you a testimonial, you need to give them something more. The least I would have expected would have been a free oil change or even a cheap keychain. Incidentally, I did not take the time for the survey because they didn't give me a valid reason. Understand that everyone is busy: we are all dealing with our day-to-day lives, working and growing our businesses, taking care of our families and our health. So if you ask for testimonial out of the blue, at least give them something of value in exchange. The more testimonials you get, the more you will sell without even having to present your products. Think of every testimonial as an automated sales person that can be shared online on social media for months and years to come.

16

HOW TO TURN ANY WEBSITE INTO A CASH-CREATING MACHINE

I said it before and I'll say it again: to be competitive in today's economy, your online presence needs to be highly effective and highly optimized, allowing you to attract visitors and convert them into leads and customers effortlessly and automatically. Let's have a deeper look at what your online presence needs to include.

Fast-loading pages

How many times have you stumbled on a website, been interested in its content, but had to wait 15-20 seconds for the first page to load? Well, you may be giving your visitors the same treatment, and that's one of the reasons why you're most probably not converting as many visitors into leads as you could be. In our day and age, people don't have the time to wait for a website to load for 20 seconds. All your pages – especially your landing pages – need to load almost instantly. Furthermore, search engines take into account the speed at which your pages load when it ranks them in the search engine results.

Mobile-responsive pages

So much of the internet traffic nowadays is based on mobile because people are literally living more and more with their cell phones. If your website is not mobile-friendly and doesn't load fast on mobile devices, you're losing money every day. To give you a few numbers on how real mobile is in our daily lives check this out:

- 75% of Americans admit bringing their cell phone to the bathroom
- 40% of shoppers consult three or more sources before buying something
- 80% of consumers use smartphone devices to buy

Mobile traffic has taken over desktop traffic, which means that people are using their phones more than their computers. If you're not using mobile-optimized websites and mobile-optimized landing pages in your business, it's time to get going now. What's even better is that most of your competition is probably late to the party too. Yet another reason for you to get mobile-friendly as soon as possible.

Just take a moment and look around you the next time you're in a restaurant, in the car, or in a public place and you'll see how many people have their heads down looking at their phones. The world is rapidly changing and if you're not ready for how people consume content and how people buy, your business will suffer tremendously.

Flash or no Flash?

Flash is a technology that brings interactivity and flashy graphics to a website. The problem is that programmers and designers who can handle Flash easily get so obsessed with the use of it that they design every single aspect of a site with it. The main disadvantage of Flash is that it can end up slowing your website down and making people click away if it's loading too slowly. If you're selling a product that needs to be displayed in full video to show its full potential – such as boats, cars, or planes – then Flash might be suitable for you. A word of warning: don't let a graphic designer create your website. Your website should be designed by a direct marketing expert. It doesn't matter how pretty your site is, it matters how much profit it generates for you!

SEO optimized pages

When you're building your online presence, all the pages on your site need to be optimized to attract the most attention from the search engines. I'm amazed by the number of businesses that have websites that are completely under-optimized and don't show up in the search engines, or can't even show up on page 1 of Google for their desired main keyword phrase. Studies have shown that 90% of people who search on Google never look past page 1, so if your website is not showing up on the first page, many potential customers don't even know you exist.

One goal per page

Look at every page on your website and ask yourself this question: "What is the sole and only action I want people to take when looking at this page?"

Every page on your website must have just one sole purpose and one "call to action" that you want visitors to take when they land on it. If you present them with too many options, they won't take any of them and will quickly leave your site due to overwhelm.

Opt-in form on each web page

We've discussed this several times so you know the importance of collecting email addresses of visitors who land on your website. Your opt-in form (also called "opt-in box") and the mention of your ethical bribe should be visible on every single of your website. This means that no matter which page a visitor looks at, he'll always be able to sign up to your email list. The best place to display your opt-in form is at the top right part of your website. The opt-in box needs to be discreet but compelling, and needs to have a strong call to action to entice the visitor to sign up.

Let me make something else clear: it's not 1995 anymore. So just saying "Subscribe to my Newsletter" is not going to work effectively. You need to be delivering MASSIVE value in your ethical bribe just to get people's attention and to convince them that you are a professional outfit worth connecting with.

Education about your market and products

Your site should include education-based articles. This will allow you to achieve two things simultaneously: educate your visitors and prospects, and generate high search engine rankings. Your articles shouldn't be sales pitch for your products and services, but should be educational and practical to your readers. Remember that you need to publish articles and feed your site with new content on a regular basis to increase your search engine rankings and always keep your online presence as fresh as possible.

Here are some ideas for attention-grabbing articles you can publish:

- 7 ways to improve your health this week
- 21 techniques to lower your golf handicap
- How we helped a client reduce their energy bill by 32%
- 3 reasons why you should wash your car every week
- 11 tips to keep your food fresh longer

Virtual real estate

How's the layout on your homepage? In terms of web usability, keep in mind that the top left part of the computer screen always attracts the most eyeballs when a new page is loading.

Have a look at your current website to find out how the top left area is used and see if you can use it more effectively. Google, Amazon and eBay spend millions testing and optimizing their sites and have found out that the viewer's eye is always attracted to the top left part of a screen, so that should be your site's most valuable asset. Don't put a huge version of your logo on your site: people just don't care about your logo. Use that space to display your navigation bars as well as an effective direct-response headline that communicates your USP in a matter of seconds.

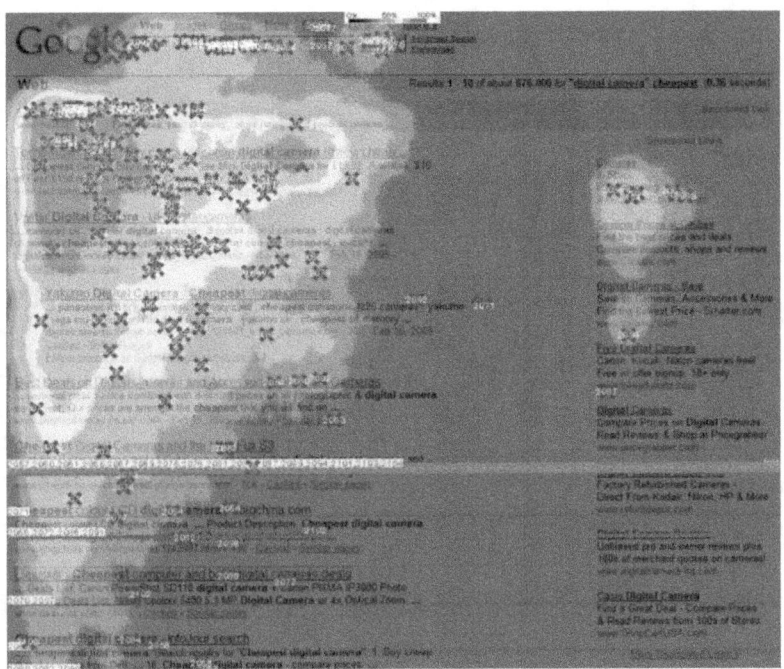

Make sure that the top left corner of your website is optimized with what you want viewers to see.

Testimonial Overload

We talked about the power of testimonials in the previous chapter, but it's such a powerful way to increase sales that I'd like to explore it further. This is something that many business owners simply disregard and it has the power to increase sales without having to do any extra promotion work. Your website needs to feature tons of testimonials collected from your customer base.

What others say about you, your company, your products, and your services is infinitely more credible than anything you can say on your own behalf.

When you make a statement, it's a claim. When your customer makes a statement about you, it's a fact. You cannot overuse testimonials. Just make sure you have permission to use the testimonials you gather from your customers. The most powerful and persuasive form of testimonials are video testimonials. If you're on a tight budget, you don't need to spend thousands of dollars hiring a professional camera crew - any pocket camera is enough to establish the credibility of your business. A good testimonial basically sounds something like "Hello, my name is Jane Doe, and since I started working with XYZ business, I've achieved XYZ results. I highly recommend him to anyone who wants to [keyword here]".

The video can be as short as 20 seconds, or can last for several minutes. People have grown to distrust "too good to be true" type of testimonials, and when a testimonial looks like it's been recorded in a professional studio with an actor who's wearing make-up and who sounds corny, it can only hurt your business. Publishing small video clips of your happy customers recorded in your store or office will make the footage look genuine, raw and more believable. People are tired of seeing actors give fake testimonials on late-night infomercial. Recording short clips with your iPhone of Smartphone of real everyday people talking about your service in a good way is much more believable.

How to Collect Testimonials

Simple: just ask for them. The majority of your satisfied customers will be happy to compliment your business. Make it a new rule from now and commit to asking for testimonials every time a happy customer does business with you. If you can't actively ask for it, instruct your staff to collect testimonials every single time they can. Ask for a video testimonial, and if some customers don't feel comfortable in front of the camera, you can have an audio microphone to record just their voice, or a text version of what they have to say about your business.

In one of my businesses that ran training seminars and bootcamps, we asked attendees to record a short video testimonial about what they thought the event and or anything they had to say about the value of what we delivered. In a matter of weeks, we collected hundreds of video testimonials that I used to build our credibility and trust in the marketplace. Once prospects saw that hundreds of people were recommending our help and services, they were eager to purchase our products and services.

Image Congruency

If you're selling high-ticket products and services, your site needs to "look the part". It's all part of delivering the strongest and best first impression as possible. Every word and picture you display on your website has the power to increase sales. If you're selling to the affluent customer or any kind of high-ticket items, you'll increase your sales considerably if your website looks expensive and high-end.

The mind has its own way of perceiving things and if you're selling million dollar houses, your website needs to look like a million-dollar house. I've seen many real estate agents who still have terrible-looking websites that are quite repulsive. This first image in the mind of the customer will stick for a long time, and it will be difficult to remove it once it's ingrained in their mind.

The 3-second rule

Remember what we mentioned in the chapter about your positioning and your USP: your marketing material and your USP need to be used on all marketing and advertising materials, and this includes, of course, your website. Visitors need to grasp your USP in the first few seconds after landing on your website. If people can't understand your USP and why they should do business with you in less than 3 seconds, you've failed to communicate your USP in a clear way.

Clean design

Google.com. One of the most famous websites on the internet, if not the most famous one of all is a model of simplicity and clarity. Very few links and one main call to action. Google is very clear in what offers the user: a search box. It doesn't have millions of links to articles, it's not cluttered, it's not complicated to use. Many business sites are overcrowded with unnecessary links, heavy graphics and too many pictures. When a visitor comes to the website, your site has to come off as a model of simplicity and clarity, like Google does. Even sites that sell thousands of items such as Amazon.com and eBay.com still look clean and focused. How does your site look?

Direct-response

I've said this several times, and I'll repeat it many more: your website needs to be direct response oriented. Visitors who land on your site should be directed to take action and do something: call your business, subscribe to your email list, or buy your product. Building your email list with prospects on your website must be one of the main – if not the main – focuses of your website.

Video Bonanza

With online video being so cheap to produce (you can shoot a solid video on your smartphone for FREE), I believe businesses would be absolutely dumb not to seize the opportunity to use video to communicate and build trust with their audience. Showing a tour of your offices, publishing videos of your products and services, as well as customer testimonials are easy and cheap ways to establish your credibility.

Automated follow-up system

As discussed in previous chapters, you must focus on collecting email addresses from your visitors and following up with them on a regular basis. Your follow-up sequence needs to have at least 10 pre-written email messages that will be sent out on a pre-defined basis with set intervals as soon as a prospect is added to your list. The longer the follow-up sequence, the higher the chances of increasing the lifetime customer value of everyone who enters your funnel.

E-commerce ready

Visitors who come to your website must have the option of instantly ordering products and services they are interested in. Your website needs to offer an E-commerce system which allows you to automate and streamline your sales process and turn your website into a 24/7 sales machine that will bring in sales even when you're on vacation or during the weekends when your staff is away from work.

A Dutch entrepreneur and close friend of mine sold a record company a few years ago to one of his competitors who now sells thousands of records online. To this day, the new owner still doesn't have a sales-oriented website and his customers can't place an order on his website! To order a record, they need to send him an email with the title they want and wire him some money for him to ship the product.

In this day and age, customers just don't have the time to go through so much hassle. If he put all his records on a sales-oriented web platform, he would instantly increase his revenue. No one has time to send an email and go back and forth for days when they can have the same product shipped to their doorstep from another merchant. He has without doubt lost hundreds of thousands of dollars over the last few years. Don't make the same costly mistake.

17

GOING HIGH FEE

For every business income goal, there is a business model to reach it. If you're just starting out and you want to make $10,000 a month, there is a model for that. If you want to make $100,000/month, there is a different business model for that. And if you want to go big and scale the business to $10 million/ month, there are business models for that too. For every income goal you're shooting for, there is a different and more specific business model that can get you there.

If other companies have done it before you, it means that there is a working model for it. Obviously, if you are currently barely breaking $1 million a year in sales, scaling to $50 million will require a much different approach, a different business model and different internal operation procedures to scale. It's the same as with racing. Some cars can only go up to 50 miles/ hour while others can go up to 500 miles/ hour. If you want to go faster, you need to use a different engine. In this chapter, we'll go over some key concepts to help scale your business in a matter of weeks and sometimes up to 1,200% in less that 90 days, like some of our clients have done.

Why cheap is deadly

If you're currently selling products and services that allow you to be flexible with pricing, the first thing I will advise you to do is to raise your prices. Unless your business runs essentially on volume, raising your prices will almost always have a positive impact on the type of customers you attract, the amount of friction that you have in your business (by decreasing it) and the overall revenue and profits in your company.

One of the first things that need to be said about pricing is that the vast majority of businesses are completely wrong in terms of how they think about pricing. They look at what the competition is doing and base their pricing based on what others do. In my opinion and after over 10 years of selling high-priced and high fee offers and helping our clients generate millions of dollars by selling high-priced offers, competing on price is a recipe for disaster.

If you look at any market, there is always a cheap option and an expensive option. One of the things that I always advise our clients to do is to immediately raise their prices and develop the necessary marketing material that can sustain the positioning of their offer in the marketplace. If you're currently is service provider such as a coach, a consultant, a trainer, a therapist or sell services by the hour, you seriously need to reevaluate your business model and stop charging by the hour. The solution is to charge by packages and creates value-based offers that help your customers get as fast as possible from where they are right now to where they want to be and offer packages at prices anywhere between $1,000 to $10,000.

I host a weekly show called "Coach's Corner" where I go in depth into all the marketing, positioning, sales, and mindset aspects of selling high-end products and services and increasing your income. If you're service provider, you definitely need to check it out, it's available on my blog MatthiasMazur.com

Doing reverse math

Once you've decided that you want to sell high fee offers and stop charging by the hour, you need to do reverse math. One of the first things that you need to keep in mind is that cheap is deadly.

Why? Because you attract the wrong type of people: cheap customers usually create the biggest headaches and demand the most attention. If you've sold anything that's cheap and if you've sold anything that's high-end, you probably noticed that the cheapest customers are the ones that demand the most hand-holding and also create the biggest issues for your customer support.

If you're providing a solid high-value service, I urge you to raise your prices to at least $1,000 dollars and preferably between $2,000 and $5,000. Some of our clients have even gone up to $10,000 dollars as a front end offer. The result of this is that you will start getting better clients and more committed clients because they've invested more in the process. And since they've paid more, they're going to pay more attention to your service and will get better results.

Why 1-on-1 services are killing your business

If your business is based on providing 1-on-1 services, it's crippling your business. Why? Because the business model you're using is a monster that you've created. The more you grow, the more you work, and the more you get tired. And more importantly, you're creating a business that is completely dependent on you: if you stop working, the income stops.

Let's say you charge $100/ hour and you're coaching clients 40 hours per week (which is a LOT). You're making $4,000 a week, which is $16,000 a month. It's a respectable income. But here's the truth: you can never grow past that.

If you charge by the hour, your income is limited to the number of hours and to the rates you're charging. And even if you increase your rates, you're always dependent on putting in more hours to make more money. The result of this is that you're a SLAVE to your business. You're trapped. What happens when you want to take a few of weeks off? No income. What happens when you get sick and you can't work for a few weeks?

You lose your income.

You've basically created an income ceiling and you have no leverage whatsoever. That's why selling HIGH FEE offers is key and why you need to stop charging by the hour.

Because the truth is, your clients don't care if you spend 5 minutes, 5 hours, or 5 months with them. Your clients just want results. If you're doing 1-on-1, the truth is no one cares about being helped for 15 hours or 15 years. If you can get your clients faster results, you MUST apply high fees and stop charging by the hour.

3 reasons why you're not charging high fees

Reason #1: You don't think what you're offering is valuable enough

If you think that what you're delivering is of high value then you need to start charging high fees. If your service doesn't deliver results for your clients, you need to improve the quality of your service. There's no way around it. But if you're delivering value, you need to be charging high fees. If you don't charge high fees, you'll always be a slave to your business.

Reason #2: You don't know HOW to do it

You KNOW other people in your market are charging more, your competition might be charging 5, 10 or maybe 50 times more than you, but you just don't know how to raise your prices and how to create marketing material and a sales process that converts prospects into high-paying customer.

Reason #3: You're afraid

Maybe you're afraid that if you raise your prices, you won't be able to attract new clients, and that the clients you have now might leave you if you increase your prices.

And in some ways, getting rid of cheap clients is a GOOD thing because then you can really focus on getting high-quality clients.

The High Fee Mindset

A segment of the market will ALWAYS happily pay more. Let's have a look at the hotels and accommodation business.

There are literally thousands of hotel chains in the world that each caters to specific demographics and segments or the market. For example, the Four Seasons Hotels cater to people who like luxury and high-end service, whereas Holiday Inn caters to people who travel on a budget. Fundamentally, both products are in the same market and offer a similar product: a warm room with a bathroom in a decent location. A night at the Holiday Inn will cost you $100, and a night the Four Seasons will cost you between 5 to 20 times more.

Let's have a look at the air travel industry. Nowadays, you can literally fly for less than $50. Budget airlines are in constant price wars, beating each other by lowering prices every day, which is great for the consumer. You can buy tickets for $50 on low-cost airlines and you can fly coach for anywhere between $100 and $500. Or you can fly business for prices between $500 and $5,000 and you can fly first class starting around $500 to $25,000. And if you really want to live the high life, you can fly private and pay approximately $5,000 to $10,000 per flight hour. Same market, different segments, different pricing.

And yes, I know some people will debate this and say that flying private is a different market than flying coach, but I trust that you understand what I'm trying to communicate here.

Let's talk about one final example where you can see a massive difference between in pricing between the cheap end of the spectrum and the high-end segment: the automobile market. You can buy a used Toyota Corolla for $500 or you can buy a brand-new Ferrari for $300,000. Fundamentally, both products will get you from A to B - and yes the Ferrari might indeed be faster. Obviously, both brands sell very different things, Toyota usually features its exceptional mileage and long-term warranty as selling points, and Ferrari sells luxury, exclusivity and feeling of belonging to an elite group of people category who are part of the "Ferrari club".

You will never see high-end brands discount their prices because of tough economic times or to get new customers. Luxury brands such as Louis Vuitton, Ferrari, Bentley, or the Four Seasons hotels will never offer their products for 50% discounts or 90% off. And that's exactly what I'm urging you to consider about your service-based business: to take the position of the most expensive and valuable brand in the market, which allows you to sell your products and services at a high price, attract the best customers who are fully committed to the service you can bring to them and who will be loyal and high-paying fans for years to come. Discounting prices as a means to get new business is one of the very worst business practices that I see being used on a common basis on a regular basis by businesses.

Reverse Math Exercise

Let's do a quick exercise to figure out how much you should charge and how many leads (prospects) you need to reach your financial goals.

First, you need to decide your income goal. Maybe you want to reach the $10,000, $50,000 or $100,000 a month in your service-based business.

Second, decide how many clients you need and what price you need to charge to reach that goal. If your goal is $20,000 per month and you want to be able to price your service at $5,000 dollars, you only need 4 clients a month. That means one client a week.

When you have a solid marketing and sales system in place such as our proprietary "Conversion Engine" that our clients use, the typical conversion rate that you'll be getting is 1 out of 5. This means that to get 4 clients who pay you $5,000, you will need to have approximately 20 leads a month, which is less than a lead a day. And if you want to scale and grow from $20,000/ month to $40,000/ month, you just need to double the amount of leads you generate. With 40 leads a month and a Conversion Engine that typically converts 1 client out of every 5 prospects, you only need 8 clients to reach $40,000/ month.

If you're a service provider and want to grow your business, I highly recommend you start raising your fees and start charging by value and by package rather than charging by the hour. If you're working by yourself and charging by the hour, it is not a scalable business model and it will force you to always work to create more income instead of having your business work for you and be able to leverage your service. Turning the service you provide into a high-perceived value offer is the fastest way to multiply your revenue in the next 30 to 60 days. The great thing about raising prices is that it will also help repel bad clients and help attract great clients who are happy to pay high fees for a high-quality service.

Additionally, you must have a steady flow of leads coming into your business and asking for your help. For this, you need to have lead generation systems in place and I highly recommend using paid advertising strategies because they generate a constant stream of prospects rather which will put an end to the "feast or famine" cycle that so many businesses suffer from. If you want more help about implementing all this in your business and how we can do it all for you, go to MatthiasMazur.com/Agency or visit ZuraMedia.com.

18

THE ART OF TURNING ANYONE INTO YOUR CUSTOMER

In this chapter, I'll share with you how to create the best possible offer in your marketplace by using the concept of "risk reversal" to eliminate the customers' risk in any transaction, thus eliminating the primary reason why most prospects don't buy from you.

Put all the weight on your shoulders

First, let's start with an example that illustrates the power of risk reversal. A father wanted to buy a puppy for his daughter. There were two for sale in his town and both puppies were equal in all aspects. The first man told the farmer he wanted $100 for his puppy – take it or leave it. The second man was selling his puppy for $250.

The second man told the father he wanted the daughter to take the puppy home for a month before making any purchasing decision. He offered to bring the puppy out to the daughter's home along with a month's worth of food to feed the puppy. He said he'd send out his own employee once a week to show the girl how to take care of the little dog. Finally, at the end of 30 days he'd drive over to the father and either take back the puppy and clean up the house – or ask, then, to be paid the $250. Which puppy do you suppose the father decided to purchase for his daughter?

Obviously, it was a no-brainer. Your customers will be thinking the same thing once you start integrating the principle of risk reversal in your business.

Whenever two parties come together to do business of any kind, one side is always asking the other (either consciously or otherwise) to take more or all of the risk.

When you take away the risk to your prospect or client, you lower the barrier to action and eliminate the primary obstacle to buying. And that's one of the techniques you must implement in your business immediately. Let your customers know that if they are dissatisfied with your product for any reason, you will give them their money back, re-do the job at no charge or whatever else you can do to show that you stand firmly behind your product or service.

If you're like most other businesses, you probably already include a guarantee of some kind when a customer purchases a product or service. The idea here is to emphasize your guarantee in every marketing piece you have, and maybe even have it stand as a sort USP to assure prospects and remove all possible fear of transaction and risk associated with the purchase in their mind. Not only do I recommend you to mention your guarantee everywhere, I also advise you to think about how you can turn a transaction and make it "better than risk-free". Smart businesses have implemented this strategy in the past few years with great success, and you'd be missing out on extra business by not to use the same concept in your sales process, especially if your product delivers what you promise.

The concept comes with an idea that I mentioned earlier, which was over delivering and doing more than what is expected from you. The more you give, the more you get. It may sound corny, but I've found it to be true and so have our clients. The more value you offer, the higher price you can charge, and the least perceived risk you present to the custom er. With customers having the ability to price-shop thousands of items online by the touch of a button, you need to bring something more to the table than your competitors do. And adding a "better than risk-free" component is an effective way of increasing your sales and profit figures. Even if some tire-kickers end up abusing your fantastic guarantee, you'll attract way more business this way than by using a common and understated guarantee.

Something else that I've noticed on several occasions in my own businesses as well as in many of my clients' businesses is that every time you increase the guarantee, profits increase too.

And because you'll be one of the only businesses (if not the only business) that takes all the risk in the transaction, you'll attract more customers who will want to do business with you because they'll simply feel safer with your conditions and will sense your commitment to helping them get the result they want. Powerful risk reversal will also allow you to push prospects sitting on the fence to buy and do business with you, giving you the opportunity of servicing them for months and years to come, earning repeat business and possibly even testimonials and good referrals that can lead to extra business.

Are you starting to see all the ways you can adapt the concept of risk reversal to eliminate uncertainty, increase sales and conversion and give your business a competitive edge? I certainly hope so. If you remove all the risk from your prospect's mind, you increase the chances of getting his business. If your product or service performs as you say it does, he will continue to buy from you again and again.

Your guarantee must be sincere and honest, and you must be able to stand by it at all times. It must have no loopholes or small font, because insincere risk reversal policy can do more harm than good.

If you already use some sort of risk reversal, try to make it stand out more by making it perfectly clear in the verbiage you use in all your communication materials and feature it in visible places in your marketing pieces. If your product or service delivers on what you promise your customers

– the longer the guarantee and the more specific the end result expectations you make, the more people will buy. I've seen it happen time and time again in different markets, online as well as offline.

Usually, longer guarantees like 60 or 90-day guarantees will increase sales over a 30-day guarantee. That's something you should start testing as soon as you can. A full year guarantee or even longer will often perform better than a 60 or 90-day guarantee. The more specifically you tell customers what "satisfaction" and the end goal looks and feels like and what they can expect after using your product or service, the more compelled they become to invest their money and themselves in what you have to offer.

The clearer and more specific guarantee you formulate, the more impact it will have on a prospect. Let's say you're selling a diet product and your current guarantee just says something like "satisfaction guaranteed". You can make it much more powerful by turning it into something like:

> "No questions asked, 90-day 100% money-back guarantee. If you don't honestly feel younger, more energetic, and healthier and if you haven't lost at least 20 pounds within the next 90 days of using our product, we don't want to keep your money. You have every right to ask for a full, no-questions-asked 100% refund anytime you wish. And if you decide you want a refund, there'll be no questions asked and no hard feelings whatsoever. We'll still part as friends".

That's a much more powerful guarantee, and it makes "satisfaction guaranteed" sound irrelevant. Think of how you can change the wording of your guarantee to make it stand apart from the crowd. When you use risk reversal, you are basically telling your prospects and customers that they will never make a bad buying decision by doing business with you. That's a powerfully persuasive point to make as it motivates everyone who's on the fence to take action. It turns people who were only slightly interested and turns them into hot prospects who are ready to buy. It makes people who were trying to decide between you and one or more of your competitors choose you without even thinking twice.

Unless your product or service seriously fails to perform – or just doesn't match the promises you've made when selling it – the number of people taking you up on a refund guarantee will be insignificant in comparison to the increased sales and profits you will make.

I've seen strong risk reversal double and triple sales without even changing the rate of customers using the guarantee and asking for a refund. If you're really worried about the increase in potential refunds, run a small test on a few initial transactions and compare the numbers. Risk reversal and guarantees should be used in all your marketing efforts. Your staff should be using risk reversal to ease the doubts or skepticism of prospects and to compel them to take action now. All your advertising and marketing material should use the power of risk reversal.

Case Studies

Risk reversal can even become an important part of your USP, and even the main component. That's exactly what Hyundai did when it came up with "America's Best Warranty." It's a 10 year/ 100,000-mile warranty that covers the engine and some additional elements of the car. This warranty is in addition to the standard new car 5 year/ 60,000-mile warranty, which covers nearly every new car component. At the time when it was introduced, it was unheard of especially for an automaker that wasn't known for reliability. Hyundai executives knew that car buyers were doubtful of Hyundai automobiles because of its reputation of producing mediocre vehicles. To overcome the perception that Hyundai cars were unreliable, they invented a guarantee stronger than any of their competitors had. Instantly, they became a market leader since nobody else could offer such a strong assurance. This move totally turned Hyundai around: customers flocked to buy their cars and other car manufacturers started implementing similar extreme guarantees just to be able to stay competitive.

Weight loss programs guarantee specific weight loss in a specific period of time.

Domino's Pizza won't charge you if your pizza arrives 30 minutes after you've ordered.

Major corporations as well as smart businesses offer these guarantees for a reason. They do it because risk reversal gives them a tremendous competitive advantage. And a strong risk reversal policy will do the same for you.

The Power of FREE

Everyone loves the idea of receiving something free. The concept of "free" is not new and has been used time and time again with great results. I'm always surprised why more businesses don't use it to attract more customers and increase their sales conversions. Do not underestimate the power of giving away low-cost but high-value gift-with-purchase items to your buyers. Including something as a "bonus" in your offer by giving something for free to your customers will allow you to craft even more powerful sales messages and irresistible offers.

Your goal must always be to create the most compelling offer in your marketplace, something that your competition isn't offering or doesn't dare to offer. Including an extra free "gift with purchase" will help you build up a reputation as "one of the good guys" in your market and will increase the likelihood of customers coming back to you for repeat purchases.

Gift with purchase offers will allow you to turn skeptical prospects into repeat customers because they'll feel like they'll be getting the best deal they can possibly get.

Subscription-based products like magazines have been using the "free gift with purchase" for decades now for one good and only reason: it works, especially if you combine it with free trial offers. Offering your customers a 30-day free trial plus a free gift when they sign up for the trial is an offer that is hard to refuse. I've personally used this model and offer several times in my businesses, so have many of our business colleagues and clients in million-dollar businesses. Think about how you can come up with such a persuasive offer that removes all the doubts and fears from your prospects. What can you offer your customers as a "free gift with purchase" when someone decides to do business with you?

If you own a tennis retail store, you could offer customers who buy one or two new rackets a box of balls and a few grips. This literally costs you a couple dollars, and has the power to bring in hundreds for every transaction you make.

"Free gift with purchase" offers work great when you do seasonal or time-limited promotions or during product launches or relaunches. You can offer an extra gift to every customer who comes in and buys during your 1-week special promotion. You could send an email broadcast to your list offering subscribers a free gift with purchase when they come to your store and buy something on a specific day. If you run a restaurant, you could offer free desserts to every couple who comes in and buys a full-course meal. The possibilities are infinite. The key is simply to add something to your current offer to make people take action now.

Take them by the hand

Another very effective tactic to turn more prospects into customers by improving your offers is by offering more hand-holding once the customer purchases. It helps the customer use the product or service better, helping him achieve better results, hence increasing the quality of the testimonial he'll be giving you after he's benefited from what you offer. For you the business owner, it will allow you to decrease refunds and customer complaints and increase your relationship with the buyer, giving you the opportunity to increase the lifetime customer value thanks to multiple purchases. Think of the hand-holding components you can add and implement them in your business immediately. As long as your product or service delivers what it promises, it will make wonders for your customers.

Sacrifice early profits

This is a concept that can put off many business owners who do not understand the bigger picture and I hope you are not one of them. If an average customer spends $500 per year with your business over a period of five years, this adds up to $2,500 in Lifetime Customer Value (LCV). If you know that every customer is worth on average $2,500, doesn't it make sense to sacrifice a few dollars on the front-end to attract new customers or keep existing customers happy and build a good relationship?

Of course it does.

Let's imagine you own a software company. Doesn't it make sense to offer a 60-day free trial to prospective customers? Giving away something for free is a strategy that will allow you to put your best foot in the door and offer something truly risk-free. You may end up with less cash flow initially, but the value of having an extra customer who has a high LCV is something that can help you turbo-charge your business.

Why not offer a free meal for every couple who walks in your restaurant? This can allow you to turn one-time visitors into long-term customers by offering them a great experience and collecting their email address at the end of the meal so you can follow-up and market to them for months and years to come. That very same couple could end up coming to your restaurant every other week for months and years, recommending your venue to their friends and organizing a big party at your place once a year resulting in thousands of dollars of extra income for you.

I hope you see the power that sacrificing early profits can have in your business over a period of months and years. This is strategic long-term thinking, not just making a quick dollar from every person that walks in your store or calls your office. Think big, think long-term - it could help you build a huge business just by giving away a $10 meal on the front-end. What can you do to WOW your customers and make a great first impression?

19

ORGASMIC FOLLOW-UPS

By now, you know the importance of collecting email addresses of people who come to your website. But that's just the beginning. You need to collect email addresses from everyone who comes in contact even remotely with your business: inbound calls you receive, addresses from people emailing you for information, customers who buy in your store, etc. Tell your staff to start asking for email addresses of everyone who contacts your business. All these addresses are from people who are interested in what you have to offer, and even if they don't make a purchase immediately, they could turn out to be worth thousands of dollars in lifetime customer value as well as referring future prospects and customers to your business.

When you ask someone for their email address, you need to communicate a direct benefit that they'll be getting by joining your list. You could offer them a coupon code, a free gift, or anything else as an ethical bribe to entice them to join your list. If you take the time to ask for visitors and prospects' email addresses every time someone reaches out to your business, you'll be building a tremendous long-term asset: a responsive email list.

Your list of prospects and customers has the power to add virtually un-limited profits and help you generate cash windfalls whenever you want to. I've seen this happen time and time again in numerous online and offline businesses and it will allow you to grow your profits at lightning speed.

Imagine this: what else has the power to reach out to targeted prospects at the push of a button, and bring in a flood of sales in a matter of hours or days at the most? Email. Nothing else has the power to make such a dramatic impact in your business as using your email list to advertise your products and service by following up on a regular basis with your leads.

My companies have sent literally millions of emails in the last few years and made as much as $100,000 in pure profit just by making an offer by email to a list of customers. Every email address you can get is worth gold.

Profitable follow-up sequence

Once a prospect is added to your email list, your goal is to build the best relationship possible by educating him about your offers and bring value to his life and his universe. This means that loading your follow-up sequence with sales messages will not do you any good.

Blasting your subscriber base with constant "special offers and deals" doesn't offer anything of value to your prospect, and people sooner or later become annoyed by your messages and you'll lose the chance of doing business with him or getting his testimonial and referrals over time. To give you a specific and personalized answer for your business, I would need to audit your marketing and sales process, but generally, I advise clients to apply the 3-for-1 formula in your email follow series.

This means that 75% of all email communication content should be edu-cational and useful to your prospect, and only 25% should be sales-ori-ented, where you mention your products and services and the benefits the prospect will get by becoming a customer or taking advantage of an offer you sell.

I'd recommend you at least create a 10-step pre-written follow-up sequence and send between one and three emails per week. This provides you several weeks of content to build a relationship with a prospect and position you in his mind.

In addition to the pre-written emails that get sent automatically, you can add occasional broadcast emails sent to the entire list to let them know about a special deal you're offering or to give them a bonus gift when they purchase something in your store on a given day. Combine follow-up series with broadcasts, and you'll establish a solid relationship with your subscribers allowing you to increase your profits in the shortest time possible.

Frequency of emails

How often should you email your list? After years of sending out millions of permission-based of emails, I've found that from the moment you send an email, it generally takes up to 72 hours for the majority of your subscribers to open and read your email. Most people don't check their email every single day. It all depends on your target market. If you sell to baby boomers, they might check their email twice a week. If you sell to teenagers, they might check their email twice an hour. But as a rule of thumb, if you email your list on Monday morning, you will get the highest percentage of views most by Wednesday, or even Thursday. This means that emailing your list twice a week is a minimum and will get them involved in your business and educated about your company and your solutions.

What send to your subscribers

The goal of email marketing is to retain your current clients and convince prospects that your solutions are what they need. To do this, it is extremely important to diversify the type of emails you send to always keep your readers on the edge of their seat.

If you usually send text articles, try to send an audio or a video every now and then.

If you have a restaurant, send your subscribers some of your favorite recipes such, wine tasting tips or even advice to choose the right appetizers.

The more you vary formats (text, audio, video) sent to your members, the more you increase the chances that they react to your message.

To get ideas about what to email your list, research forums online and find common questions asked by your market, or simply ask your subscribers what they want to receive from you. You might be surprised by their questions.

Doing research online is very simple. Go to Google and enter "keyword + question" or "keyword + problem". For example: "questions asked by people who go to pizzerias".

Once you get results on Google search, analyze the ones that come up most often, which will give you ideas for the type of paper, audio or video to send to your subscribers. You can also contact your prospects directly and ask them directly what they want to receive from you.

Best days to send email

Over the years and after data I gathered from thousands of email campaigns, we've discovered that the best days to send a mailing to your list are on Tuesdays, Wednesdays and Thursdays. Those days get the highest response. This means that they are more likely to read your content and click on your links, helping you get the most response. On Mondays, everyone is still recovering from the weekend and trying to keep up with the mail they got during two days out of office. On Friday, people are already too busy looking forward to the weekend.

Consistency is Key

If you're running an email newsletter (which you absolutely MUST), make sure you keep the look and feel consistent from email to email. By keeping the look and feel consistent, you help to build and strengthen your brand and your image. Stick to one main template so your subscribers know what to look for and what to expect.

Build curiosity with the subject line

When your email arrives in your subscriber's inbox, you generally have about half a second to catch their attention with the subject line of your email. After this, they will either delete your email or ignore it. In your subject line, you need to arouse so much curiosity by that they can't do anything else but click on your email and read it. For example, instead of using the subject line "Health Newsletter Issue #1", use "A secret way to burn more fat". But getting people to open your emails is just part of your challenge because you need people to:

1.   Receive the email in the first place (email deliverability has become a major issue in the last few years)
2.   Read the subject line
3.   Open the email
4.   Read the email in full
5.   Click the link in the email
6.   Land on your website
7.   Buy the offer/ take action on your website

As you can see – there are many potential hurdles in the way of you getting people to click the links in your emails and purchase from you. The key to this is to practice and also to ensure there is a smooth transition and a common theme from the email's subject line to the email's content to the link of your web page to the page the reader is sent to. Any slight disconnect in any of these and you risk losing people's attention and trust.

Cliffhanger concept

Popular email clients such as Gmail and Hotmail show a preview of the email's content when it arrives in your inbox. This is why the first few lines of your email are vital and must grab the attention of your subscribers. If the first few lines are dull, they won't bother reading your email.

People have an incredibly short attention span and everyone is in a hurry these days. One of the best ways to increase consumption of your emails is to use what we call the "cliffhanger concept". It's a concept widely used in TV series that make you want to know what's going to happen next.

Television networks use it to keep the viewers' interest from week to week, and also apply the concept during movies by placing advertisement breaks just before critical moments in movies when you just need to know what's going to happen next.

Use this concept in your emails: always have some curiosity-building content at the very top of your email, as this is the part that will show in the preview window of your subscribers email program. If it's interesting enough, your subscriber will open your email and continue on reading.

Test and track results
When creating marketing emails, avoid sending heavy-loaded graphics and pictures because many email providers don't download and show images by default, which makes your email look blank and empty. Most autoresponder tools allow you to gather results of your email campaigns with the number of emails opened, links clicked, and number of people who've unsubscribed, allowing you to compare the click-through stats and see which one worked best.

Footer information
At the end of your emails, you can list links to your different products and services. That way, when someone reads your email, he'll always have option of accessing your products or services, giving you the opportunity to increase your sales just by adding a few lines and links at the end of each email you send.

Piggyback on news and trends
A great way to gain credibility and build a deep bond with your readers is to piggyback off the news and trends that are happening in the world or in your marketplace. A good example of this would be sending an email during a major sports event like the Superbowl, offering a discounted sale of 10% on your stock and title your email as "Superbowl Sale". You can adapt this to any kind of event, national holiday or special day throughout the year.

Have a clear call to action

Your emails must have a specific goal: drive traffic to a page, get a call back from your reader, direct him to a sales page, etc. Whatever your goal is, it has to be clearly stated in your email. Don't make the mistake of being sloppy in your call to action. If you want the readers to take a specific, tell them what exactly what to do. Be specific and upfront about the action you want the reader to take: "Click here to order", "Reply to this email for a free gift" and "Call 1-800-XXXXXX today for more information" are examples of clear calls-to-action.

Friendly tone

Always write with a friendly tone as if you were talking to a friend. Don't use a legal jargon or technically-advanced terms because readers don't want to feel like you're trying to impress them or belittling them. Just be clear and understandable and keep it simple. Your subscribers are human beings, and no one likes to get an email with complicated verbiage.

Ultimately, email marketing has the power to change your business for the best and massively increase your profits. Start implementing these strategies today and I can guarantee you'll see a massive change in the next 60 days or less.

20

THE POWER OF MOBILE MARKETING

You've learnt about the power of email marketing and I hope you will be using it on a daily basis to attract new customers and increase sales. Let's have a closer look at a channel still has incredible growth potential and hasn't been taken advantage of by many businesses yet: mobile and text-message marketing.

What is Mobile Marketing?

Mobile marketing involves communicating with prospects and customers via mobile devices. It can be used in the same way as email marketing and works in a similar way in terms of relationship building and prospect conversion. There are many ways of adapting mobile marketing to your business, but we'll be covering mainly text and image messages. Cheaper than traditional direct mail and offering a much higher response, mobile marketing provides all the benefits of email marketing but with a much higher open rate.

Facts and figures you need to know

In the United States, SMS (text message) technology was not widely used until only a few years ago - but it is estimated that 6 billion text messag-

Plus, 90% of text messages are read within 3 minutes and responded to within the hour - compared to email communication which could go unread for days. Here are a few numbers to help you grasp the power and the reach that mobile marketing currently has, and why you absolutely need to start using it.

- More than 30 countries exceeded the 100% mobile device to population ratio. Among them are Russia, Italy, the United Kingdom, Spain, Hong Kong, and Israel.
- 91% of the population of the United States owns and uses a mobile phone, which represents approximately 290 million people.
- 60% of the world's population (4.6 billion) uses a mobile device.
- China has over 815 million mobile subscribers.
- 98% of all handsets in the United States have text message capabilities.
- 68.7 million American citizens use SMS and text services on a regular basis.
- Only 10% of SMS messages are spam (compared to over 90% of email).

Mobile marketing is MASSIVE and still overlooked by the vast majority of businesses. Corporations are starting to play around with the concept, but many are still dabbling with it and don't really know how to use it, which is great news for you. This gives you a tremendous opportunity, and I predict that entrepreneurs who quickly harness the power of mobile marketing and implement it in their marketing strategy will be able to outplay their competition in the next 12 to 24 months. And the beauty is you don't need to transform anything in your business to make use of mobile marketing, you just need to apply direct-response strategies we've laid out for you in this book.

Add mobile to your marketing strategy

As you start collecting email addresses from your prospects and customers, start collecting cell phone numbers too. This way, you'll be able to contact people by sending SMS broadcasts to all your leads. And since

98% of text messages get open and read (which is 10-20 times higher than email open rates), this will allow you to harness the power of an additional communication channel with your prospects and customers. The cost of sending out an SMS depends on the volume of messages that you send, but will generally be somewhere between $0.05 to $0.20 per text message sent. Peanuts.

I recommend you give something for free when you ask prospects and customers for their cell phone number by using the same ethical bribe principal we covered earlier. The "give before you ask" concept will do wonders if you give something valuable to your subscribers when they join your mailing lists (email and text message). This could be a white-paper or an online video delivered by email or even a free drink on their visit to your store or restaurant.

Remember that there is no magic pill in business. The only way to achieve tremendous growth is by implementing different strategies and tactics that contribute to converting as many prospects to customers, increasing the value of each transaction, and making sure your customers are purchasing more frequently.

It's all about building relationships
Mobile marketing is really all about building a long-term relationship with your prospects and customers. The beauty of this is that you can automate many things and keep track of your customers' habits in a systemized way. Any business can track when customers last came in and can send them a text message if they've disappeared for a few months. It's also an effective tool to increase customer satisfaction and repeat transactions since you can reach out to your buyers in a matter of seconds and even have automated text messages that get sent out at pre-determined times. Everything can be automated.

Maximize Mobile Benefits
When you send out a text message broadcast to your cell phone subscribers' list, you can include your phone number for them to call your business for more information about one of your products or services.

For example, if you're holding a special discounted price sale this week, you can reach out by text message and give them a special code they can use when they buy on your website or in your store. You can also give them a special phone number they can call to have VIP treatment by your staff.

Mobile and text message marketing is the ultimate permission-based form of marketing because you're contacting prospects and customers on the only device they carry with them literally everywhere. Oh and here's a fun fact: 75% of people use their phone on the toilet. So yes, you can literally reach them everywhere.

Very few businesses are making good use of mobile marketing, so if you implement a good text message strategy to fuel your marketing campaigns in addition to email marketing, it will give you a boost over your competition.

21

THE FOLLOW-UP MATRIX

By now, you should have picked up at least 10 ideas that can dramatically increase your sales and profits. But we're not done yet. Let's stay on the topic of following up with your prospects and customers as this strategy alone will add geometric growth to your business.

Studies have shown time and time again that a prospect needs to see your sales message at least 5 to 10 times before even considering making a purchase. Yet most businesses stop their follow-up sequence after 2 or 3 contacts, leaving piles of money on the table. Don't make the same costly mistake. Remember the 3 main ways of increasing your business are the following:

1. Increase the number of customers.
2. Increase the size of each initial transaction.
3. Increase the number of repeat sales from each customer.

In the last chapters, we covered extensively the first element: attracting new customers. In this part, we're going to have a deeper look at how you can convert more prospects into customers. You've probably heard time and time again about the importance of following up with your leads once they mention their interest in your product or service. To increase the conversion rate of people who do business with you, it's vital you implement a solid follow-up system using as many different types of media you can: physical mail, email, telemarketing, SMS text messaging, and even face-to-face if possible. Obviously, some businesses don't lend themselves to face-to-face sales, which is perfectly fine. Many of our clients don't even see their customers until AFTER they've paid for their service, so don't feel intimidated by all the strategies I'm laying out for you. Use these strategies as a buffet: pick and choose the ones that work the best for YOUR business.

Depending on your business, some types of media might be more or less adapted to your target market. Don't make the mistake of looking at what all your competitors are doing and simply doing the same – you goal is to be different than everyone else, so you need to do things differently to stand out in the marketplace and create breakthroughs in your business. If you do what you've always done, you'll always get the same results you've been getting in the past and up to now. If you want different and better results, you need to execute things differently.

The Follow-up Matrix

A follow-up matrix is a system that allows you to maximize the conversion of your prospects into customers by implementing a multimedia and multistep follow-up sequence once a lead comes in contact with your business. Every time someone comes in your store, calls for information about a product, subscribes to your online newsletter, or purchases something from your business, he's entered into your follow-up matrix. An effective multistep follow-up matrix could look like this if you're in the weight-loss market:

Day 1: prospect enters your follow-up matrix.
Day 1: receives a free report by email about "How to Lose 10 Pounds in 2 Weeks" with links to your products inside the report.
Day 5: receives an email about a special offer with a 10% discount if he calls or walks in your business.
Day 10: receives a free audio and transcription by email of an interview conducted with a weight-loss specialist about "The 10 Lies of Weight-loss".

Day 15: receives an email requesting him to call your business to take advantage of a special offer.

Day 20: receives a direct mail letter with testimonials from past customers who purchased your solution.

Day 25: receives a postcard with a coupon to one of your products.

Day 30: receives an SMS with a time-limited offer.

Day 35: receives an email with an article you wrote featured in the local press.

Day 40: receives an email and SMS with a 48-hour deal taking place on your website.

Day 45: receives a direct mail piece with sales letter urging him to order your product.

Day 50: receives an email with a link to a free video about "How to Lose Fat by Eating Right".

Day 60: receives a call from your team asking why he hasn't taken advantage of one of your offers, and offering him a special discount if he orders on the phone.

That's an example of a solid 13-step multistep follow-up matrix, meaning that a lead will receive information from your business for 60 days following his interest. It includes emails, direct mails, SMS text messages, and phone marketing. If a lead purchases something on day 20, he's removed of this follow-up matrix and is placed on another list, specially created to make customers increase the frequency of transactions they do with your business.

Using a variety of different mediums will considerably increase your sales conversions because people operate in different ways and are triggered by different formats. Some people prefer text, some people like videos, others prefer listening to audios, while others prefer print media like physical mail. Some like to order online while others prefer to speak on the phone with someone to make sure they're receiving personal treatment. If you're only using one type of media in your follow-up sequence, I can guarantee you'll increase your conversions if you add different types of media to your follow-up matrix.

What happens after the 60 days are over if a prospect hasn't bought yet? Simple: add more steps to your follow-up matrix. Add better offers, more value, more education for the subscribers, and make use of more risk reversal in your offer.

Don't be shy about the follow-up matrix you implement in your business as it is there for one main reason: convert prospects into buyers. The longer the follow-up sequence, the more chances you have of converting a prospect into a buyer. Don't be afraid of creating a follow-up sequence that is too long. In our experience, no follow-up is long enough. If someone hasn't bought after 60 days of follow-up, it won't cost you anything to put that lead in an email autoresponder and have an extra 200-day sequence to keep the lead warm and try to convert him into a customer.

I've seen this happen time and time again in many different industries: increasing the number of follow-up messages always increases sales. Every single time. If you're using direct mail as a way of following up with your leads, you can add an email autoresponder sequence to keep in touch with the non-buyers after your direct mail campaign is over. That way, it won't cost you anything more than the low monthly fee for your autoresponder to stay active. Every business can and must implement an effective system to keep in touch with leads for weeks and months. Take a few moments now to think about your current follow-up system, and how you can integrate a full-blown follow-up matrix in your business.

22

THE CONVERSION ENGINE

One of the keys I always share with clients is that your business needs to operate like a vending machine. You need to predictably be able to put in $1 and consistently get $2, $5 $10 or even $20 every single time. And that's exactly what a "Conversion Engine" does for you. If you don't have any systems in place, you cannot grow. Ask yourself:

- What do people see when they approach your business, your website?
- Where do they sign up?
- What are the marketing messages you expose them to?
- What sequences do you have in place?

This must be as systemized as a vending machine if you want peace of mind and predictable income.

When my company started selling high-end packages in 2008, we started focusing on two major things: lead generation mechanisms and conversion mechanisms. A conversion mechanism is simply a way to convert prospects into customers, which means turning non-buyers into buyers. If you currently don't have a predictable system of transforming prospects into buyers, you don't have a scalable business.

After testing, tweaking and improving our sales and marketing process, we've generated tens of millions of dollars in additional revenue for our companies and clients by deploying full-blown campaigns and turn-key businesses. All this has been possible thanks to what we now call a "Conversion Engine". Let me share with you the two-step sales process that composes a Conversion Engine.

The number one component is webinars. And the second component is known as strategy sessions. Let's have look at both of these components.

Key #1: Webinars

Webinars are by far THE most powerful presentation tool to systemize your lead nurturing and your lead selection.

- It has to be a great presentation of what you do.
- It has to be well crafted.
- It has to tell people how you help them.
- It has to tell people what they can expect of you.
- And it has to communicate what kind of people you can't help.

Webinars are great because they are easy for your audience to consume and you can deliver a ton of value in an under an hour. Obviously, there is a science behind it.

So that's the first key. Use webinars to communicate your value and what kind of product or service you're offering so people know exactly what you do before you talk to them. It's the perfect lead-qualification process. Like I said, my companies have done thousands of webinars over the past few years and generated millions of dollars as a result, and we've tested a ton of different things. And the best structure we found is a webinar that follows this kind of direction.

Minutes 0 to 5:

- Introduce yourself.
- Talk about the theme of the webinar.
- Explain how attendees will benefit from the webinar.
- Mention who you are and what brings you to the present webinar. Briefly discuss your life story, your experience on the matter, your passion, etc.

Minutes 5 to 35:

- Go deep into the content of your presentation
- Find about 3 to 7 topics that you want to share with the attendees. This can include statistics and stories of your industry. Every topic would take 5 to 10 minutes to cover.

Here's an example of webinar if you're in the weight-loss industry. The webinar would cover 5 topics regarding contents on weight loss industry:

1. Myths and legends of the weight loss industry. (5 minutes)
2. Foods to avoid and best foods to eat. (5 minutes)
3. Daily tweaks in eating habits to lose weight in the next 7 days. (5 minutes)
4. Good versus bad workouts and exercises. (5 minutes)
5. Your client results and general health advice. (5 minutes)

Every point would take approximately 5-10 minutes to cover, and that brings you to about 30-45 minutes.

Towards the end of your webinar and after you've delivered the content, offer attendees a way to sign up for a personal consultation if they're interested in reaching their health goals to have a conversation with you 1-on-1 to find out if you can help them personally and have them enroll in your high-fee program.

Of course, as you can imagine, there are a lot of small details that go into crafting a high-performing webinar in terms of marketing, messaging, framing and positioning your authority and services, etc.

But like I said, we've tested a lot of different things in webinars, and that webinar structure gets us the best results.

Key #2: Having a 1-on-1 Conversation

The goal of the first component - a webinar – is to deliver very, very qualified and high value leads to you for you to have a 1-on-1 phone consultation with. The goal is to only speak with leads that are qualified and people who have gone through your marketing message, who have been properly marketed to and who have requested your help.

There's nothing worse than talking to a prospect that doesn't really know what you do, doesn't know about your expertise, your client case studies, etc. That way, you'll never spend an hour talking to skeptical or an unqualified prospect again. Let your competition do those annoying calls while you just talk to people who have gone through a full marketing message that you crafted and who are already inclined to buying what you offer.

As with webinars, there is a science behind converting leads into clients, and we can help you with that. Combining webinars and strategy sessions is gold. It's brought in tens of millions of dollars for our companies and fortunes for clients. Having a Conversion Engine allows you to simply send people to your online video presentation (ideally a webinar, which can be pre-recorded and automated), which delivers your best marketing material and offers viewers a chance to sign up for a 1-on-1 consultation (also known as a "strategy session") with you or your sales team. It works like this:

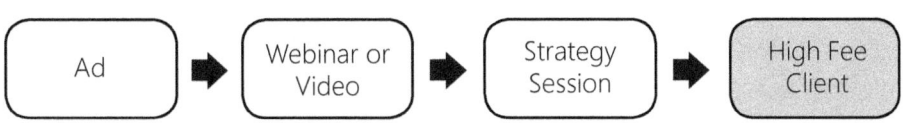

The key is to ONLY talk to people AFTER they've gone through the entire presentation, meaning they know what you offer and are interested in how you can help them solve their problems. If you've put together a good webinar in the way we structure it for our clients, you will generally convert 1 out of 5 people you talk to at a price between $1,000 and $10,000. Those are the numbers that we typically see for our clients and in our own businesses, and they are very much predictable.

If you have a customer, fan, or subscriber base, deploying a Conversion Engine can realistically add an extra $100,000 to $1,000,000 in the next 30 days to your business, like it has for our clients time and time again. And if you're starting from scratch, it's the fastest way to blow past the 7-figure mark with the lowest amount of work and stress, and the highest amount of free time, allowing you to do everything and anything else that you want to do in life rather than be a slave to your business.

23

THE 8 FIGURE SALES SCRIPT

In this chapter, I'd like to share in detail the exact telephone scripts that we've been using in my companies for since 2008, which have generated multiple millions of dollars in revenue for my own businesses and at least an extra $50 million for our clients and sales teams I've trained. But first, let me tell you from experience how we started selling on the phone and why this has the power to literally transform the way you do business.

When I was running one of my first businesses selling training courses about internet marketing and internet sales to small business owners in the French market in 2006, online advertising was still in its infancy in Europe. Although many advertising networks had grown significantly in the English-speaking markets, the European markets were still developing. That meant that we weren't really able to generate large amounts of new leads through paid advertising for that specific business, which pushed us to explore ways to generate more revenue per customers.

Remember the 3 ways to grown and transform a business? Number 1: get new customers. Since that was difficult in the French market at that time, we had to use rules number 2 and 3: getting more revenue per customer and increasing the frequency of transactions.

One day, I started exploring the idea of contacting our customers on the phone and offering a high-end training program that would be in the form of an online and physical seminar. Since we were running a test, we limited the number of seats available to only 15, and what happened was absolutely fascinating. In less than a week, we sold out 15 seats at a full price of $5,000. That was an extra $75,000 in revenue from a completely new income stream.

From that moment on, I knew that using the phone to increase sales - especially high-end sales - was a complete game changer. I started hiring more sales agents and training them on our proprietary sales method-ologies over the next few years and expanded the operation to several countries and languages. Over the years, I've hired over 150 sales agents and trained hundreds more for our clients. I've taught our sales meth-odologies to rooms full of sales experts and witnessed them generate anywhere between $50,000 to 7 figures in extra business in the following days.

I can legitimately say that I've pretty much seen everything there is to see in terms of phone sales, phone scripts, small phone teams and large-scale phone rooms and even boiler room operations - the good, the bad and the downright ugly.

When I refer to "selling on the phone", this has nothing to do with both-ering people at home and 7 PM to try to sell magazine subscriptions or "magic diet pills". The structure we have in place and that we put together for our ZuraMedia clients (where we handle all the sales for them) creates an AMAZING experience for their customers. And even when customers can't afford the offers we make, there is never any bitterness or lost love.

Over the years, I've written over 50 sales scripts in over 20 different in-dustries, selling products anywhere between $1 trials to $50,000 prod-ucts and services, all using the phone.

I've refined the selling process and tested and tweaked pretty much ev-erything that you can imagine to increase sales. In this chapter I'm going to go over several key elements and processes that work best and give you the exact sale scripts that we use every day in my company to sell products and services up to $100,000 on the phone.

As I mentioned earlier in the book, one of the services we provide and help clients with is handling all of their phone sales and focusing mainly on helping service providers (coaches, consultants, therapists, trainers, etc.) who sell high-end packages. The outline I'll be sharing over the next few pages has the power to add at least another $100,000 to your business in the next quarter. But if you decide to take this seriously, it can had several million dollars over the next few months and years as you grow your business and start using this process. Let's get into it.

Golden Rules for phone sales

Let's have a look at a few guidelines that need to be considered when selling on the phone.

More expensive products require more marketing and sales efforts

As you might imagine, it generally takes longer to convert a $10,000 sale than a $1 trial. Although this might seem completely logical, it needs to be addressed because it might take you or your sales team several contacts to close more expensive deals. But with the methodology we use, we generally are able to convert cold leads into sales at price points between 1000 and $10,000 with a one call close, or a 2-call close at most. I'll be showing you the exact script that we use for each case.

It takes time

If you've never done phone sales before, you might not convert sales at the very beginning. As with anything, there is a learning curve and converting your first prospects into clients - especially if they've never heard of you - might be a challenge. The more you do it, the more you'll get familiar with the process and the more sales you'll make. My rule of thumb is to always invest between 1 to 4 months to start mastering the sales process and to get familiar with the sales scripts. If you're hiring new phone reps to make sales for you, keep in mind that it can take them anywhere between 14 to 60 days to become fully knowledgeable about the sale script, the sales dynamic, your specific customers' psychology, the rebuttals to be fully confident in closing deals for you.

It's incredibly effective

Converting prospects into customers using the phone is the number 1 way to generate revenue if you're not able to sell face-to-face. If you're running a global business selling to people across the country or across the world, selling on the phone is the most effective way to convert prospects into high-end customers. If you've never sold on the phone and you have products or services that can be sold for a minimum of $5000, using the phone as a conversion method will transform your business. We've seen numerous cases where our students and clients have added an extra $20,000 in monthly revenue and up to as much as $500,000 per month in extra revenue to their business using phone sales the way we do it.

20% is the norm

If you're using the phone to sell at the moment and not getting the results you're looking for, you're doing it wrong. If you're not closing at least 20% of your prospects into high-end sales, the sales process you have in place is flawed. By using our marketing and sales process, converting 20% of leads into customers is the norm.

You must use a script

If you're reluctant to using scripts or if you've never had a sales script in your life, I can tell you with the utmost certainty that you're leaving a fortune on the table. I don't care if you have 10, 20 or 50 years of sales experience, you need to work with the script and have your script in front of you at all times. Every single phone agent I've hired that tells me they don't like to use scripts either learns how to use our script or needs to get a new job after a few days. Can you imagine the best actors in the world shooting a movie without a script? It's impossible. That's why everyone – even the greats like Anthony Hopkins, Al Pacino and Michael Caine who've been acting for decades - always have a script within arm's length. Why? Simply because having the script printed in front of you is reassuring and gives you a clear direction during the conversation. It forces you to focus on the outcome and guaranteed that you'll never wonder what comes next.

A sale is made on every phone call

The desired outcome of the phone conversation as the phone sales conversation is to close the sale and make money. Too often, amateur sales people think that sales calls or just a way to create a relationship with your prospects. That's completely wrong. The one and only goal of contacting someone on the phone for an appointment is to determine if there's a fit: if the client can benefit from what you have to offer. If there's a fit, you MUST focus on closing the sale. Spending hours on the phone with prospects without asking for the sale and without closing the deal is a waste of time and energy. It doesn't allow the customer use your product and it doesn't help your bottom-line either.

To have high conversions, you need the right marketing process

The big secret as to why we manage to get such high conversions on phone sales is because of we only talk to leads that have been properly marketed to BEFORE we get on the phone with them. Sales companies that don't market extensively to their prospects to put them in the right state of mind before the call waste enormous amounts of resources on the call. And that's the big secret to succeeding at phone sales. You need to rock-solid and heavy-lifting marketing process in place to prequalify leads and disarm any objections that might come up during the sales process, and only get on the phone with people that have been exposed to your marketing material before reaching out to you.

Go high-end or go home

If you want to maximize your results in phone sales, you need to sell high-end packages. I've personally made thousands of sales calls and closed hundreds of deals myself, and continue to close deals on the phone and in person every week. Like I said earlier, my companies have sold products between $50 and $50,000 on the phone. And I can tell you from experience that selling a $500 offer on the phone takes the same amount of energy as selling a $25,000 offer. That's why I always recommend to our clients to offer a high-end package for a bare minimum of $5,000. That would be the lowest price point I recommend when selling on the phone if you want to get a massive ROI on your time spent. With the right marketing process in place, you can close a few sales every week by yourself. And once you have a flawless conversion process in place, the only thing you can focus on is generating leads to increase revenue.

Outsource if you don't like selling

If you don't like marketing or sales but love delivering your product or service to your marketplace, we can help. Even though you can find the exact phone script that we use every single day in our business, you might not want to make phone sales every day yourself.

In that case, we can take over your entire marketing and sales process, we can do all the lead generation for you and even make phone sales for you. Yes, we can take care of everything for you: create custom-made highly targeted lead generation campaigns to generate new leads for your offers, and then my professional sales team can contact your leads on your behalf and sell high-end products or services for you. It's a complete turn-key solution that enables you to never worry about lead generation or sales ever again. We do everything for you, you just deliver your service.

For this, there are a few conditions that you need to satisfy. First of all, you need to be delivering a stellar product or service. That means that you need to have successful case studies of clients you have helped and to have directly benefited from your services. The second condition is that you need to be offering or willing to offer a high-end product or service. This means that your product must be priced at approximately at a minimum of $5000. If you currently don't have a high-end offer, we can work together to brainstorm an offer that would satisfy that pricing condition. And thirdly, you must be able to service between 10 to 50 clients per month. If you can satisfy those three conditions and would like us to take over your marketing and sales complete completely, reach out to us and let's talk. Go to MatthiasMazur.com/apply.

Your product is a vehicle

Whatever product you're selling at the moment: if you're selling industrial solutions to tech companies, B2B consulting services to small businesses, consumer products B2C or anything else, you need to understand that ultimately, your buyers don't care at all about your products. That's right: they don't care AT ALL about what you are delivering. The only thing your buyers care about is solving their problems and taking care of the issues they're experiencing. If you know how to present an offer in an appealing way, which speaks directly to how get rid of their problems, you will make sales. If you have the best product in the world that you don't know how to sell, you won't make a dime. Your product or service is just a bridge from your customer's current situation to your customer's desired outcome. For example, if you're selling a diet solution, it doesn't matter if it comes in the form of a pill, a drink, or a book. Your target market wants to lose weight. And whether they have to sing songs, dance around in their living room or buy a pink hat that makes them lose weight, they will do it as long as it solves the main problem and gets them closer to their desired outcome. Keep this in mind at all times: your product is merely a vehicle from the customer's current situation to the customer's desired outcome and takes them from where they are right now to where they ultimately want to be.

Ask questions to sell more

I'm baffled by the amount of amateur salespeople who think that selling consists in talking fast and smoothly. The best salespeople I've met and trained are always the ones that speak the least and listen the most. Good sales people ask questions. Weak salespeople talk without listening to what customer is trying to say. If you want to really understand what customers want, you need to start asking the right questions and actively listening.

Everyone buys for different reasons

If you don't know why your customer wants to buy and what his core issue is deep down, you'll always struggle in sales. You'll notice that the script that we use (and that I share word-for-word in this chapter) relies heavily on questions. And that's because to get high conversions, you need to understand the deep fears and desires of the person you're talking to. You'll also notice that presenting an offer generally has nothing to do with the bells and whistles or how many colors your widget comes with. Presenting an offer has everything to do with how you explain to the customer how your solution will directly benefit and solve his issues. And the only way to understand what your prospect wants is to ask questions, speak less, actively listen and take notes.

Find the real issue

This is a huge one. People don't buy Ferraris to have a red car or to drive fast. They can buy a used Toyota and put a new engine in it and drive as fast as a Ferrari. There are dozens of cars that can beat a Ferrari's speed. Every transaction that takes place in the world is always triggered by a deep and emotional reason. Oftentimes, people buy a Ferrari because they want the feeling of finally having "made it" and belonging to a group of people who are rich enough to buy a Ferrari. Maybe they've seen their favorite actor drive around in a Ferrari and they want to feel like him. Maybe they've watched Formula One races since they were kids and loved to see Ferrari win and now they want to own one. Emotions guide everything we do and every transaction that takes place in the world. That's why it's so important to ask questions and dig deep into your customer's issues to really understand what the problem is.

Go deep

Usually, people won't openly disclose their fears and the core reasons why they're interested in the product you're offering in the first few minutes of the conversation, because it makes them feel naked and vulnerable. Let's say you're selling a solution that increases speed of production for B2B companies. Your prospect might tell you that their core issue is that they're falling behind on orders and they need to keep up with production or that their core employees are not working fast enough.

These are all valid, yet rational reasons. But the deep reason might be that your prospect - a director of operations in that business - needs to hit certain quotas and milestones to prove to his board of directors that they made the right choice in promoting him so he can get bonus and to take his family on vacation next Christmas. Or maybe he needs to hit a certain number of sales to be able to just keep his job next year.

What people tell you verbally usually isn't the real answer, and it can take some time over the conversation to dig deep into what the core reptilian issue is. Often times, it has to do with very deeply rooted elements about self-belief, their self-confidence, the way others see them, and the way they see themselves in the world. That's why when someone says that they bought a new car because it has effective mile mileage, it's just the rational reason that they're using to back up their emotional decision. Your goal on the phone or in any sales situation is to find the core emotional issue and speak directly to that. You need to find what is hidden under the surface under the tip of the iceberg. If you don't know how to ask the right questions, your prospect will only tell you about his rational reasons, which will make it much tougher for you to get the sale. To increase sales, you need to get down to the emotional reasons why your prospect reached out to you and was interested in your solutions in the first place. Get down to what lies beneath the surface and your sales will soar.

The best phone sales process

In 2008, I was looking for ways to increase revenue in my company and had to do it with limited ways of online advertising, as I mentioned earlier. I remember seeing a seminar in the United States being promoted on the internet that was selling for $5,000. In France, no one had ever dared to sell a seminar at what was considered a "high" price point. But I told myself "if people are doing it in the English-speaking market, why couldn't I do it in the French market?" So one morning, I signed up for a paid Skype number, downloaded all the phone numbers of our customers and started calling one after the other.

I had no idea what I was doing, but I set my goal on selling a $5,000 event and accept only 15 attendees. That was the first key to sales: I knew that in order to be able to command high price (seminars in the French markets were selling for $500 at most, so 10 times less than my offer), I had to be able to justify it with a higher degree of service and by limiting the amount of spots available. I considered that campaign a test and didn't even tell my staff. I just called all out customers over a period of a few days and set a deadline for that that Friday.

On Thursday evening, I had personally sold all 15 spots at $5,000. That was the one of the biggest turning points in my business career. The script I was using at the time was so basic (just a few questions on a piece of paper), but it worked because I was really trying to do my best to understand the customers' needs and the real reasons why they were interested in our solutions in the first place. When I saw the results of that I had generated by myself just by calling a few customers had done business with us over the past 18 months, it blew me away. I knew I had gold in my hands, and I started expanding my sales team and investing all my time in studying everything I could about sales.

That year, I probably read at least 250 sales books and thousands since then. And by reading the books from all the major "sales gurus" and "sales consultants", I started noticing that 99% of the material in those books is complete junk. Why? Simply because since I was actively involved in selling and training my sales team every day, I knew that most of what was written in those sales books - most of which you can find in bookstores - was far from the reality of the sales world and did not apply to real life experience. It really struck me that most of these experts had not sold anything themselves and had just decided to write a book about some theories they thought could be interesting... even though they couldn't sell a bottle of water to a crowd of thirsty people in the desert to save their lives.

I'm a very pragmatic and "get it done" type of entrepreneur, so anything too theoretical doesn't resonate with me. That's why I dropped out of college after only three months: I was bored by how teachers were teaching us theoretical concepts that never applied to the real world. That's also why I make fun of most MBAs and students who graduate with business degrees from fancy overpriced business schools, but have zero real life experience and would crash a company if they applied the theories they were taught in school.

I firmly believe that if you haven't sold anything in your life, you should not be allowed to write a book about sales. Fortunately, I've sold my fair share of products and services in different markets, from industrial machinery to online training courses and software that wasn't even developed at the time it was sold.

I've also hired and paid large sums of money to sales consultants, whose names you would recognize if you've bought a few books about entrepreneurship and sales. At that point, I noticed that very few people are actually willing to share their money-making scripts and sales processes. Because I run ZuraMedia, a marketing, sales and social media agency that offers turnkey solutions for our clients, I have no problem sharing every piece of information I have in me. If you'd like to do this all by yourself, by all means do it. And then, reach out to me on social media and tell me how much money you've made (or get me some VIP tickets to go see my Ottawa Senators). If you don't want to make phone sales yourself but know that adding a phone sales operation to your business would be a major game changer, we can do it for you.

After tens of thousands of sales calls, after writing over 50 scripts for dozens of industries and testing hundreds of variables, I've concluded that the most effective way to sell products and services on the phone is usually by using one of the two following processes.

The Magic 3-step Process

What we've found to be the most effective is to get prospects to raise their hands and reach out to you for help. The psychology behind someone reaching out to you versus you contacting them (without having any prior relationship) is incredibly powerful and increases revenue by over 300% in phone sales in several markets that we tested. That means that we've routinely generated 3 times more revenue per call when a prospect reached out to us (as an inbound call) compared to when we initiate calls (through an outbound call).

This is literally one of the biggest tweaks that you can make if you'd like to increase sales by phone. Implement a mechanism so your prospects or followers can raise their hands by sending you a message or filling out an application to request a conversation with you. When someone asks for help, the sales dynamic is such that you are perceived as the expert diagnosing and recommending treatment if needed.

To elicit a response, there are several mechanisms you can use. If you have an email list of subscribers or customers, the most effective way to generate sales (literally this week) is to send one of the two following emails. You can use these emails word-for-word or you can tweak them as you wish. You might not get thousands of responses, but the responses you will get by using the following templates usually converts anywhere between 20% to 50% into high-end sales for products and services priced between $1,000 and $10,000.

Here are 2 emails we use to generate responses that convert into high-end sales:

Email 1:

Subject line: Need help?

Hello,

If you're looking to [insert market's desire here], I've set aside some time over the next few days to have a personal 1-on-1 strategy session to discuss how to reach your goals faster.

If you're interested, reply back to this email with your best phone number and a couple time slots to call you at, and I'll be in touch.

Speak soon,

Signature

P.S.: I only have a few spaces available and this email is being sent to [number] subscribers, so reply as soon as you can.

Email 2:

Subject line: Let's talk

Hello,

As a way of helping serious [your target market] reach their goals faster and find more [target market's goals], I've set aside some time this week to talk to a handful of our clients.

If you're still struggling to [insert target market's goal], let's talk and see how we can speed things up.

Reply back to this email with your best phone number and a couple time slots to call you at, and I'll be in touch.

Signature

P.S.: I only have a few spaces available and this email is being sent to [number] subscribers, so reply as soon as you can.

Simple and sweet. Your goal in that first email is not to sell anything. It's just to have a few people on your list to raise their hands and pre-qualify themselves.

The ideal process we've found to work the best is composed of 3 steps:

1.   Send your list one of the emails above to generate interest and phone numbers.
2.   Send those people to an "Objection Crusher" page.
3.   Have a 1-on-1 conversation on the phone.

Let's have a look at those 3 steps in more detail.

Step 1
If you have a list of subscribers or customers, send them one of the emails

above. If you don't have an email list but have a following on your Facebook page, you can re-work one of those emails into a Facebook post and ask your followers to send you their numbers by private message.

Step 2

When they reply, send them to a special page on your website that features case studies and testimonials of some of your best customers have had. This is what I call the "Objection Crusher page". Remember what I said about only talking to people who have been properly marketed to? This is where all the heavy lifting is done. You want people to be in the right state of mind and open to your advice and offer during the 1-on-1 conversation get. One of the main reasons why people don't buy in general is because they don't believe the seller or don't believe that the solution being sold can really help them. By sending them to a page that has testimonials, articles that you wrote in major publications or trade journals, endorsements by different people in market or a copy of a recent interview you gave, you're able to disarm most of the objections that people can have.

And on that page, you want to feature what I call an "Objection Crusher". The objection crusher is one of the most effective and under-the-radar sales tools I have used in my businesses and implemented for my clients and is the reason why this 3-step process works so well. The objection crusher is a recording (an audio or video interview) that addresses the 10 to 20 main objections that your target market has when choosing a provider and buying solutions in your market.

For example, if you sell a service to help people lose weight, list the 10 to 20 top objections people have about losing weight. Here are a few examples:

- I've tried to lose weight in the past and it hasn't worked.
- I've tried crash diets and I haven't lost weight.
- My metabolism is too slow so whatever I do I don't lose weight.
- I tried taking pills and it doesn't work.
- My neighbor told me that he saw a TV show saying that it's

impossible to lose weight when you're over 50 years old
- Is it possible to really lose weight even if you have a 9-to-5 job?
- Losing weight costs too much money.
- Etc.

Those are some of the questions that people looking for ways to lose weight ask themselves. And if you don't address those in your marketing sequence before getting on the phone with them, those unanswered objections will decrease sales. But if you compile all those objections and do a 20-minute recording called "20 Weight-loss Myths" answering those questions, you destroy and crush their objections even before they come up during your conversation. The Objection Crusher page is one of the most important keys in the sales process because it's educational and it frames the right information in the customer's mind without pitching anything.

This is how our clients are able to convert prospects into customers for services anywhere between $1,000 and $25,000 on the phone in conversations that last less than 45 minutes, because all the heavy-lifting is done before the phone call.

If you currently don't have an Objection Crusher page, you can put one together in less than 48 hours. It will be one of the most valuable pages you have on your site.

That way, you will only be talking to people who have raised their hands and who have gone through the marketing material. Then, when comes the time of your phone consultation, all the main objections will have been handled beforehand, which gives you the opportunity to really focus on digging into your customer's problems and seeing if there's a fit for your services.

In the case of a one call close, this is the script that we use.

Step 3: The script for a one-call close
Okay, let's get down to the money. With much anticipation, I'm now go-

ing to reveal the scripts in detail. We will go through it as follows: first, I will give you the script in its entirety, and in the next section, I will rip the script apart section by section with comments and share with you why things are structured the way they are. I'll discuss customer psychology, sales psychology and how to say things to have maximum impact when you're delivering the script on the phone.

Here's the script in its full form. You can download a copy of it on my blog: MatthiasMazur.com/script

You: Hi [prospect's first name], this is [your first name] calling from [your company here]. Is this a good time for our Strategy Session?

Great! Congratulations on reaching out to us. What we'll do during this call is really clarify your goals and see how we can help you reach those goals as fast as possible and start [insert target market goals here].

This is how it's going to work: I'll ask you a few questions to find out more about your current situation and see, and I'll tell you what we've got going on over here, so feel free to ask questions anytime you'd like during the call. Does that make sense?

Before we start, I'll be very candid and transparent: the majority of people who reach out to us are not a good fit for what we do. Sometimes it's because they're not serious enough or be-cause [insert common excuses target market makes]. So if for some reason it's not a fit, I'll give you specific reason so you know where we stand. Sounds good?

Ok, great!

1.   So tell me, what made you decide to reach out to us in the first place?
2.   What do you do at the moment?

3. Let's dig into what's going on at the moment on your end: what kind of results/ weight lost/ sales volume have you generated over the last quarter?

4. Let's talk about your goals... How much [insert target market desire] on a weekly/ monthly/ quarterly basis over the next 12 months?

    a. Okay, so if we had a conversation 12 months from now and you had [insert prospect's goals here: lost 50 pounds/ doubled your sales/ found th love of your life], would that be a victory for you?

5. Why are looking to solve these problems now?

6. What's the main obstacle that has kept you from making achieving your goals until now? I need you to be perfectly honest because I can only help you if I really know what's been keeping you from reaching your goals.

7. We talked about your main objective as it relates to [insert target market desire here]. But when I talk to people who reach out for help, there are usually secondary goals that will be positively affected once you achieve [insert prospect's main goal here]. For some, it's being able to have more free time/ more income/ more self-confidence/ a better relationship. What are some of the collateral areas that will benefit you reaching your goal?

8. Ok... let's fast-forward a bit... paint me a picture of how life will look like once you've reached [insert prospect's goals here]?

(Pause for a few seconds)

Ok, let's go back and recap...

At the moment, you're [insert prospect's current situation here] and you're looking to reach [insert prospect's desired outcome here] in the next [insert time frame].
The main objective is to get to [insert 12-month goal here].

So far, you've had issues with [insert prospect's challenges and why he hasn't reached his goal yet] and you said you've strug gled with [insert issues here].

Let me ask this... how soon are you looking to get these issues taken care of and start reaching your goals?

If the prospect is NOT a fit for your solution:

I appreciate everything you've shared with me on this call, but based on the situation and more specifically [insert the reason why the customer is not a good fit], I don't think there is a fit at this particular time. [End call politely.]

If the prospect is a fit for your solution:

Ok, based on everything you've told me, I think there's definitely something we can do together to help you reach those goals.

Let me tell you a bit more of what we do.

We're putting together...

[Continue into a simple and direct presentation of your offer, re lating to what the prospect has told you about his situation. Tailor the offer based on his needs.]

There, that's it. That phone sales script has generated tens of millions of dollars over the last few years for our clients and my own companies. It's the closest thing to gold and it's been tested and refined dozens of times to get to its current and most effective form. Use it and adapt it slightly to fit your style and you'll see how well it converts.

Now that you have the script, let's dissect it line by line to see why it's so effective.

Dissecting the Script

> *Hi [prospect's first name], this is [your first name] calling from [your company here]. Is this a good time for our Strategy Session?*

This first line is simple and sweet and dramatically different from a cold-calling situation. Because people have requested a conversation with you, they will most likely be ready and extremely happy to have you on the phone.

> *Great! Congratulations on reaching out to us. What we'll do during this call is really clarify your goals and see how we can help you reach those goals as fast as possible and start [insert target market goals here].*
>
> *This is how it's going to work: I'll ask you a few questions to find out more about your current situation and see, and I'll tell you what we've got going on over here, so feel free to ask questions anytime you'd like during the call. Does that make sense?*

This section is CRUCIAL to set the tone for the call and implies to the prospect that you are in control and you are the one setting the pace for the conversation. Selling on the phone is all about setting and maintaining control and direction over the conversation. If your target market's goal is to lose weight, insert that into last sentence: "... *help you reach those goals as fast as possible and start losing weight, getting back in shape and feeling great again."*

That statement also implies that you have a solution to help them solve their issues, but don't mention ANYTHING about your product or service here. At this stage, you don't know anything about the prospect and this is simply a way to set the intention for the call, giving you control over the conversation.

> *Before we start, I'll be very candid and transparent: the*

majority of people who reach out to us are not a good fit for what we do. Sometimes it's because they're not serious enough or because [insert common excuses target market makes]. So if for some reason it's not a fit, I'll give you specific reason so you know where we stand. Sounds good?

This section uses an extremely effective sales technique known as "take-away selling". This section implies that demand for your help and solutions is greater than the supply, which immediately and positions you as an in-demand solutions provider. You can rearrange this paragraph to suit your style, but this is exact wording our clients and my own companies use to sell multi 6-figure solutions. The key is to convey that you don't do business with everyone who reaches out to you and that you are selective on who you can service. Let's get into the magical 8 questions.

1.   *So tell me, what made you decide to reach out to us in the first place?*

This first question focuses immediately on the reason why your prospect reached out in the first place. Amateur salespeople pitch their products immediately, but the best salespeople ask questions and gather data. This is where you start gathering insights into what makes the prospect tick and what his pain points are.

2.   *What do you do at the moment?*

This question helps you to start gathering information about the prospect's situation. This can be altered into "how big is your organization at the moment?" or "what systems do you currently have in place to track your sales?" if you're selling B2B.

3.   *Let's dig into what's going on at the moment on your end: what kind of results/ weight lost/ sales volume have you generated over the last quarter?*

This is where you start getting deep into the prospect's current situation and gathering as much information as possible about where he's currently at. If you've done a good job setting up the conversation, the prospect will feel safe in sharing his issues and challenges. I refer to this question as "Point A": the prospect's current situation. This section usually takes between 5 to 10 minutes (sometimes more depending on the scope of the problem he's facing). Spend time digging into the answers the prospect gives you and ask additional questions to narrow down the exact issues he's experiencing. For example: if the prospect says *"we're facing a sales slump since the last quarter"*, go deeper and ask *"what are your sales on an average quarter?"*, *"how were sales the quarter before that?"*, *"did you feel any changes in your staff's motivation?"*, etc.

When you hear the issue, you need to go deeper to really understand what's going on. Think of this as you being the doctor and asking questions about the person's pain and symptoms. The deeper you dig into the prospect's pains and problems, the better you understand his situation and the better you can position your offer based on his issues (and make a LOT more sales).

> 4.   *Let's talk about your goals... How much [insert target market desire] on a weekly/ monthly/ quarterly basis over the next 12 months?*
>
>   a.   *Okay, so if we had a conversation 12 months from now and you had [insert prospect's goals here: lost 50 pounds/ doubled your sales/ found he love of your life], would that be a victory for you?*

Now that you have a deep understanding of the prospects pain and issues after exploring question number 3, this is where you gather information about his desired goals and outcome. In the previous question, you gathered intelligence about his current state, "Point A" and now you gather information about his is the desired state, "Point B". This magic of this entire sales script and sales dynamic relies on shining a light and making the prospect realize the distance between his current situation, "Point A", and his desired outcome, "Point B". The more clearly you can make the prospect realize the immense gap between Point A and Point B, the better you can position your offer and the more sales you will make.

The second part of this question is absolutely crucial because it paints the picture in the prospects mind about reaching how different life can be in only 12 months time. It doesn't necessarily mean that he will reach all his goals in that time frame (maybe sooner, maybe later), but it implies that it is possible. The fact that you ask that question now makes it a possibility. When asking this question, you'll usually notice that prospects are almost reassured and happy about the possibility of reaching their objective.

5.   Why are looking to solve these problems now?

This is a huge one because it's where you start creating "implied urgency". It's an extremely powerful question because you make the prospect almost sell himself into why he needs to start taking the steps to solve his problems now versus postponing his decision. The worst thing that can happen in sales is when people say *"I'll get back to you"*, or *"let me think about it"* or *"it's not the right time"*.

Narrowing down on this question implies that they understand that they need to take care of the issue NOW, rather than waiting and delaying it. You'll notice that prospects that will actually sell themselves and convince themselves about why they need to take the necessary steps into solving their problem sooner rather than later.

6.   What's the main obstacle that has kept you from making achieving your goals until now? I need you to be perfectly honest because I can only help you if I really know what's been keeping you from reaching your goals.

Question number 6 allows you to get deeper in the prospects mind and understand why he hasn't reached his goals yet. When asking this question, you might hear a lot of superficial answers and even excuses. Don't fall for them.

Your goal is to really get down to the REAL root cause of why he's experiencing issues and why he hasn't taken care of them yet. Usually, the first couple of reasons he mentions verbally are the tip of the iceberg and he might be embarrassed to disclose the real reason(s). If you can get to the real reason, it will make your life infinitely easier and increase sales when you make the offer.

7.   *We talked about your main objective as it relates to [insert target market desire here]. But when I talk to people who reach out for help, there are usually secondary goals that will be positively affected once you achieve [insert prospect's main goal here]. For some, it's being able to have more free time/ more income/ more self-confidence/ a better relationship. What are some of the collateral areas that will benefit you reaching your goal?*

Question 7 is another way for you to gain information about what drives your prospect. If you're selling B2B, you might hear prospects saying that they want to "increase sales" or "increase employee productivity". But the true benefit of increasing sales might be to please the CEO or the investors to get a raise at the end of the year. This might give your prospect more free time to enjoy with his family, fewer hours spent at the office, or an extra week off every year.

If you're selling B2C and your prospect is in the weight-loss market, the collateral benefits of losing weight might make him feel more attractive, gain self-confidence to start going out more or even being able to walk confidently when he's at the beach with friends.

8.   *Ok... let's fast-forward a bit... paint me a picture of how life will look like once you've reached [insert prospect's goals here]?*

This final question is the icing on the cake and the final opportunity for you to understand exactly what the prospect really wants and how life will look like when his problems are solved. In this question, you want the prospect to paint a picture of how life will be like once he's reached his desired goals. Go deep in this question, ask him about everything related to the main benefits, asked about the collateral benefits of reaching his goal: how his income will be affected, his health, family, time for hobbies, etc.

As you can notice, we haven't mentioned anything about a product or a solution at this stage. This entire section is about gathering intelligence and information and generally takes between 20 to 30 minutes. It allows you to determine if your solution can be a fit and how to position it in relation to the prospects issues.

(Pause for a few seconds)

Ok, let's go back and recap...

At the moment you're [insert prospect's current situation here] and you're looking to reach [insert customer's desired outcome here] in the next [insert time frame].
The main objective is to get to [insert 12-month goal here].
So far, you've had issues with [insert prospect's challenges and why he hasn't reached his goal yet] and you said you've struggled with [insert issues here].

After asking all the questions, pause for a few seconds to review your notes and summarize out loud in a few sentences the main highlights of what your prospect told you. The goal of this is to make him hear the exact words he used to make him realize the importance of the situation, the pain and problems he's facing and the gap between his current situation (Point A) and his desired outcome (Point B). It's like placing a giant mirror in front of the prospect.

Let me ask this... how soon are you looking to get these issues taken care of and start reaching your goals?

This question allows you to determine if the prospect is truly serious to get his issues solved and to get rid of the pain he's currently experiencing. Make no mistake: people buy to solve problems. Even when someone buys a Bentley, it's to scratch the itch and satisfy the desire of owning a high-caliber car. If you've done a good job during the questions section and made them realize the massive gap between Point A and Point B, 90% of your prospects will tell you that they want and need to take care of their issues as soon as possible, now. Once you've done a good job by gathering information and playing back word-for-word what the prospect told you by summarizing his situation, you can determine if there is a fit for your solution or not.

If the prospect is NOT a fit for your solution:

I appreciate everything you've shared with me on this call, but based on the situation and more specifically [insert the reason why the customer is not a good fit], I don't think there is a fit at this particular time. [End call politely.]

If the prospect is a fit for your solution:

Ok, based on everything you've told me, I think there's definite ly something we can do together to help you reach those goals.

Let me tell you a bit more of what we do.

We're putting together...

[Continue into a simple and direct presentation of your offer, relating to what the prospect has told you about his situation. Tailor the offer based on his needs.]

Again, keep in mind that we haven't mentioned anything about the solution or service until this point. If the prospect asks you during the intelligence-gathering process about your product or solution, politely say that you need to get more information to establish if there is actually a solution that can be offered or not. Don't go into the pitch without having gathered information. That would be like a doctor prescribing medication or surgery without having asked gathered enough information about the pain and symptoms.

Once you follow the scripts and have all the information necessary and have summarized the prospect situation, you can then decide to go into a presentation about your offer. Make sure you position your offer in relation to what the prospect said. Everyone buys for different reasons, and now that you have all the intelligence about your prospect's situation, it is vital to position your pitch based on HIS specific state. Once you've have presented your solution, you can then ask for the order and close the deal there and then.

Many people think that sales is un uncomfortable exercise of manipulation and trickery, I firmly believe that even though manipulation is indeed part of sales and everyday life to some extent, sales can be very fun if you follow the script and just help the prospect realize the disconnect between his current situation and his desired outcome. And by creating a sense that things need to change FAST, it makes the prospect realize that he can't postpone his decision-making process indefinitely.

There you go, that is the script that has brought in tens of millions of dollars in extra revenue for our clients and our own businesses. Use it, it works.

The script for a two-call close

Now that we've dissected the process and script for a one-call close, let's have a look at how the two-call close works best. A two-call close is generally used when you have two departments in your company: an appointment setting team and a sales team. The appointment setter's job is to filter and qualify leads so that the sales team only interacts with prospects that are qualified and have a basic understanding of the solution you can provide. We generally define a lead as "qualified" if it (A) has interest in a solution you are offering and (B) a budget available to make a decision. In some instances, you might require additional conditions to be met for a "qualified" lead if you're selling more specific solutions and require to be talking to the CEO or the board of directors, etc.

If you have a secretary or someone who can filter your calls, it makes sense to use a two-call close because the leads that will be interacting with the sales team will be much more qualified. The worst thing for a sales team is to interact with unqualified prospects, because it's a massive waste of time and energy for them. Many sales managers make the mistake of dumping massive amounts of leads on their quota-carrying salespeople in the hopes of finding the diamonds in the rough, but the best process that we've tested and gotten massive results with is by implementing a two-call close. Again, it all depends on the infrastructure you have available in your company. Some businesses don't have the luxury of having an appointment setting team and a quota-carrying sales team. Whatever you do, select one of the best processes for you, and make the most out of it. Keep in mind that each "team" can consist of only one appointment setter and one closer (quota-carrying salesperson).

Appointment-setting Script

Now, let's have a look at the script used by an appointment setter. The goal of the script is simply to reach out to prospects that have mentioned their interest and define if they are qualified to be passed on to your sales team.

Here it is:

> Hi [prospect's first name], this is [your first name] calling from [company name here]. How are you doing?
>
> Great! Congratulations on reaching out to us. What we'll do during this quick call is go over a few things to have a better understanding of your situation and see if we can help you see [insert target market goals here].
>
> This is how it's going to work: I'll ask you a few questions to find out more about your current situation and I'll tell you what we've got going on over here, so feel free to ask questions any time. Does that make sense?

For the introduction, you want to sound sharp, clear and authoritative and polite of course. This intro accomplishes the same goals as does the intro on the one-call close by implying urgency and scarcity. It also shows that you're in control of the call and that you're leading the prospects. Remember that control during a sales conversation is extremely important.

[Current situation]

1. *First of all, tell me a little bit about yourself/ your company. What made you decide to reach out to us in the first place?*
2. *What are the top 2 issues you're looking to solve at this time?*

In this section, you're gathering information about the prospect situation. You're not looking to sell your product, you're not looking to impress, you're just looking to gather information and determine if there might be a fit for a conversation with your quota-carrying sales team (closer team). Let me repeat that again: you are not selling anything on this call. You are qualifying the lead to determine if the prospect is qualified for a conversation with your sales team.

[Budget]

I speak with [insert prospect's profession] every day that are looking for ways to [insert prospect's goal] and I find that they fall in one of three categories:

- *Group A: People/ businesses that generate between $100,000 and $1,000,000+ per month.*
- *Group B: People/ businesses that generate between $20,000 and $100,000 per month.*
- *Group C: People/ businesses that generate under $20,000 per month.*

Now, just out of curiosity, if you had to pick one of those 3 groups, which one describes you best?

In this section, your goal is to determine the prospect's budget or revenue. Since we can't ask directly "how much money do you have available to invest with us now?", you need to go about it in a more tactful way. You can adapt these categories as to fit your industry and your prospects' average level of revenue/income, but the purpose is to determine a category in which they fit in. This is simply to avoid wasting the sales team's time with someone who has absolutely no budget available.

If the prospect is unqualified, uninterested or has no budget available, end of the call politely.

(Pause for a few seconds)

Ok, based on what you've told me, what I'd like to do is schedule a one-on-one appointment/ Strategy Session with one of our [Orientation Specialists/ Service Consultants/ etc.] who will how you a few things and walk you through how to [reach prospect's goals] that you mentioned.

Again, we're not looking to offer any type of solution or product during this call. Do not mention anything about your offers, your pricing, etc. The goal of this call is to determine if the prospect is qualified and to set an appointment if possible.

By the way: never referred to your sales team as a "sales team" or "salesperson". Use different terms such as "Orientation Specialist", "Service Consultant", "Success Advisor", etc.

Before that call, there's a little "homework" you need to do, and it's critical you go over it before your call with [insert sales person name] and it takes less than 15 minutes.
I'll be emailing you the details just after the call, it's a special training that our CEO/ founder put together to give you more details about us, and it's vital that you listen to it before that session.

Can I count on you to go through that material and do that for me?

Remember the marketing material and the Objection Crusher page? This is exactly what you'll be sending the prospects so that he watches everything before the strategy session with your quota-carrying sales person.

> *Ok great! I can see [insert sales person name] is available [day] [date] [time], does that work for you? The call will take between 20 to 30 minutes.*
>
> *Perfect, I just booked your session. Be ready for the call and be in a calm place with a computer, [insert sales person name] might be showing a few things online.*
>
> *Great, it was a pleasure talking to you and I wish you the best of luck. Make sure you check your email in the next few minutes and go over the links I'll be sending you. Have a great day!*

Once you set the appointment, your job is done. As soon as you hang up, send the lead the email containing the details and the links to the marketing material so he can review your Objection Crusher page and be in the right state of mind before the call with your sales team. Once you're done, do not engage in any unnecessary small talk. Keep it professional and end the call.

This initial call generally takes less than 10 minutes and results in amazing conversions for the sales team.

It's the first impression that your company makes on your prospect, so it needs to be very professional. Generally, one appointment setter can set anywhere between 5 to 10 qualified appointments a day. A closer (quota-carrying salesperson) can generally handle anywhere between 5 to 10 appointments a day if we consider that a sales call last generally between 30 to 60 minutes. Our best appointment setters generate consistently between 10 to 12 qualified appointments per day and our top performing sales people routinely handle between 8 to 12 presentations conversations per day.

Closer Script for Quota-carrying Salespeople

Now, let's have a look at the script used by your sales team when an appointment has been set. You'll notice that is it that it is pretty much exactly the same as the script used on a one call close, so I won't be dissecting it line by line. Go back to the previous section to see my comments in detail.

If the appointment setter did a good job and followed the script, the appointments should be incredibly well-qualified because they've gone through the entire sales process. They've seen your marketing material, they've raised their hands to get more information, they've had an initial screening conversation and have been qualified by your appointment setters and now they're in the last phase of the conversion process.

Generally, you will see that 30% to 75% of the prospects you speak to after they've been qualified by and appointment setter will turn into sales. That's a predictable statistic that we've seen over and over again in dozens of markets after tens of thousands of calls over the last 10 years. Here's the script for the quota-carrying sales team:

You: Hi [prospect's first name], this is [your first name] calling from [your company here]. Is this a good time for our Strategy Session?

Great! Congratulations on reaching out to us. [Insert appointment setter name] told me about your conversation. So what we'll do during this call is dig deeper in what's going on, clarify your goals and see how we can help you reach those goals asfast as possible and start [insert target market goals here].

This is how it's going to work: I'll ask you a few questions to find out more about your current situation and see, and if there's a fit, I'll tell you exactly about how we can help, so feel free to ask questions any time you'd like during the call. Does that make sense?

Before we start, I'll be very candid and transparent: the majority of people who reach out to us are not a good fit for what we do. Sometimes it's because they're not serious enough or because [insert common excuses target market makes]. So if for some reason it's not a fit, I'll give you specific reason so you know where we stand. Sounds good?

Ok great!

1. So tell me, what made you decide to reach out to us in the first place?
2. What do you do at the moment?
3. Let's dig into what's going on at the moment on your end: what kind of results/ weight lost/ sales volume have you generated over the last quarter?
4. Let's talk about your goals... How much [insert target market desire] on a weekly/ monthly/ quarterly basis over the next 12 months?
   a. Okay, so if we had a conversation 12 months from now and you had [insert prospect's goals here: lost 50 pounds/ doubled your sales/ found the love of your life], would that be a victory for you?
5. Why are looking to solve these problems now?
6. What's the main obstacle that has kept you from making achieving your goals until now? I need you to be perfectly honest because I can only help you if I really know what's been keeping you from reaching your goals.
7. We talked about your main objective as it relates to [insert target market desire here]. But when I talk to people who reach out for help, there are usually secondary goals that will be positively affected once you achieve [insert prospect's main goal here]. For some, it's being able to have more free time/ more income/ more self-confidence/ a better relationship. What are some of the collateral areas that will benefit you reaching your goal?
8. Ok... let's fast-forward a bit... paint me a picture of how life

will look like once you've reached [insert prospect's goals here]?

(Pause for a few seconds)

Ok, let's go back and recap...

At the moment you're [insert prospect's current situation here] and you're looking to reach [insert prospect's desired outcome here] in the next [insert time frame].
The main objective is to get to [insert 12-month goal here].

So far, you've had issues with [insert prospect's challenges and why he hasn't reached his goal yet] and you said you've struggled with [insert issues here].

Let me ask this... how soon are you looking to get these issues taken care of and start reaching your goals?

If the prospect is NOT a fit for your solution:

I appreciate everything you've shared with me on this call, but based on the situation and more specifically [insert the reason why the customer is not a good fit], I don't think there is a fit at this particular time. [End call politely.]

If the prospect is a fit for your solution:

Ok, based on everything you've told me, I think there's definitely something we can do together to help you reach those goals.

Let me tell you a bit more of what we do.

We're putting together...

[Continue into a simple and direct presentation of your offer, re lating to what the prospect has told you about his situation. Tailor the offer based on his needs.]

There you have it. The holy grail of phone sales.

If you're a service provider or sell any kind of products, using these scripts will totally transform your business. We've seen clients go from $10,000/ month to $100,000/ month in a matter of weeks and some clients going from $50,000/ month to over $1 million/ month in sales just by using the exact script and process I gave you.

The reason why this works so well is because when you create a process where all your leads are marketed to before reaching out to you and your sales team, you're getting the best of both worlds: heavy-lifting marketing (the Objection Crusher page crushes all the objections, shows testimonials and establishes indisputable authority) combined with the best sales scripts in the world.

This is not guesswork. This is very predictable and has the power to totally transform everything you do. After you make your first few sales, reach out to me and let me know about your results, I would love to hear about them.

I could sell these scripts for $10,000 in a fancy sales program, but I'm giving them away in this book because I want to impact as many entrepreneurs and businesses as possible. If you love the process but don't want to do everything by yourself, reach out to us because we can do everything for you as we do for our clients.

We can create (or revamp) your branding and marketing material, generate ongoing leads for you, and make all your phone sales for you. You just focus on delivering your service to clients. That's the essence of the revolutionary hands-free and full-service agency I created, and it's helped clients generate millions of dollars, totally hands-free.

Find more information on:
MatthiasMazur.com/Agency or visit ZuraMedia.com.

24

MONEY MAXIMIZATION METHODS

In this chapter, we'll cover several ways to help maximize your revenue even more by adding a few simple things in your sales process that can be implemented literally in the next 24 hours. If you have an existing business that does between $100,000 and $10,000,000 per year, this chapter can increase your revenue anywhere between 25% and 500% in the next 90 days.

Low-hanging fruit
The best time to make a sale is when your customer is in a "buying state of mind" and is just about to order or has just ordered. As much as 20% to 60% of your customers will take advantage of an additional offer if it brings increased value to their situation and if it's presented in the right way. In this chapter, I'll share how to offer upsells to customers doing business with you, which will help you increase customer satisfaction and the value of every transaction.

The Art of "Upselling"
Upselling is a sales technique that consists of making an offer to your customer to purchase an additional item, upgrade or add-on, which

gives you – the business owner - the opportunity to increase the value of each sale you make. For example, a computer hardware seller might offer customers a yearly software update at a 50% discount at the point of purchase. A hair salon might suggest that when you have a haircut, you also buy some kind of product or spray from them. These are purchases that increase the buyer's experience and provide him with "more" of what you have to offer. The benefit for your business is that this can be extremely profitable if presented the right way.

Why upselling is so profitable

Consider this example: a customer buys a computer for $2000. With that kind of price point, there's very little resistance to accepting a $10 monthly service for a "computer crash protection service" that protects the customer from any bad surprises he may encounter with his machine. For you, however, that additional sale is significant, because over 24 months, it adds up to a $240 extra per sale, with a huge profit margin.

Some would say that a $240 sale on a $2000 computer is a minimal increase in the overall sale. But if it only takes 30 seconds to make the $240 sales, why not take the time to make that amount of money? The fact that it's attached to a $2000 sale is irrelevant to the buyer because it secures his investment and makes sure he doesn't get an issue with his new computer. Upselling is one of the most profitable tactics and best uses of your time in your business.

Upselling should be easy

The best part of upselling is that it's very easy to integrate into your daily operations. Because it's done when someone has decided to make an initial purchase, that customer is in a buying mindset. You've already established a relationship, identified needs, presented the benefits, asked for the order and handled objections. Upselling is just presenting an additional add-on offer presented with a "by-the-way" tone. This is something you should instruct your team to do every single time someone purchases something in your business. Think of when you buy something at McDonald's: they cashier is trained to offer you something extra like:

"would you like fries or a dessert with that?"

When it comes to applying upsells in your business, the 3 biggest mistakes are the following:

- Your staff doesn't mention the upsell on a systematic and consistent basis.
- The salesperson comes across as being pushy and un pleasant.
- The offer is made in an unconvincing manner, so the customer generally refuses.

Effective upselling strategies

You've got to assume that the customer will naturally want what you have to offer, and it needs to be presented in a benefit-oriented way. The customer doesn't want to "buy" another product or service. He wants the added benefits of the upsell, so you have to make the benefits stand out clearly when you or your sales team is presenting the upsell. Focus on customer's needs - not yours. It is totally irrelevant whether or not this purchase suits your desires; what is relevant is whether it suits the customer's desires.

Always create a "better" option

To illustrate the power of upselling, let's have a closer look at a few examples in different industries that target different demographics and different price points. All these industries rely heavily on upsells and upgrades to generate profits and sell products and services that are suitable for low budgets as well as high budgets.

Remember the last time you went to buy a car or to check out a new car. The basic model, which advertised on TV commercials and billboards to the general public is usually not the car you end up buying. The car you end up buying often is generally several thousand dollars more expensive than the model advertised. That's because instead of simply selling cars, most dealers offer their customers the opportunity to "add on" extra gadgets like an improved sound system, security devices, a sunroof, a navigational system, an extended warranty and all kinds of extra options to the basic purchase.

The dealers know for a fact that what car buyers want isn't just a new set of wheels and seats, but a personalized transportation vehicle that will satisfy their desires and make them feel good when they're stuck in traffic, rain, or late for a meeting at a venue they can't find without a GPS. Customers aren't just buying convenience and a commodity. They're buying a sense of well-being, a feeling of ownership, independence and even pride. More than just a simple purchase, they're making a statement about themselves with the car and the options they choose. It's all a part of the end result the client desires.

If the customers don't add the extra options they're presented before finalizing the purchase, they would have to pay more later on to add those extra options. Upselling enriches both parties: the business (higher profit margins on every transaction without having to attract a new buyer), and the customer (who gets and more customized experience).

The airline industry also makes heavy use of the upsell and upgrade concept. If you've booked a flight through the internet, you've probably been presented with several different ways to "upgrade your reservation": more cabin space, front-row seating, priority boarding, extra hand luggage, checked luggage, special items on board, cancellation insurance policies, etc. When you see flights advertised for $200, you can quickly end up paying $500 if you select a few extra options. That's an immediate increase in revenue and it all happens when you book online, at the click of a few buttons. Low-cost airlines excel in this upgrade concept and many companies survive mainly thanks to the upsells they offer to passengers who book a flight advertised as dirt-cheap on billboards and on television.

Look at what McDonald's does when you order something at the counter. You rarely get away with what you just came in for as the cashier will suggest that you upgrade to a larger size or get extra fries or extra dessert, "for just 50 cents more".

The upgrade fee seems small in comparison to the price you're paying for the main product, making it a very persuasive offer that most customers rarely resist. This in turn generates millions for McDonald's in extra revenue.

Starbucks has the "Tall", "Grande", and "Venti" sizes of drinks. They've done an effective job positioning the "Grande" as the standard' option, which is actually an upsell from the "Tall".

Another example of an upsell would be a faster computer than the one you initially chose. A gym membership with a personal trainer rather than the basic plan which only includes the use of equipment. It could also be a cell phone plan with more minutes than you originally planned to buy.

Amazon.com has implemented upsells as part of their business model with incredible success, presenting the customer with several options when he buys using the verbiage of "Other people who have ordered X have also ordered Y".

Being an entrepreneur, my "business mind" is constantly turned on. When I walk into a store, I instantly see how well or how poorly the sales process and operations are, along with the hidden opportunities that are not being maximized. Here's an interesting story.

I travel a lot and like to eat healthy. I happened to walk into a local GNC store where they sell food and vitamin supplements. I recently went to three different GNC stores in San Francisco, New York, and in Turkey and always have a good experience analyzing how they use strategic upselling. In all three branches, which are thousands of miles apart, all the salespeople were highly effective in presenting multiple upsell offers at the time of my purchase. I was always prompted with at least two (sometimes three) different upsells for various products, extra refills, and products that complimented my initial purchase.

Making the Upsell Irresistible
An upsell must be perceived by the customer as an irresistible offer. Unfortunately, few businesses take advantage of the use of upselling, and

those who do use it rarely implement in a systematic and consistent way. Upselling takes very little effort and will make a dramatic increase on your bottom line. If your business offers a $20 upsell and 50 customers take advantage of it every week, you've just added an extra $52,000 a year to your bottom line, most of which is profit only. And what was the cost of offering the upsell? Just a few seconds of you or your staff's time.

You'll need to instruct your staff to integrate upsells in everything you offer. You can have the best sales system in your market, but it's useless if the people dealing with customers are not presenting them on a consistent basis. It's your responsibility to be very firm with your staff when you tell them to start offering upsells to your customers. Don't tolerate salespeople who fail to implement this tactic consistently.

How to increase your upsell conversions

The key to making upsells work in your business is to present them to the customer assuming he'll take advantage of it. It has to be presented in a confident way, and needs to be simply irresistible. The value the buyer will receive must be far greater than the price he's paying. Instruct your salespeople to convey the notion that most customers take the upsell and that it's perfectly normal for a customer to choose to upgrade too. To accomplish that, the upsell has to be presented in a low-key, in a "by the way" type of fashion, giving the customer the feeling you're doing him a favor and getting him a better deal.

When we work with clients, we spend time going through their current sales process, products and services to understand what can be offered as an upsell and exactly how it should be presented. Remember, the result can be tens or even hundreds of thousands of dollars in pure profit for your business in a very short amount of time.

I urge you to look at ways to implement these powerful profit strategies in your business. If necessary, contact your current customers to offer them the upsell and track the conversion rate you're getting with the offer you're using. A good upsell offer should have no trouble converting between 20 and 60 percent of the time. Integrating regular and consistent upsells to your marketing mix is the key to increasing the size of every transaction you make.

Back to your business

Take a few moments and ask yourself what are your best-selling products or services. Ask yourself: "What additional product or service can I offer my customers at the point of purchase to give them a greater experience?"

Try offering three times the average volume being purchased for twice the price. The idea behind this is "buy 2, get 1 free". If you are selling a widget, package three together. If you sell a service in monthly or yearly increments, offer 3-month and 3-year options. If you're selling software, try offering a monthly or yearly update package at a discounted rate. Wherever possible, let customers buy more volume at the time of purchase.

Package your product or service for a longer period of time. Any service can be turned into a monthly or yearly offer, from software maintenance to personal trainer sessions. Nearly every consumable product can be provided in a year's supply delivered every month. Many gifts can be turned into a "gift-of-the-month" club experience.

Offer your product or service with recurring charges like insurance and magazine subscriptions are sold. If you offer something truly valuable to your customers, they will want access to your widget on an ongoing and recurring basis.

What upsell to offer your customers

Ultimately, there are two types of upsells: one-time fee upsells, and rebill upsells. If you can provide a valuable product or service every month, quarter or year to your customer, you have all the reasons in the world to add a rebill upsell, even if it's to the tune of $5 or $10 per month. This is something I've implemented in several of my businesses and that generates predictable revenue month after month. Ask yourself what upsell you can integrate that can allow you to charge a customer on a residual basis, providing him with ongoing value and benefits.

A word of caution about rebill offers: do NOT attempt to hide the rebill nature of your offer in legal jargon on page 7 of your terms and conditions in grey font on a hidden page on your website. Always be upfront about the fact that you will be charging your customer every month/ quarter/ year and. If not, customers will eventually find out about it, will call their banks and chargeback any "hidden" transactions that you might not have mentioned clearly during the sales process, which will result in bank fees and penalties on your end. And if you don't handle these cases extremely courteously and give prompt refunds to complaints you receive for rebill charges even if the customer has signed a written agreement with you, be ready to suffer the consequences of bad word-of-mouth and massive amounts of complaints on social media.

Rebill upsells will allow your business to grow in an exponential way by providing you month after month with a massive source of predictable revenue, which increases the lifetime customer value of your buyers. Just keep in mind to do them the right way. Don't do silly stuff. It's not worth the hassle.

One-time fee upsells are great and will undoubtedly increase your bottom line too. It can be as simple as a complimentary product that already sell, a "buy 2 get 1 free" type of offer, a "50% off any additional product" type of offer, and so on. Be creative in your upsell process and brainstorm ways to offer the most incredible value to your buyers.

Take a few moments to think of all the products and services you can provide customers and all the extra products or services you can start offering as part of an upsell package. Think of any services your client could benefit from after purchasing your product or service such as tech support, extended warranties, annual or semi-annual maintenance, pick-up and delivery services, done-for-them services, etc.

The bottom line is that you should always have an upsell. It can simply be a "premium" or a "better" offer and should be presented to your customer in a consistent way, sale after sale, day after day. I can guarantee this strategy alone has the power to transform your business into a highly profitable enterprise in a very short amount of time.

25

SHOW ME THE MONEY!

When you ask most business owners to list their assets, they quickly mention items such as their equipment, furniture, the location of their store or their inventory. But one of the greatest assets to your business is your customer list and more specifically what is called the "lifetime customer value" (or "LCV" in short). Lifetime customer value is defined as the total value in monetary terms your average customer will bring you during the entire period that he is likely to do business with you. In other words, it defines how much money a customer spends with you in his lifetime.

My agency advises and helps CEOs and businesses from all sizes – start-ups and solopreneurs to billion-dollar brands – and it always baffles me that many don't have a clue about the lifetime customer value in their business. To most, what matters is increasing revenue by continuously acquiring one-shot customers, which is considerable harder than increasing the number of transactions a customer makes with your business over the weeks, months and years following his initial purchase. Attracting a new customer will cost you 5 to 20 times more than bringing one of your past customers back to you. Here's how to calculate your LCV:

Let's say you currently have 2,000 customers and your revenue was

$700,000 in the last 18 months. This means that your lifetime customer value is: $700,000 (divided by) 2,000 = $350.

What this means is that over a lifespan of a year and a half, each customer is worth $350 to your business.

Why is this so important to your business?
For several reasons. The first one being that if you know that a customer is worth on average $350 to your business, you have a moral obligation to convert as many prospects into customers in the first place by removing the risk a prospect is facing when presented with an offer from you.

Most businesses make it too difficult for prospects to start using their products and services in the first place. If you make it easier for people to do business with you, more people will start a buying relationship with you. And if you deliver a great experience and good value to your customers, they will keep coming back to you. This will in turn allow you to convert customers into lifelong customers, helping you increase their lifetime customer value and maximizing your profits. That's why taking all the risk from the prospect's shoulders and implementing a strong risk reversal guarantee will allow you convert many more prospects into buyers. The faster you get a buying relationship started, the higher the chances of getting that customer to buy more from you.

How much would it be worth to your business if you could bring in an extra 30 customers every month starting today? Even if you don't make a single dollar on the initial transaction, you'll be able to make enormous amounts of profit if you make them come back over the months and years without having to spend any extra money on advertising and lead generation. Acquiring customers at a break-even point or at a slight loss and making big profits on the back-end is one of the most overlooked profit-generating methods you can use. Lifetime customer value is important to you and your business for the following reasons:

When you know the lifetime value of your customers, you can determine how much time, effort and money you can afford to invest to acquire new customers. In other words, you can invest more today to collect much larger profits in the future.

Every time you do an advertising or marketing campaign, you need to track your ads to know how much you're spending to attract a new customer. Many business owners have no clue about the advertising they do: they don't track how many prospects and customers were generated from that campaign and they don't know how much money on average a customer spends with their business in their lifetime. Basically, they're throwing money at something they can't track and don't know what the specific outcome is.

Once you start realizing that customers are worth infinitely more than just the initial purchase and are actually an ongoing stream of revenue as opposed to a one-shot sale, you can completely refocus your marketing efforts on attracting new customers at a slight loss if necessary.

Instead of constantly struggling to go after more and more new customers, you can focus on keeping your existing customers longer and offering them more things to buy.

Here are two elements that you must implement into your business as soon as possible:

1. Implement a customer retention and appreciation program, including frequent contact and communication via a newsletter, greeting cards, email, direct mail, and even phone calls. I do this in several of my businesses where my staff will personally contact all my customers by phone to keep in touch and ask them how they're doing. This alone has been responsible for hundreds of thousands of dollars in extra revenue.

2. Go after past customers who haven't bought in a while. Setup a system to track every customer's activity. Whenever a customer goes without buying anything for a long period of time, send them an email, a text message or a postcard with a compelling offer, coupon, free gift, or just pick up the phone and call to find out why that person is no longer purchasing from your business.

You need to have a perfect understanding of the lifetime customer value in your business because it's the key to growth in your company. It will allow you to acquire more customers than your competition by making attractive and irresistible offers and it will dramatically increase your bottom-line through more repeat sales and turn your current business into a profit-generating machine faster than you can imagine.

Understand that repeat sales are the key to your business flourishing in the long-term and having a flawless customer service team that offers the best experience and support to your buyers is a must in today's environment.

To excel in customer service, every member of your team has to understand, accept, and live it as a priority in every single contact they have with prospects and customers.

Is the Customer Always Right?

This brings us to the old adage used in sales and customer service that says that "the customer is always right". I firmly believe that the customer is not always right. Some customers (thankfully only a minority) are darn wrong and will never be satisfied no matter what you do for them. Every now and then, it makes more sense to refuse doing business with a customer who loves to create problems, because you'd much rather spend time dealing with happy customers than with someone who just drains time and energy from you and your team.

In some instances (although very rarely), I've had to get rid of problem-causing customers as well as fire difficult clients. Some people will just never be satisfied, and I have no desire to waste time with people who are disrespectful or impolite with me or my staff. Life is too short for that. Sometimes, it's simply easier to terminate a relationship with a customer than to spend hours trying to keep up with nonsense or to resell them on the relationship

Remember that ultimately, you run your business the way it suits you. You make the rules and decide who you accept to work with and offer service to.

Have a system for handling complaints

An angry, irate, unsatisfied customer on the loose can and often will cause you considerable damage. With the rise of the internet, it's very easy for anyone to accuse you of things you've never done and bad-mouthing has become much easier. That's why you need to have a system for handling and solving complaints diplomatically and with the least amount of pain for the parties involved.

In summary, you must know how much an average customer is worth to your business during his lifetime of purchasing from your company. Once you find out your current lifetime customer value, it will allow you to figure out how much you can invest in acquiring new leads and customers with your advertising and marketing.

26

HOW TO BREAK THROUGH BUSINESS BARRIERS

In this chapter, we'll have a deeper look on how to achieve major break-throughs in your business. In this instance, I define a breakthrough as an important discovery and a clear (and often sudden) understanding of a complex situation. It's how businesses often go from average (or good) to great.

Breakthroughs are a set of dramatic improvements in various areas of your business that lead to increased customer satisfaction and retention, higher revenues and profits, and overall greater success.

Breakthroughs allow you to double or triple your revenue faster than ever before and with the same effort or less. Breakthroughs let you max-imize the productivity of your business, allowing it to perform with fewer costs while producing higher returns and higher customer satisfaction. Breakthroughs let you outplay, outrun, outwit, outlast, outsell, and out-perform your competition without them knowing what hit them.

Stepping out

If you've been in business for any period of time, you know how over-whelming and time-consuming the day-to-day tasks can become. It's very common for entrepreneurs and executives to pull off all-nighters and 80-hour workweeks. But in my experience, it is more important to take the time to step out of your business on a regular basis in order to be able to recognize what strategies can be implemented to increase productivity, efficiency, and overall profit.

Many entrepreneurs don't take the time to step out of their daily activities and get so caught up in the daily tasks of their business trying to put out small fires that they don't see the forest that's behind it.

If you're used to working more than you'd like for weeks without being able to generate a noticeable increase in sales and profits, you need to take a moment and step out of your business for a few days. This will allow you to see your business with a different perspective, and you'll end up having several realizations that will allow you to achieve greater growth in your business.

I grew up trained as a professional athlete and have always been known to be a workhorse. My tendency is always to do more than what I re-quired, and that's also why I've been able to accomplish so much at an age where most of my peers are just starting their first job.

Personally, I have to force myself to take days off every month to get away from my businesses to reflect on how things are going, what can be improved, how the overall strategy is getting executed, how effective are the tactics we have in place, and what we can implement to grow to the next level. During those days off, I don't check emails or sales and don't have contact with my staff. I do this on purpose to help my mind get away from all the activities that occur on a daily basis, and I usually end up getting several key insights on a professional, but also on a per-sonal level.

Those days are the ones that give me the best ideas and allow me to get a bird's-eye view of the current situation of my businesses. Ideally,

I'd recommend you take one day every week to step out and get away from your business and immerse yourself in a completely new environment and do things you usually don't do. If you can't afford to take a day off every week, try to take at least two days off per month. I guarantee you those days will literally be the most profitable days of your business, because breakthroughs are often achieved when the mind far from the daily business occupations.

Here are steps you can take that will help you achieve breakthroughs in your business:

Try viewing your business, product and service through the eyes of a new potential customer. How does a new prospect perceive your business, product or service? What can you improve?

Identify all the time-consuming tasks that you're still doing yourself but that don't result in direct profit and delegate them. Your goal is to spend time creating systems that generate extra revenue and profits. What tasks are taking you too much time on a daily basis?

Come up with new ways of increasing first-time purchases by implementing risk reversal, and think of how you can implement that in your business right away.

Find the reasons why customers do business with you in the first place and use that information in your marketing and advertising materials to convert more prospects into buyers. Can that reason become your main USP?

Ask your staff to collect evidence as to why prospects still haven't done business with you and ask yourself how you can remove the barrier of entry to increase your front-end conversions. The key to new customers lies in how you convert your existing prospects into more sales.

Remember the last time you were in direct contact with an unhappy customer. What could you have done to minimize his frustration and turn him into a loyal long-term customer?

What can you give your customers as a gift for thanking them of doing business with you? It could be a discount on a related product, a free book or report, or whatever you can offer that can benefit them even if you need to spend a few extra dollars. Good deeds go a long way, and you'll increase the quality of the relationship you have with your customer base.

How can you differentiate yourself from your competition with a powerful USP? What can you offer that no one else in your marketplace currently offers?

When is the last time you congratulated your staff for the good things they did? Most business owners are quick to notice the small mistakes of their staff rather than congratulate them for the good things they do.

What can you do to increase the customer's experience after a sale and make him feel glad he did business with you? What unannounced gift or bonus can you offer to thank him for his purchase?

Ask your staff

A high-end nightclub in Switzerland I used to spend time at in my early twenties closed a few years ago. Less than 24 months before shutting down, the club was generating around $150,000-$300,000 per month in revenue, with a healthy chunk of profit. When the club was doing well, Saturday nights would bring in up to $50,000. But in its last few months, the club was sometimes generating less than $20,000, and eventually had to close for obvious economic reasons.

The irony of this is that the club was perceived as probably the most luxurious club of my city (Lausanne, approximately 150,000 residents). I was curious as to why the place went from being the hottest place in the area and most exclusive venue and then lost its edge and sunk in less than 12 months. Over the years, I became friends with several of the staff members, most of which were working there when the place was doing great and were the first to witness the attendance and numbers crumble.

At the closing party, I asked them what they thought of the way things had turned out and what could have been done differently. Surprisingly, every single person I talked to - bouncers, event planners, and waiters - came up with at least five ideas the club could have done to get its momentum back. They were the ones who were in direct contact with the customers. After hearing all the ideas the staff came up with, I asked them if they'd had a chance to share their ideas with management. They all said no. Apparently, management "wasn't interested" in what their employees' suggestions. That's a true story that illustrates how a multi-million dollar business could have saved itself from shutting down had they simply asked their staff for ideas.

The lesson from this story is simple: get feedback from the people on your team who are in direct contact with your customers: the people who are in the field, at the counters, on the phone, presenting your products and services. If you run a big organization with several layers of management, you'll find it very useful to receive frequent updates and reports from the people who are in contact with your customers.

The Pink Elephant Syndrome

Managers have a tendency of glorifying accomplishments and not delivering the raw truth of what's really going on. Don't let layers of management obstruct the flow of information, and hold regular meetings with your staff on a weekly basis. Ask for their input and what they would do to increase revenue and sales. Schedule a meeting this week and ask your staff the following questions:

- What do you feel is holding you back from performing at optimum level?
- If you could change one thing about our company, what would it be?
- How do you feel the company and your team are doing?
- Do you receive sufficient feedback about your performance?
- What's the biggest challenge you run into on a daily basis at work?
- What is most satisfying about your job?
- What is least satisfying about your job?

- What would you change about your job?
- Do you feel you receive enough training to do your job effectively?
- How can I, or the firm, help you reach your career goals?
- Do you have any suggestions that would allow us to convert more prospects into customers?
- Do you have any suggestions that would deliver more value to the customer?
- Do you have any suggestions as to how we could improve the customer's experience?

Don't judge or criticize their opinions, let your ego on the side and take notes on what your team says. Give every person in the room a chance to speak up and make suggestions. You'll be amazed by the information and the ideas your staff will come up with during that 30-minute weekly meeting. Another way of getting input from your people is to simply email them a questionnaire and ask them to fill it out and send it back. If your organization employs a large number of workers, make sure to get raw feedback from the people who work in direct contact with your customers: tech support people, salespeople, customer service teams, etc. Don't always trust your managers to relay the information – ask the workers directly for honest feedback and reward them for their honesty and for the time they spent answering the questions.

Undercover Boss

Undercover Boss is a great TV show that deserves your attention for the business lessons you can get out of it. The show is based on a senior executive of a company - oftentimes the CEO himself - going undercover with a fictional name and back story as an entry-level employee in his own company to investigate how the company really works and identify how it can be improved. The executive generally spends a week working in different areas of the company and in most cases a different location each day. Each episode is smartly structured and allows the executive to see and experience what's really going on "in the field" of his organization. Keep in mind most of the companies on the show usually employ thousands of people, so it's often impossible for the workers to recognize the CEO. At the end of his week, the boss reveals his true identity and summons the employees he worked with and gives them his honest opinion, often rewarding them through promotions and financial rewards.

If you don't employ thousands of people, you can still use the same concept by asking a friend to call your business and ask for extra information about a product or service and simply test the scripts, attitude, politeness, and seeing how your staff handles incoming calls, how they upsell your products and services after an initial purchase, etc.

Work to stop working

This is an interesting concept that I often discuss during my weekly web shows and at the conferences I speak at. The idea behind is to do everything you can to set up systems in your business to start removing yourself from the daily tasks in your business. Next time you do something in your business, ask yourself what you can do reduce the number of hours you spend at your desk to have more time off and to enjoy life and everything it has to offer. If you had one month to completely replace yourself from your business, what would you do differently? What would you automate? What would you systemize?

Many business owners get caught up in the daily tasks and unfortunately spend their entire lives working inside their business, forgetting why they started a business in the first place! If you're like the majority of business owners out there, you've started your business to have more time off and be the master of your destiny. Are you making the most of the time you initially thought you'd have? Or are you stuck in the day-to-day tasks and putting out fires in your company?

How 22 Year-Olds Run a Billion Dollar Business

One of the world's most successful businesses, McDonald's, is operated by late teenagers and people in their early twenties. Maybe not literally, but at least the majority of its employees dealing directly with customers are extremely young. Each McDonald's store turns over $2 million every year on average, and the average age of a branch manager is under 25 years old, while the average age of an employee is around 16 years old. The success of McDonald's depends on everyone in the business following a highly detailed system in place that leaves nothing to luck.

This is one of the key elements in running a highly profitable business. Franchises have long understood that to be able to generate such high revenue and remain profitable while being operated by employees from all walks of life (including people who haven't finished high school), they would need to have a system that's so effective that their branches would work even if the workers are unqualified or have trouble communicating in fluent English.

Think of your business as a movie set. On a set, you have a number of actors, and in order for the performance to be a success, each actor needs to follow his script. At McDonald's, when a 16-year old worker at the counter asks you "would you like fries with that?", he's applying the system. McDonald's knows that if every employee offers upsells when a customer is making a purchase, it increases its bottom-line.

Think of your own business: what systems can you create and implement to streamline product development, product fulfillment, and marketing and sales?

If you've been to a Disney theme park, you've probably noticed that all the shops are located right at the entrance of the park. Why? Because after a day of fun at the park, that's where children ask their parents for a new T-shirt, a new box of crayons, a statue, and other souvenirs. They have it down to a system.

Highly successful and profitable businesses know that systems drive the business more than people do. Of course, having great people working for you is a tremendous asset and will considerably increase your results, but having systems in place allows you to generate predictable actions and results that are highly measurable. Your task, as a business owner, is to develop systems for your business that maximize your profits.

Sharpening the saw

In "The 7 Habits of Highly Effective People", author Stephen Covey shares an interesting story that illustrates a highly important point. A young man was struggling in the woods to saw down a tree. An old farmer came by, watched for a while, and then quietly said, "What are you doing?"

"Can't you see?" the man impatiently replied, "I'm sawing down this tree."

"You look exhausted," said the farmer. "How long have you been at it?"

"Over five hours, and I'm beat," replied the man. "This is hard work."

"That saw looks pretty dull," said the farmer. "Why don't you take a break for a few minutes and sharpen it? I'm sure it would go a lot faster."

"I don't have time to sharpen the saw," the man says emphatically. "I'm too busy sawing!"

That story illustrates how caught up you can get in your daily tasks and why it's important to take the time sharpen your own saw on a regular basis. It is pretty obvious that if the young man had taken a few minutes to sharpen his saw, he would have been able to save a lot of time afterwards.

When is the last time you've taken a step away from your business and learn a new skill to grow your business? When is the last time you've taken time to meet with some like-minded businesspeople and mastermind about the future of your industry? When is the last time you asked a consultant for advice on how you can increase your profits?

Take a few moments to think of how you can sharpen your saw to be more effective in your business. Brainstorm ideas and see what you can start implementing today to achieve exponential results.

Continuous education

Just because you run a business doesn't mean you should ignore developing new skills and increasing your knowledge. By continuously educating yourself, you'll be able to solve problems faster when times become more challenging. Another benefit is that studying and improving your skills will allow you to stay on the cutting edge in your industry, which will in turn increase the likelihood of experiencing breakthroughs in your business. Whether you run a 500-employee company or a one-man operation run from a home office, it's vital that you always keep educating yourself.

That's why I highly recommend you to do everything you can to be on the forefront of innovation and always be one step ahead of your competition. Many of your competitors won't take the time to sharpen their saw by educating themselves further because they are too busy putting out fires in their daily businesses. Be smart: take the time to improve your education. It will add serious growth to your bottom-line.

27

PREPONDERANCE OF PROOF

Lying politicians, corrupt government officials, below par news agencies and cheating professional athletes are now part of the daily news landscape. Society has become more and more skeptical. Chances are your prospects don't believe you. Even worse, they don't believe your product or service delivers on what you promise.

Proof to the Rescue

One element that will increase dramatically your sales and allow you to convert more prospects into customers is to induce maximum proof in everything you do, and emphasize social proof in your communication materials such as your marketing and advertising pieces. Let's have a closer look at what social proof is and how can it can help you accomplish your goals faster in growing your company.

Social Proof Mania

Social proof is a phenomenon that occurs in social situations when people are unable to determine an appropriate mode of behavior. In a given situation, the tendency is for people to follow what other people do. Social influence, in general, can lead newcomers to join a large group of people in what is often referred to as "herd behavior".

There's a psychological explanation on social proof, but the basics come down to the theory that "if you see someone doing something and that person survived the experience, it's relatively safe to assume that you can also do what they did and survive too".

A few years ago, I read an interesting story concerning a so-called "mystery disease" in a school in England. A total of 53 students and teachers were taken to the hospital after suddenly developing sickness and headaches. Oddly enough, the doctors couldn't find anything wrong with the patients.

A clinical psychologist later declared: "When one person feels ill, it is not uncommon for others around them to have the same symptoms. It is not hypochondria; the symptoms can be quite real. Mass hysteria is a likely explanation for what happened at the school."

And it was all fueled by one main element: social proof.

As Robert Cialdini, one of the world's most recognized persuasion and influence researchers wrote in his book Influence: "people will do things that they see other people are doing".

If a man is associated to a group attractive women, his perceived social value and attractiveness is enhanced. The thinking pattern in this case would be "if all those women seem to really like him, there must be something about him that is of high interest and high value".

If a man is constantly getting rejected by women, his social value will be judged negatively. The thinking pattern is then "I just saw him being rejected by many women, there is probably a good reason why women don't like him".

Similarly, someone who has been unemployed for a long time often has a hard time finding a new job. Potential employers often attribute (mistakenly) the person's lack of employment to the candidate's lack of motivation and skills. Similarly, a person who is in high demand like a CEO often continues to receive many attractive job offers even if his performance is ordinary.

Nightclubs, bars and restaurant owners often use social proof to increase the perceived popularity of their venues by deliberately reducing the rate at which people are allowed to enter, thus causing the line to be longer. People passing by the venue might perceive the long line as a signal of the place's desirability and may wait in the line merely because "if all these people are waiting, the place must be good". Theaters sometimes use hired staff and place them in the audience instructing them to start clapping at specific times during the show, so the rest of the audience follows.

Very few people want to go first. After all, no one really likes to be the guinea pig. No one likes to be the first to get burnt. That is why we use social proof to make decisions: it is our personal gauge of risk. Your business's goal is to use social proof strategies to let prospects know that risk is minimal, and that others have gone ahead with the transaction and that it's safe.
When you surf th
e web for reviews of a movie or a book you're interested in, you're looking for social proof. If people around you are talking about a new movie that just came out, it might intrigue you and you'll probably take the time to see it yourself or at least to check out a review online.

Start paying attention to how social proof is used in business and in daily communication and think of how you can implement small tactics to let your customers know that "it's okay to do business with you."

Where to Get Social Proof
Most of the time, you just ask for it. You can create social proof by asking people to check out your product or service and give a testimonial about their experience with it. You can survey your past customers, and ask them for their opinion and communicate those statements to your prospects.

You can also aim for people who already have an established reputation in your marketplace, yet might not be in direct competition with you. They might already have built up solid trust with their audience and clients and might be open to collaborating with you on a mutually beneficial joint venture. Piggybacking on their existing credibility will generate instant buzz and trust for your own business.

Statistics as evidence of social proof

Another effective technique you can add to your marketing is communicating numbers and percentages your customers get by doing business with you. For example, if 50% of your customers refer other people to your business, that's social proof because it shows that your business is trustworthy and it shows your customers appreciate you enough to want their circle of friends to enjoy the benefits you have to offer. And by all means: publish the numbers that make your business look good everywhere you can: on Facebook, on Twitter, on your website, in your store, on your business card, etc.

I recently rented a car in Los Angeles and the rental office used the power of social proof in a very unique and interesting way. When you entered their office, you could see literally thousands of Polaroid pictures on their walls of happy past customers. The rental agency would give customers a $20 discount when you returned your car in exchange for a picture of a review posted on Yelp or on Facebook. The result was indisputable proof: hundreds (if not thousands) of pictures of happy customers on their office walls. That's a great way of putting new prospects at ease and reassuring them that they've been around for a long time and deliver a good service. Social proof is showing that someone out there likes you – the more people, the better. Testimonials go a long way and are free to display online. I always recommend having and displaying as much proof as possible so prospects can't question the fact that you deliver on your promise and that your service works. Implementing social proof and testimonials is one of the best ways to build trust in your market and convert more prospects into customers.

Another effective technique to increase social proof is to have a section on your website where your visitors can post a question for others to see and have someone of your staff answer it on a short 30-90 second video. I've used this technique in several of my businesses with great efficiency and I've always had an increase in sales in the weeks following a "Questions & Answers" video campaign. Creating an interactive way for prospects to have answers to their questions will position you as a trusted advisor rather than as a salesperson. Creating content has become so cheap: you can literally shoot a video in a matter of seconds with your Smartphone. And people love to feel valued and to see that you took a company FINALLY took the time to answer their question. Why not take advantage of the power of free content?

28

RESIDUAL REVENUE RICHES

In this chapter, we're going to uncover an income stream that has the potential to solve (almost) all your revenue headaches, increase profits, turn cold prospects into hot customers and increase lifetime customer value. It's an powerful technique that smart companies use in markets like insurance, media, publishing, health, and personal development. If you get nothing out of this book but simply implement this one technique, I can guarantee that your business can generate increased profits in a very short period of time.

The Incredible Power of Predictable Income

Residual revenue is based on one simple but extremely powerful principle: make one sale, and generate income month after month. The fitness industry works on a continuity marketing model: once you sign up for a gym, your credit card gets charged month after month until you cancel. Usually, it's a small nominal fee like $10-$100, which makes it rather painless on the monthly credit card statement even if you haven't had time to go to the gym that month or are out of the country. Dietary supplements use the same model and will oftentimes offer you to join a monthly membership program where you get shipped vitamin supplies every 30 days, and your credit card gets billed month after month until you cancel. This means that you could present your customers with an offer in January to join your continuity program, and they might still be paying you several months after that initial purchase without requiring you to resell them anything else.

This model is extremely powerful and should be integrated in some shape or form into any business. The beauty of it is that almost any industry and type of business can implement a continuity model and generate solid predictable income month after month. Let's talk numbers.

Let's say you have a free 30-day trial that leads to a $39.95/ month re-billing plan. Let's assume that you're able to get 200 new customers to take a free trial every month. This means that every month, you have 200 new people who enter your continuity program and who could end up staying a member of your program for several months. After 12 months, 2,400 customers will have taken advantage of your free trial, and if you offer good value and a good reason to stick to your membership pro-gram, you could have several hundred customers paying you $29.95/ month. If you manage to retain only 25% members per year, you would have close to $24,000 in monthly recurring revenue that your business generates on autopilot, creating an additional income stream that brings in up to over $285,000 per year.

Gym memberships often have hundreds and even thousands of mem-bers signed up, yet only 5-20% of them actively use the gym. Rest as-sured that the other 80-95% of the members are getting charged month after month too, bringing in predictable and residual cash flow.

Instead of selling products and services on a one-time sale basis, think of how you can implement a continuity program in your business in the next 4 to 8 weeks. I have both been involved in launching and running several continuity programs in my businesses as well as in our clients' businesses that have added up to millions of dollars in extra revenue over the last few years, and I can tell you this: implementing an additional income source of recurring revenue in your business can be one of the most exciting and profitable business decisions you'll ever make.

You will find it much more profitable to sell to one customer once and keep him happy over time than to go out and find new customers repeatedly for a one-time product sale. Many companies have been offering continuity programs for years:

- Proactive does it with a face cleanser.
- Doubleday Book Club does it with books.
- Microsoft does it with software.
- Columbia House does it with DVDs.
- Insurance companies and gyms have been doing it for decades.
- Phone companies and internet service providers are making billions every year with it.

These companies offer an option where subscribers pay a set fee each month and receive something new in return (books, DVDs, software updates, internet access, telephone communications, etc.). I've belonged to one of these continuity programs at some point in my life, and chances are, you have too. The model works and the cash flow involved is big. How can you incorporate this recurring revenue model into your business? Here are the 5 most common continuity program models to consider for your business:

Retainer model. Attorneys and accountants have done this for years. Their clients go on a regular retainer and the client can contact the attorney/ accountant as defined by the agreement of the retainer. Consultants, coaches, and virtual assistants offer this option too as a way of providing services over an extended period of time.

Subscription-based publications. In this model, a publisher is providing new content and information to its members via the internet or a print publication. I've personally had several publishing businesses and still have customers paying up to $150 every month to receive insider information we publish. Some of the members joined 18 months ago, which means that such a customer is worth $2,700 to my business from that monthly stream alone.

Extra support. If you're selling software or hardware of any kind, this is something you can easily implement to generate a new stream of income. You can offer a dedicated phone number your customers can call if they have any questions or problems with your product and benefit from continuous updates and discounts on other products you sell.

Auto shipping method. If you sell a consumable good, you could create a continuity program by offering a free 30-day trial so customers receive a full month's supply of your product for free. Then, they are placed into a monthly rebilling cycle where they get the product shipped automatically to their house every month, allowing you to charge their credit card on a monthly basis. This can be applied to products like dietary supplements, cleaning products, or make-up and grooming products for example.

Club, Inner Circle or VIP Program. This is a model that coaches, consultants, and speakers often use to generate healthy residual income. This offers members of the program access to the mastermind leader in the form of consulting conference calls, printed newsletters, or live seminars and events.

7 Ways to Attract Members

There are several ways to grow your continuity program. Let's have a look at the best ways to market your residual program.

Sweepstakes offers. They are a great way to increase front-end response. The idea is that everyone who joins your continuity program enters a sweepstakes contest. This generally works well for low-end monthly rebilling programs like magazine based memberships.

"2 for 1 concept". Offering more of the product can increase response like a "12 months of membership for the price of 9".

Free trial offer. This is the without doubt one of the best ways to position and sell a continuity program. The key is to develop a strong back-end strategy that allows you to upsell the customer as soon as he's made a choice of taking advantage of your free trial program.

Fixed-term offer. If you have a product or service that can be sold in a fixed amount of time, say for example 6 months, it allows your members to know what to look forward to and know that there's an end in sight.

Gift with purchase. Offer a gift when a new subscriber buys into your continuity program or takes a free 30-day trial. Sports Illustrated has done this by offering free jerseys of your favorite team when you purchase a subscription to one if its magazines.

Forced or tied-in continuity. In this model, you link your main program and your continuity program together. When someone buys your basic product or service, you can either attach the continuity program to it by default, which is called "forced continuity", meaning that the customer cannot get the main product without taking a free trial of your residual program. In a "tied-in" model, you can position the continuity offer as an upsell which still ties it your main product or service.

Premium offer. When you create a continuity program, always try to come up with an "upgrade option" or a premium continuity offer at a higher price point. From our testing and experience, you will usually end up with 10-30% of the members who will choose the more expensive membership option, bringing in more cash flow to your business.

How to keep members

One of the keys to growing your residual income is to focus not only on acquiring new members, but also on keeping them subscribed for as long as possible. Of course, it would be unrealistic to think that every member who joins your program will stay a member for his entire life. The key is to create and deliver the best value to your members as possible and send them unannounced bonus gifts every now and then just for being part of your program. A way of knowing your membership numbers is by analyzing your attrition rate.

The attrition rate (or churn rate) is a measure of how many customers or members leave over a certain period of time. It is a good way to measure growth for subscription services: if the growth rate is higher than the attrition rate, then the company grows. Attrition rates in continuity models vary greatly depending on the price of the monthly fee, the service provided, the level of communication and the satisfaction your members get out of it.

The Power of FREE: the experiment

In his book Predictably Irrational, author Dan Ariely describes a series of experiments he performed during his time at the Massachusetts Institute of Technology, a prestigious establishment full of smart and bright students near Boston in the United States. He offered subjects something desirable – chocolate – at a variety of prices. Two types of chocolate were used – a Hershey's Kiss and a Lindt Swiss chocolate truffle. While the Kiss is an inexpensive and common treat, a Lindt truffle is a far tastier chocolate that is also more expensive.

The first experiment offered subjects a truffle for 15 cents or a Kiss for 1 cent. This resulted in 73% of the people choosing the truffle, while 27% went with the Kiss.

In the second experiment, the price was reduced by one cent on each product – the truffle was offered at 14 cents, and the Kiss was free. Although the price differential remained the same, the behavior of the subjects changed dramatically: 69% chose the free chocolate, and only 31% bought the bargain-priced truffle.

To find out if the appeal of the free Kiss was based on convenience (not having any change, having to hunt around in a purse for coins, etc.), the experiment was repeated in a cafeteria food line where the cost of the chocolate could be easily added to the total purchase. Even with the elimination of paying inconvenience, the free Kiss was still the overwhelming choice.

Ariely explains that in essence, a free item carries no risk and represents the proverbial low-hanging fruit: a resource that can be obtained with near-zero effort. Picture this: if you were living years ago in a cave and had enough food supply stored, you'd be unlikely to go actively looking for more food. But if you were walking back to your cave and found a perfect apple hanging over the path in easy reach, you'd most certainly be tempted to pick it anyway and think about what to do with it later. That apple would be, in essence, "free" and would not involve climbing, traveling, fighting or any kind of physically-consuming effort.

Free Trial Offers

"Free" has transformed thousands of struggling businesses into highly profitable machines because the cost of choosing something for "free" carries very low risk for a prospect. There's virtually no barrier to transaction, no obstacle. You can use this concept in your own business by creating a free offer and monetizing it with a continuity program as well as a solid back-end range of products you can immediately upsell to increase revenue. Once a customer has accepted a free trial, he's also much more likely to buy a paid product or service since he's said "yes" by taking the free trial.

Like I mentioned a few chapters back, make absolutely sure you disclose clearly on your order page in readable font that the customer will be charged every month for the service he's signing up for. Don't try to stiff people by not disclosing the rebill terms clearly because that can get you into major legal issues with your payment processor, the Better Business Bureau and might even get you an unwanted letter from your local Attorney General. So make sure you do things the right way and deliver a solid service that people are happy to pay for.

The bottom-line is that in most businesses, having an extra source of residual and predictable income can totally transform a business and take it from average to highly profitable. I've seen it happen time and time again in our clients' businesses. Big companies have been doing it for decades and are making billions of dollars every month using this simple but highly powerful model. The beauty is that it is something simple in essence that you can implement in your business fast and that can produce income in the next 60 days. If your business is making sales but is struggling to produce profits, this method has the power to transform your entire organization and turn it into a profit-producing champion.

29

TAKE YOUR PARTNER BY THE HAND... (THEN GET RICH!)

In order to live, an organism needs energy. While some organisms are able to supply enough food for themselves, other organisms depend directly or indirectly on other organisms to survive and feed of them. Meet the oxpecker, a bird with special benefits that lives mostly in the African desert, and that feeds exclusively on the backs of large mammals. These little birds can be found around buffalos, rhinoceroses, giraffes, impalas and other game. They climb on their hosts, searching for ticks and blood-sucking flies, which they gladly eat whenever they're hungry. This does not bother the host animal, and is mutually beneficial for both the bird and its host. And it's a great example of a successful host-parasite relationship.

Over the years, businesses spend enormous sums of money on advertising, marketing and lead generation efforts to build a database of loyal prospects and customers.

Customer acquisition costs huge amounts of money, and costs keep increasing year after year as marketers get more competitive and smarter.

Most businesses invest their marketing dollars to target large audiences of demographics knowing they won't be able to convert anything more than a tiny fraction into customers and even less into frequent buyers. And even if it does indeed produce results and profits, going after cold audiences is the toughest and most expensive way of generating new business.

But what if you could reduce - or downright eliminate – the costs of advertising and lead-generation and only spend your time and money on people who are better prepared to listen to your message?

The good news is that there are ways to generate ultra-targeted leads and customers by using the power of partnerships with other non-competing businesses. You can create alliances with other businesses who have already invested time, effort and advertising money attracting customers who would gladly do business with you.

This gives you the advantage of being able to access brand new and untapped customer databases with the permission and cooperation of the business that acquired those leads and customers in the first place.

This process is known as setting up a strategic alliance in the form of win-win deals for all parties involved. It basically works like this: Company A agrees to let Company B deliver a sales message to Company A's prospects and customers. Company A encourages its customers to purchase Company B's product.

Open your wallet and look at your credit cards. Most likely, you have a Visa or a MasterCard that displays a partner of, like an airline company, a department store or a car rental that allows you to turn your dollars spent into frequent flyer miles and other bonuses.

When you subscribe to magazines like The Economist or Fortune, you end up receiving direct mail every few weeks from other publications like Time Magazine or The Financial Times. That's a power partnership at work.

Putting together power partnerships can quickly bring you more customers and more revenue. I've built an entire multi-million dollar business from scratch using joint ventures and strategic partnerships, so believe me when I say that it can make your business strive with no advertising costs. It's basically a win-win situation for every party: you get extra business at no cost, and your partner gets credit and commissions for recommending your good products and services to his prospects and customers.

How to setup Power Partnerships

Most of the time, you have underutilized contacts and resources in your very own cell phone and contact directory. You probably know several people who might help you put together profitable and business-changing partnerships. Who do you know that sells a related product or service that is not in direct competition with yours?

Once you've got a list of a few people on paper, call and ask them to introduce your product or service to their audience. Give them as much information on your products, testimonials of your past customers who have benefited from the product or service, etc.

Locate businesses that have customers who are predisposed to your product or service. For example, if you're in the catering business, you could partner with a cleaning company or an event planning company. Each business should give an endorsement to your product or service and in return they would receive a certain percentage of the sales you make to their list. Successful strategic alliances usually comprise of the following features a **clear benefit to both companies and the customers.** Both companies increase the sale of products, their visibility and strengthen their brands by joining forces.

How to approach a potential partner

Joining forces with partners can bring in revenue as soon as this week if you approach them the right way. The first question to ask your potential strategic partners is simple. Take the time to call the person the other company and ask him if he would like to make $10,000, $30,000, $50,000 or more in a very short period of time with absolutely no effort, no risk and no investment on his part. This question is a no-brainer, and any serious businessman will want to know more about what you have to offer.

Then, point out the following facts:

- Your product or service is non-competitive to what he is selling. Approach the potential partner and explain to him that any extra revenue your deal generates is virtually found money. This is especially appealing to businesses who own large databases of "one-time" buyers.
- The partnership won't take away any revenue he would make on his own.
- The deal will bring in a healthy chunk of profits with minimal risk.
- He doesn't need to do anything nor spend extra money. If he does wish to participate on a financial level, he's welcome to do so, but it is not a requirement.
- You will provide him with all the information and marketing pieces needed for the joint venture. You will take care of the copywriting, printing, and distribution of all that is needed.
- All the orders can be sent to his company so he knows that nothing is getting done behind his back. This element alone is what tips potential partners to agree to the deal, because most are afraid of losing control or getting "used". This way, they can verify the transactions from start to finish.
- Stress the fact that the whole operation is basically hands-free for him, and that it will result in pure profits for both parties, and strengthen his relationship with his prospect and customer base.

This is a method I've used for years with great success, which virtually doesn't cost you anything, and can and will produce great results. To increase the conversions, you can even offer to craft a few extras for your partner's customers by creating an irresistible offer with more value, a longer guarantee, an early-bird discount if they act fast, or split payments over a few months to make your product or service more affordable.

When negotiating the terms, avoid calling in your lawyers. Deal in person with the other business owner as it will make things much more direct. Once a deal is reached, be sure to put the main points on paper and ask him to agree to the terms so you both avoid running into miscommunications that could end up hurting your companies.

Also, know that if you're approaching a larger company, they might want to receive a better deal than just 50-50. Be ready to reduce your take, and think of this operation as "found money" and acquiring new leads and customers into your business that you can then turn into lifetime customers. Every customer you generate from this deal can eventually be worth thousands of dollars in pure profit for your company. Sacrifice early profits for long-term growth. Remember that you're not spending any money on lead generation, and that your only costs are attached to creating the marketing material such as a sales letter, stamps, envelopes, etc.

Approaching a Potential Partner

When you approach the other company, you have to basically "sell" the idea of the partnership and make it clear why it's in their interest to make this happen. If possible, try to quote some sales figures to show what is possible, without overdoing it either as you don't want him to be disappointed if the conversions are low. Just give an honest estimate of the sales and profits you expect to generate from the deal. Present the offer to make it appealing to the other party, and remember to always answer the question "what's in it for them?".

This method basically allows you and your future joint venture partners to maximize your assets and leverage what you have of most important: your prospect and customer lists.

What's in it for the host

Here are a few points that will benefit the host. If you're the host, understand that you basically cannot lose by doing this kind of deal. If you're the one approaching a host, make sure to stress these benefits when you're trying to persuade a potential partner:

- You are both making money you otherwise wouldn't have made.
- You're generating new streams of cash flow without any advertising cost.
- You're increasing the lifetime customer value of the customer base as well as converting prospects into new customers.
- You're leveraging the investments you've made for lead acquisition over the past years.
- You're creating long-term revenue streams that can generate income for years to come with very little effort on both parties.
- You tap into your hidden marketing assets by sharing resources that were just sitting in your current businesses.
- You create a long-term relationship with another company which can allow you to attract new partners and new business after your first deal goes well.
- The host company is making easy money just by endorsing a product or service.

Create an irresistible offer

This is vital and will allow you to maximize the results of every strategic alliance you start. It's crucial that the end customer feels that he's getting an irresistible offer, and that both parties have gone out of their way to provide the most exceptional deal. Think of this as creating goodwill in your company and building your business into a brand that really cares about its prospects and customers – to the point that you arrange sweet deals for them. They have to feel like you're "hooking them up" with a great offer and that you're doing it in their best interest.

Splits

When I share my thoughts about power partnerships and deal-making during keynotes in front of audiences, I always ask "who would agree to start a deal if your strategic partner is taking 90% of the revenue and you're doing all the work?"

Very few hands go up. This is interesting, because what the majority of people say to themselves is "why would I let the other party get away with 90% of the money?" whereas the reality is that the 10% you'll be gaining can be worth tens or even hundreds of thousands of dollars in the long run. Let's have a closer look.

Let's say you create a direct response marketing piece, take care of the printing and shipping costs, and mail it to 10,000 customers the host is giving you access to. Your cost for this is $8,000.

Out of 10,000 letters sent out to customers, you generate 300 sales at $200 per sale. Your revenue is $60,000. The host keeps 90%, which adds up to $54,000, leaving you with $6,000. But in reality, you've made much more than $6,000. What you've done is acquire 200 brand new fresh customers out of a single one-shot mailing. With the strategies and techniques you've discovered in this book, you know how to maximize the lifetime customer value of people who do business with you. Let's say your LCV is $800. Of those 200 new customers, you've potentially generated $160,000 in extra business, all with one mailing. So, is spending $8,000 in printing costs and giving away 90% of the sales revenue to your host still profitable for you if your lifetime customer value is $800? You decide.

Get started TODAY

Make a list of products and services that complement your current offers. Then make a list of all your contacts in the business world that have authority in their companies or even run their own businesses. Then make a third list composed of businesses that sell products or services that complement what you're selling.

Contact the businesses you've listed and share the idea with the decision-maker, the CEO or the owner of the company. Explain your plan and go over the points listed in this chapter to make every potential partner understand that the deal is a win-win situation for every party. The beauty with the model of power partnerships is that one or two deals can increase your profits in a matter of weeks with little to no risk at all.

30

BECOME A PRODUCTIVITY MONSTER

Being a business owner has its benefits but can also have its disadvantage since no one is above you to give you orders and hold you accountable. That is why it is essential to manage your time and energy efficiently to get the biggest leverage possible for every minute you put into you business. This chapter is divided in two sections:

1. Time management: how to manage your time during the day.
2. Energy management: how to manage fatigue and energy in order to complete your tasks quicker and more efficiently.

Energy management

Whether you're a billionaire, an Olympian athlete, an artist, an entrepreneur, rich or struggling financially, we all have the same number of hours at our disposal: 168 hours every week. How is it possible that some people accomplish so much more during these hours than other people? The answer lies in the way they manage their time and energy.

Minutes of productivity

A fascinating study was conducted among 500 CEOs of some of the largest companies in the United States. The study showed that these CEOs – who run billion-dollar corporations – only have 28 productive minutes on an average day. Furthermore, the study also revealed that they only had at best 45 minutes of total productivity without interruption: no phones, no interruptions from colleagues, no appointments, etc.

Time Thieves

We all have them in our lives: those people that constantly (willingly or not) try to interrupt us from getting things done. Once they've chosen a target, they slow down at nothing and are very creative in their ways of contacting you: daily phones (sometimes several times a day) with no real purpose conversation, texts and instant messages, etc. Make sure you establish rules for yourself on how you handle your time and who you allow yourself to talk to when you're busy working on a task. Live your life based on YOUR time management desires, not someone else's.

Time Vampires

Every business has them: that one employee that always asks if you "have a minute to discuss something" because they "had a question". The problem is, they interrupt you several times a day for the most futile reasons before even searching on Google for an answer. And we all know what happens when you say "yes": 15 minutes later, you're still talking. The problem is that those interruptions don't last "2 minutes" or even 15 minutes. They last much longer and have effects on your work quality because your brain disconnects from what you were doing before being interrupted. Studies show that it can take between 13 and 16 minutes to recover and get to the same level of focus you were at before being interrupted.

To counter those requests for "a quick chat" and "2-minute conversations", simply answer that you're busy working on something and will reach out when you're done. You're the CEO, so you make the rules about how you handle your time.

When you show that your time is valuable, people around you will begin to respect it. It is crucial to protect your time and make yourself unavailable to surprises when you're working on something that really needs your full attention. Become unavailable, set your phone to flight mode, and watch your productivity soar.

How to deal with meetings

I firmly believe that 90% of meetings are a massive waste of time and often generate very little results. Before taking your next meeting: ask yourself the following questions:

- Is this meeting really necessary?
- How does it contribute to the growth of what I'm doing?
- Is it really necessary to have a physical meeting if a virtual meeting (Skype for instance) is possible? This can save you considerable time.

To save time, use these three tips for your next meetings:

1. Schedule the appointment just before or just after lunch. This gives you an excuse to cut the meeting short if it drags on without any purpose.
2. List the topics to be covered in advance and know exactly what you want to cover during the meeting. This will prevent you from getting lost and forget the goals of the meeting.
3. Have a tangible outcome for the meeting. This can be a decision for a project for a new strategy or a new product, etc. At the end of the appointment, there must be a concrete decision that leads to a future development, or not.

How to be a productivity monster

Over the years, I've figured out ways to maximize my productivity. At this stage of my business career, I can write a book in 2 days, shoot almost 10 hours of video in a day and make hundreds of phone calls a day if needed. Here are some of the techniques I use to achieve maximum productivity.

When I'm focusing on work that needs my full attention, I put my phone in flight and disconnect from the internet. I don't give anybody a chance to interrupt me. It's important for your staff to be resourceful and figure out solutions on their own without always coming to you for questions. Entrepreneurs have a tendency to want to put out the "daily fires" in business, but if you spend your day dealing with the small issues, you will never have time to accomplish anything. From experience, I can also tell you that 90% of the "small fires" that happen aren't urgent, can be figured out at a later date and don't require an immediate response. If no one can find you, no one can disturb you.

Disregard incoming phone calls and instant messages when you're working on a task and are fully focused. I don't allow anything to break my concentration when I'm in the middle of something. The phone is a great tool for sales and communication, but can destroy your productivity. When I'm working, I rarely - if ever - pick up a phone call. My staff knows I'm not to be disturbed and they respect that. Once finished tasks, then I can relax and do other things.

Don't feel obligated to return phone calls. Just because someone tried calling you doesn't mean you need to pick up the phone or return a call there and then. Manage your time the way YOU want to manage it and make the callback when you're done with your tasks.

Email danger
Treat email the way I just described treating incoming phone calls: reply when you are done with your tasks, not when the email comes in. Just because technology has become fast doesn't mean that you need to reply immediately. I usually reply to email once or twice a day at most and allocate 15-20 minutes to email. If I don't have time to reply to emails in that timeframe (I receive anywhere between 100-200 emails every day), I don't reply.

10 Techniques to Become a Master of Time

Here are 10 simple techniques I use every day to be a productive monster and get a lot done without increasing my stress level.

1. Answer the phone only when absolutely necessary and keep phone calls shorts.

2. Schedule meetings ahead of time and have clear agenda and a finite time frame for the length of the meeting.

3. Be punctual and do not cheat yourself. If you're supposed to start a task at 8:45, starts at 8:45. Not at 8:30, not at 9:00.

4. Use simple to-do lists. Focus on the main goals that need to be accomplished and plan on potential delays. I like planning tasks on a weekly basis because it allows for unplanned delays (like internet issues, technical delays, holidays, etc.) to be worked into the schedule if needed.

5. Work in blocks of time of 90 to 120 minutes. Switch your phone off, disconnect from the internet or go somewhere that doesn't have any Wi-Fi. I can guarantee that you'll become much more productive and work faster.

6. Create the best environments to perform at peak productivity. Some work environments are much more productive than others. If you feel you can't get any work done in a specific place, find a place that gives you the best energy possible.

7. Reduce surprises and plan your day block by block. The less you leave your schedule to luck, the less you will be interrupted.

8. Use your downtime to learn new things. Preload your phone with interesting podcasts, and documentaries that you would like to watch or listen to or burn them on CDs to listen to in your car. I remember listening to thousands of hours of training and business education when I was starting out in business and still a teenager when I traveling on pro tennis tour. I would preload and burn CDs and listen to them during my long drives and flights and when I was at the airport or even during tour-

naments in my downtime.
9. Manage your hours and do things when others are busy. If you need to run errands, plan your schedule strategically so you only so you don't run into big crowds.
10. Plan your time off. Everyone needs to relax and recharge their batteries and have fun.

The world owes you nothing!

I often hear people saying "I deserve better", "I should make this amount of money" or "I deserve to be number one". But the reality is that the world owes you absolutely nothing. Entitlement is the biggest disease in today's society and makes smart people miss opportunities that they could benefit from if they have the right attitude and were willing to put in the work. There are over 7 billion people on earth, why would the world owe you anything?

The reality is that it's up to you to create your future, your career and your life. You can't rely on preferential treatment. Many people who are struggling in their businesses spend time complaining and finding excuses not to progress. Rather than complain, just get to work, execute ideas and strategies and get results. You don't know how to fix things on your website? Get someone else to do it for you or find a tutorial on YouTube. Be resourceful and think in solutions rather than finding excuses all over the place. All successful people, athletes, entrepreneurs, artists are often those who firmly believe that nothing is due and that they need to create their own luck.

Energy management

Energy management goes hand-in-hand with time management. To be productive, you need to be able to manage your time but also the amount of energy you have at your disposal. By "energy", I'm referring to "the level and the ability a system has to change its state". If you're running on fumes 24 hours a day, there's no way you can reach a higher level in your business. If you try running a marathon without being rested, you'll get injured in the first few miles.

The best way to maximize your energy is to operate in blocks of time and to be fully present and whatever it is you are doing in the present moment. I treat this as "work blocks" and "rest blocks". For visual representation, consider that every slot is either black or white. This is a concept that I picked up from Tony Schwartz in his book "The Power of Full Engagements", which is a fantastic piece of work that I highly recommend. It summarizes and defines exactly what I was taught and trained throughout my tennis years about managing one's energy and time during training and competition and even during points in when you're playing a match to make sure you always perform at the best of your abilities.

The main concept is that when you work, you work. And when you're resting, you allow yourself to rest completely. The key with energy management is that energy does not increase according to demand, but demand increases following work. I'm sure you noticed that the more you work, the more you feel you have to work because there are always more items on your things to get done. The problem with work is that your energy decreases as work gets done, and if you don't strategically plan for moments of rest and relaxation, this often leads to the phenomenon of burnout and exhaustion.

As an entrepreneur who is always on the move and involved in so many different areas from business to investments to movies, I will admit that I have reached exhaustion several times in my life, and it is not a fun situation to be in. The difference between time management and energy management is that time is finite, whereas energy can be increased depending on the task you are doing.

Tony Schwartz says that we need 4 sources of energy to function at our best.

1. **Physical energy**, represented by diet, fitness, physical recovery, rest and sleep.
2. **Emotional energy**, or the sense of accomplishment and being useful and excited. If you don't feel excited and motivated by what you do, you will find it difficult to realize your projects and push through when times get tough.
3. **Mental energy**, or the ability to focus and concentrate

for long periods of time on a single activity. This is endurance work and is a skill that needs to be developed to reach greatness and success.

4. **Spiritual energy**, which is the passion that governs what we do, our reason and the motivation to succeed in our ventures.

It is essential to recharge these four "cylinders" of energy whenever possible and always work on training and improving them. You can train your mental energy by extending your work slots and by pushing your boundaries. At this stage of my entrepreneurial career and having been trained for over a decade as a pro athlete, I'm able to go for 3 to 4 hours nonstop without feeling any loss of concentration of focus.

The importance of habits and rituals

We would like to believe that we are all masters of our destiny, but studies show that over 90% of what we do is done automatically. Human beings operate largely through habits and routine. The most obvious example that you can see is by watching great athletes.

Take the example of tennis players. Every tennis player has specific rituals that they have trained for years and sometimes decades to help them get focused regardless of how tired they are, how bad the weather is or how different the food is from one country to the next. After training for years, things become so ingrained that they become automated. There is no room for luck, every athlete knows that they must be trained as machines yet still be able to react in the moment and make small adjustments when needed. Tennis is an extremely complex and interesting sport because it requires so much on a physical yet also on a mental level. The best tennis players in the world all have very distinct ways of getting in the zone, preparing for games, preparing for points, etc. You need to develop your own rituals to perform at peak productivity.

Creating a ritual

I recommend that you start by analyzing the rituals that you have in life. First, become aware of what you're already doing. Then, try add a new ritual from today onwards for the next 30 days, even if you think the ritual is basic. I remember that after I retired from tennis in 2007 after a string of health issues, I gained over 10 kg (over 20 pounds) because I just wasn't training 20 hours a week anymore and wasn't burning as many calories. When I became aware of the need to lose weight and get back in shape, one of the decisions that I took was to shift my eating habits and start off the day by drinking a full bottle of water to rehydrate my body after a night's sleep. That could be your first new ritual, as simple as that. In the first few, it was difficult because I had to think about it. Now, it's a habit and is part of my morning routine. Create a simple habit for yourself and stick to it for 30 days.

The importance of recovery

Modern society tends to suggest that we have become machines that are made to work continuously. For some reason, working 80 hour weeks is somewhat regarded as a good thing, and working only 20 hours a week is frowned upon as being lazy. As Tony Schwartz highlights in his book, our bodies are made of rhythmic elements, heartbeats, emotions, sleep cycles, etc. We are not machines that can run without resting.

However, to dominate your industry and business, you need to do the necessary to push your circle of comfort and become more productive, or work on what currently might be your weaknesses. This is how our body develops its muscles. When you lift weights at the gym, you place stress on muscles. To grow, your muscle needs to be stressed so that the tissues can slightly rip. After working out, your body needs rest because it is during the recovery period that your muscles actually increase in size and resistance.

Rest makes your body stronger, because it allows the muscles that you have broken down to heal and recover. Rest allows you to recover so you can be strong, and be able to increase weights and the number of sets and reps for future gains. That's why it's important to push your limits and challenge yourself to accomplish more but also allow yourself to recover and fully replenish.

The importance of the start of the day

One thing that has had a tremendous impact on my level of happiness and productivity in business and in life in general is the way I start off every day. I have my own rules, and I suggest highly recommend that you create rules for yourself. My rules are as follows:

- When I wake-up, I don't do anything that puts me in a reactive mode. Mornings are focused on my health and my mind. When I wake up, I drink a liter of water and workout for approximately 45 minutes to an hour and a half. This could be going to the gym, playing some ice hockey, or just a going on a nice hike.
- I then have a green smoothie with spinach, broccoli, frozen berries, ginger and superfood ingredients such as maca, chia seeds, matcha and bunch of other healthy ingredients.
- I don't take any meetings in the morning and don't reply to any emails or work-related messages. Until 10 AM, I focus on myself because it gives me the time to really step out of the business every single day and it helps my mind find solutions for the ventures I'm involved in.

Sport plays a huge role in my life and has become a daily need for me because it makes me feel good about my body and grateful for everything I can do with it. Interestingly enough, all my best ideas and breakthroughs I've had always come when I'm away from the business. By manufacturing a morning routine where I force myself every single day to step away from the business and focus on my health, I have created an environment where good ideas pop up in my mind every single day. That's why I recommend that you create your own morning routine and work on creating the best environment possible.

Engineer a routine that allows you to be in a creative and proactive environments rather than being reactive. Outline your ideal morning routine and start doing it every single day and commit yourself to doing it every single day for the next 30 days. Why 30 days? Simply because studies show that is the average time it takes to internalize new habits.

To reach the next level in anything you're doing, you must work on your time management and energy management skills. Avoid the gray area: don't rest when you're supposed to work and don't work when you're supposed to rest. Time is your most precious commodity, so treat it as such. For more about this, I highly recommend reading "The Power of Full Engagement" by Tony Schwartz.

31

WHAT NEXT?

We have come a long way together and this can the end or the beginning. You now have a blueprint and dozens of practical strategies to boost your profits in the next 60 days. But growing a highly-profitable business is no walk in the park. And even though I've laid out a ton of money-making ideas in this book, and I realize there might be an enormous gap between where your business currently stands and where you'd like your business to be in terms of automation, revenue and impact on the marketplace.

If you've taken the time to go through this book, you are a smart entrepreneur and you know that reading a book alone will not help you achieve the results you need. The reality is that almost every single successful entrepreneur and business owner I've met and who has achieved an incredible level of success understand that execution is the key to everything.

That is why our clients have asked us to offer complete turnkey solutions where they don't have to go through the process of learning everything, mastering branding and social media, hiring programmers, hiring and training a sales team, etc.

If you'd like to have a conversation on how we can help you with all this, reach out to us. Go to MatthiasMazur.com/Agency to find more information or visit ZuraMedia.com.

Two Types of people

When I was 12 years old, I remember getting a letter from the Swiss Tennis Federation telling me that I had not been selected me to be part of the Swiss national tennis team. I remember opening the letter in front of my dad and literally crying my eyes out because I felt like I had failed everyone. Looking back on it, it's actually quite funny.

But it did give me something incredibly powerful. It gave me the desire to win and to prove people wrong. I started working three times more than the other players in my category and a couple years later, I won the Swiss national championships and became number 1 in the country.

The only thing that made that big jump possible was my dedication to putting in more work every single day and finding solutions better than what other players did. Unfortunately, my dream of making it to the Grand Slams and having a long professional career did not pan out the way I had hoped because of several health issues that forced me to look elsewhere to accomplish my sky-high ambitions. Entrepreneurship and building businesses was a natural alternative.

When I started my first internet company, a lot of the people around me questioned my move. I was still a teenager and many of my friends made fun of me and kept asking me repeatedly what "gave me the right" to start a company since I "didn't have any training or degrees in business".

But what they didn't know is that when they were drinking and partying on weekends, I was working. I took the work ethic I produced as a pro athlete and applied to business. I worked Friday nights and entire weekends with countless sleepless nights. That was the price to pay.

Building businesses in Europe and more specifically Switzerland is very different than building businesses in America, the public opinion piece. People don't see entrepreneurship as a rational choice. Ten years ago, they saw it as an escape and even as an anomaly until Hollywood made business look "cool" with movies such as The Social Network and Jobs. That is why I felt the need to move out of Switzerland very quickly, as I felt suffocated by the lack of opportunities in the country in the online tech space. Mind you, this was 10 years ago.

And that is my message to you. If you want to make things happen, if you want to grow your business, if you want to transform your life, you have all the tools necessary in this book. When I set out to write this book, I wanted to make it to "the end-all-be-all" of marketing. Even though I have several other books in the works and scheduled to come out soon, I wanted this one to be the main reference point and the one people readers refer to for years to come. I could have written a lame book like most entrepreneurs do. But I'm a perfectionist and I wanted to write the best damn book I could and to put everything in it.

I would love to help you transform your business even more, and I know that even though I put all my strategies in it, you might need more help to make things happen. I understand that not everybody understands marketing, advertising, creating angles and irresistible offers, generating leads on a daily basis and managing and training a sales team. I know that not everybody has the time or the desire to spend hours every week working on their online brand and handling their social media presence.

Even though it is a necessity in today's environment, the reality is that you might be jammed with things to do and just don't have the time to add new things to your plate. If all this resonates with you and you want to make things happen, you know that you have the power to take more space in your market and you want to double, triple or even 10X your revenue like some of our clients do, I urge you to reach out to us to see how we can help.

This is my life's work, and that is why I am attaching my personal name to everything I do in business with my marketing and sales agency, ZuraMedia. I will be here for years to come and we will continue to help brands generate more exposure with social media, help businesses generate unlimited leads every day, close sales and make millions of dollars for our clients. If you'd like us to take your business to the next level without only teaching you what to do but by actually DOING it your marketing, your branding and your sales for you, reach out to us on MatthiasMazur.com/agency or go to ZuraMedia.com.

If you liked this book - which I hope you have - it would mean the world to me if you reached out to me on social media or left a nice review on Amazon. I love connecting with entrepreneurs who are ambitious yet insightful enough to be grateful and aware of the incredible fortune we have to be alive in this day and age. I'm grateful you took the time to read this book I'm grateful that amongst the millions of other books out there, you decided to pick this one.

The Talent Myth

When I was 12, hearing tennis coaches say that I didn't have enough "talent" gave me so much motivation to work harder and smarter than others that it soon became part of my identity and my DNA. Outwork and outcompete others. Be the workhorse. Work hard and work smart. Dominate.

So whatever area you're involved in, I don't believe in talent anymore. I believe in keeping an open mind, being open to change, being humble enough to recognize what you need to learn and who you need to listen. Being smart enough to put in MORE work than others and to continue and to keep pushing when others stop.

When you watch Roger Federer play tennis, everything seems so easy. Journalists and pundits say that he was born to be a tennis legend, born to be number 1. What a bunch of B.S.

I know this because I saw how he trained day in and day out; I saw his focus and his dedication when I was training at the National Tennis Federation when I got recruited by his tennis coach at age 16. I saw the hundreds of hours he put into training, conditioning and mental work. His talent is obviously huge, but many other players came and went with even more talent than him. Talent alone might have got him to the top 100 players in the world, but his work and dedication took him to the number 1 spot and to holding the record for the most Grand Slams Championships won.

The Gift and the Curse of the Book

Writing a book is always a beautiful yet frustrating undertaking, because the reality is that 99.9% of the population will not read it. And even those who do buy a book often don't even get halfway through. That is why if you made it to this point, I would love to hear from you. I would love it if you implemented the strategies that I outlined. Think of this book as a big buffet: choose the strategies you like and refer back to the other sections when your business situation lends itself to new growth. Start with one or two strategies this month.

A Word about Gratitude

As much as we as entrepreneurs are focused on growth, dominating markets, increasing revenue and putting out daily fires, it is important to look within and be grateful for the things we have. It is vital to take the time to disconnect from the daily grind and to be grateful for the loved ones we still have, knowing that anything can happen from one moment to the next.

One of my favorite quotes of all time is by John Lennon who said "life is what happens to you while you're busy making other plans". That is one of the most beautiful things I have ever read and it's stuck with me ever since. In the daily hustle - hiring and building teams, getting rid of bad employees, managing cash flow, coming up with new.creative marketing campaigns, being so ultra-connected through phones and computers and fighting to always be ahead of the marketplace, we sometimes tend to forget what really matters at the end of the day.

Spending time with loved ones and being grateful for everything we have. If you woke up this morning with a roof over your head and being able to walk and move with no pain, you are one of the fortunate few and you're already privileged. Take care of yourself, take care of your health, take care of your family, take care of your mind. Make time to eat well and to stay in shape. Make time to work out or engage in fun hobbies - health is always the number one asset. I've had several health struggles in my life, and nothing is more humbling than being unable to use your body in the most basic ways.

Now, it is my turn to be grateful and to thank you from the bottom of my heart for giving me the opportunity to share some of my experience throughout these pages. I wish you nothing but the best and I'll see you at the top.

Best,

Matthias Mazur

Connect with me on social media:

Website: MatthiasMazur.com
Facebook: Facebook.com/MatthiasMazur
Twitter: Twitter.com/MattMazur
Instagram: Instagram.com/MatthiasMazur
LinkedIn: Linkedin.com/in/MatthiasMazur
Snapchat: MatthiasMazur
Medium: Medium.com/@MattMazur
Tumblr: MatthiasMazur.tumblr.com

INDEX

Yahoo, 113, 135, 144
Yellow pages, 74, 99,
repeat sales, 32, 48, 50, 52, 24, 67,
104, 202, 256,

Matthias Mazur and ZuraMedia

After sharing his marketing, sales and business growth strategies and concepts with thousands of entrepreneurs and companies of all size since 2005 and speaking at dozens of conferences and workshops in Europe and North America, Matthias started noticing that entrepreneurs often didn't enjoy the process of branding, creating marketing material, advertising, generating leads, making sales and promoting themselves.

That is why he created ZuraMedia, an online marketing, sales & social media agency that helps clients with turnkey and hands-free solutions to increase exposure, leads and sales using heavy-hitting internet marketing and sales strategies.

Matthias is also available on a limited basis for speaking engagements.

For more information on how Matthias can increase your business with online marketing strategies, go to:

www.ZuraMedia.com
Or visit:
MatthiasMazur.com

Connect with Matthias on Social Media:

Website: MatthiasMazur.com
Facebook: Facebook.com/MatthiasMazur
Twitter: Twitter.com/MattMazur
Instagram: Instagram.com/MatthiasMazur
LinkedIn: Linkedin.com/in/MatthiasMazur
Snapchat: MatthiasMazur
Medium: Medium.com/@MattMazur
Tumblr: MatthiasMazur.tumblr.com